COMPARATIVE POLITIC

Comparative politics

New directions in theory and method

Hans Keman (ed.)

VU University Press
Amsterdam 1993

VU University Press is an imprint of:
VU Boekhandel/Uitgeverij bv
De Boelelaan 1105
1081 HV Amsterdam
The Netherlands

tel. (020) - 644 43 55
fax (020) - 646 27 19

cover design by D PS, Amsterdam
printed by Haveka, Alblasserdam

isbn 90-5383-163-0 cip
nugi 654

© VU University Press, Amsterdam, 1993.
All rights reserved. No part of this book may be reproduced, stored in a retrieval system, or transmitted, in any form or by any means, electronic, mechanical, photocopying, recording, or otherwise, without the prior written permission of the holder of the copyright.

Acknowledgments

The preparation and publication of this book has been made possible by the generous support of both the *Vrije Universiteit* (and in particular the Rector Magnificus, Prof. Cees Datema, who showed a personal and keen interest in the Symposium that laid the foundation for this book) and the *Graduate School of Political Science* in the Netherlands. The *Vereniging voor Christelijk Wetenschappelijk Onderwijs Vrije Universiteit* and the *Graduate School of Political Science* contributed financially to this enterprise. Support was also given by the Faculty of *Social-Cultural Sciences* and the Department of *Political Science & Public Administration* (and in particular its Head: Prof. Wim Noomen).

Apart from the contributors to the volume a number of colleagues participated in the discussions we had during the Symposium and their contributions certainly helped to improve our arguments. These included Prof. Stefano Bartolini (Geneva), Dr. Kees van Kersbergen (VU Amsterdam), Prof. Peter Mair (Leyden), and Dr. Peter Nannestad (Aarhus).

The swift and neat production of this book would not have been possible without the invaluable assistance of Roos Siwalette, Albert Santing and Jaap Woldendorp. The latter also played an indispensable role in organizing the symposium and kept track of the whereabouts of both the contributors and their manuscripts notwithstanding my inclination to disorganization. Finally, I would like to thank Margriet Helder who helped to design the cover of the book.

I am most grateful to all mentioned here.

Hans Keman
Haarlem/Amsterdam, December 1992

CONTENTS

Introduction: Comparative Politics: 1
New Directions in Theory and Method
Hans Keman

PART I: *Comparative Politics and Political Science*

1. The Development of the Study of Comparative Politics   11
   Hans Daalder
2. Comparative Politics: 31
   A Distinctive Approach to Political Science?
   Hans Keman
3. Comparative Studies of Elections and Political Science   59
   Cees van der Eijk

PART II: *Institutions, Actors and Rationality*

4. Rational Choice as Comparative Theory: 81
   Beyond Economic Self Interest
   Ian Budge
5. Institutional Difference, Concepts of Actors,   101
   and the Rationality of Politics
   Roland Czada
6. Restrictions in the Political Control of Science   121
   Dietmar Braun

PART III: *Comparative Political Research*

7. Policy Network Analysis: 143
   A Tool for Comparative Political Research
   Adrienne Windhoff-Héritier
8. The Politics of Managing the Mixed Economy   161
   Hans Keman
9. The Political Trinity: 191
   Liberty, Equality and Fraternity
   Jan-Erik Lane & Svante Ersson

Bibliography   219

About the Editor and the Contributors   244

LIST of TABLES and FIGURES

Table 2.1	The Comparative Approach	56
Figure 4.1	Unimodal Model of Party Competition	84
Figure 4.2	Polymodal Model of Party Competition	84
Figure 6.1	The Credibility Cycle of the Scientist	127
Table 8.1	Economic Development in 18 OECD-Countries	171
Table 8.2	Relationships between Economic Performance and Economic Policy	172
Figure 8.1	Strategies of Economic Management	173
Table 8.3	The Combined Impact of Monetary Restrictive and Tax Spending Strategies on Economic Performance	174
Table 8.4	Relations between Policy Actors and Conflict Dimensions	176
Table 8.5a	The Impact of Parties in Parliament	177
Table 8.5b	Party Control of Government	179
Table 8.5c	Party Behavior in Coalitions	180
Table 8.5d	Left Wing Party Control, Trade Unionism and Economic Policy Formation	181
Table 8.6	Party Control of Government, Institutional Arrangements and Choice of Economic Policy	183
Table 8.7	Politics and Policies of Economic Management (1965-1972)	187
Table 8.8	Politics and Policies of Economic Management (1975-1979)	187
Table 8.9	Politics and Policies of Economic Management (1980-1988)	188
Table 9.1	Liberty around the World	193
Table 9.2	The Size of the Public Sector	196
Table 9.3	The Redistributive State	198
Table 9.4	Income Inequality	199
Figure 9.1	The Kuznets' Curve: Income distribution and Affluence	200
Table 9.5	Level of Affluence	201
Table 9.6	Economic Growth: average yearly rates	203
Table 9.7	Average Growth Rates 1965-1989	204
Figure 9.2	Human Development Index and Level of Economic Affluence	207
Table 9.8	Ethnic and Religious Homogeneity versus Heterogeneity	210
Table 9.9	Ethnic Fragmentation	211
Table 9.10	Religious Fragmentation	212
Table 9.11	Consistency of Trinity Values	214

Comparative Politics:
New Directions in Theory and Method

Hans Keman

Comparative politics as a distinctive field within political science is receiving more and more attention today. One can find articles in the leading journals which have a comparative focus, employ cross-national data, or discuss theoretical issues from a comparative perspective. Paradoxically this development has generated growing concerns *within* this field of Political Science as well as doubts about it as an approach *per se*. One would have expected more convergence in both theory and method, and a more or less undisputed 'place under the sun'. Yet, this is apparently not the case. The concerns and doubts with respect to comparative politics are directed to its 'distinctiveness' as an approach to 'politics'.

It appears a suitable moment therefore to publish a book that aims at a re-appraisal of the state of affairs and an appreciation of the recent developments in comparative politics. Such an undertaking appears to be particularly necessary if doubts are increasingly raised about the usefulness of this approach and the soundness of its methodology by comparative political scientists *themselves* (Przeworski, 1987; Ragin, 1987; Castles, 1989; Mayer, 1989).
Furthermore, it is a worthwhile enterprise since considerable confusion exists among political scientists about what comparative politics and comparative research is all about. Hence there is an apparent need for clarification and explanation of this sub-discipline and its applicability to a number of topics within political science as a whole.

The publication of this volume will hopefully have a positive and fruitful effect on the understanding and the employment of comparative political research. For it appears that this field is not quite accepted in political sciences, as is the case for instance in the Netherlands, and is often plagued with misunderstandings about its theoretical endeavors, methodological implications and its potential for political science in general[1]. The paradox is that, although it is taught at most Departments, comparative politics is hardly acknowledged as a *distinctive* part (and parcel) of political science.

It should be noted from the outset, however, that this book is not primarily meant to introduce and to justify comparative politics. On the contrary, this book attempts to combine two objectives which are of importance for the development of this (sub-)discipline within political science: on the one hand it is intended as an introduction to comparative politics and should therefore be of interest to all students of comparative politics. On the other hand, the contributions can be seen as 'up-dating' of the field by discussing recent developments in theory and method. To this end the book is divided into three parts and in each part three themes will be addressed that represent the main topics of debate in comparative politics today.

1. *Themes*

The basic ideas underlying this volume are the clarification of comparative politics as a field of political science, the elaboration of its theoretical potential for political science, and the discussion of the methodology of comparative political research. However, the contributors do not only wish to inform the reader in general on the present state of the art, but also intend to further and to enhance new and promising developments of the comparative approach to political science. The contributions to this volume will cover the following topics:

---

[1] This does not imply that comparative politics is unknown or not practiced in the Netherlands, on the contrary. See for instance: Rosenthal, 1978; Bertrand, 1981; Daalder, 1987; Keman, 1988; Daalder/Irwin, 1989; Hoetjes, 1990; van Kersbergen, 1991.

1.1 The Development of Comparative Politics

In order to discuss the present 'state of affairs' properly comparative politics as a field of Political Science will be introduced in most of the chapters by illuminating its development as a sub-discipline, in particular since the late fifties. This 'stocktaking' will *inter alia* focus on the theoretical questions asked. For instance the issue of the development of a 'grand' or universal concept versus more culturally specific conceptualizations will be discussed (Sartori, 1970).

Another concern is the shifting of the object of study that can be observed. It is worthwhile to reflect, for example, on the basic unit of analysis. Is it still the nation-state? Or should we rather look at political processes of integration (e.g. supra-national bodies) and at processes of regional and functional devolution? Or should we devote (again) more attention to the core actors in politics, such as political parties and interest groups?

In addition the methods of investigation that have shaped the present 'state of the art' will be scrutinized. For the logic of the comparative method and its consequences in terms of data-collection and related techniques of (primarily statistical) analysis, which formed a seemingly undisputed core of comparative politics in the early seventies (Holt/Turner, 1970), is today under siege. For example the question whether or not a 'case-oriented' (or: historical-cum-qualitative) approach must be preferred to a 'variable-related' (or: synchronic-cum-quantitative) design is a topic of debate (Ragin, 1991; Baldwin, 1990). Whatever view may be correct on these matters, it is obvious that they have to be discussed in full.

1.2 Diverging Directions in Comparative Politics

One can observe various developments in which the specific 'mix' of theoretical and methodological concerns are a topic of considerable debate. Firstly, it can be observed that the object of study has changed, including the meaning of comparison. On the one hand, a tendency towards 'middle-range' theorizing has become the objective and with it a research design that is confined to the number of 'relevant' cases (i.e. limiting the 'universe of discourse'; Rokkan, 1975). On the other hand there has been a development towards emphasizing 'politics' as the core object instead of (implicitly) considering political phenomena as a result of socio-cultural *specifica differentia* or being dependent on socio-economic dynamics and circumstances (e.g. Milner, 1989). Hence 'politics' as the subject of investigation appeared to become 'de-politicized' as an explanatory variable and comparative analysis served the purpose of illustrating similarities rather than stressing the search for causal relations (Przeworski, 1987; Lane/Ersson, 1990).

A divergent development can then be noticed in recent attempts to "bring politics back in" and to develop alternative research designs. In a way this divergence has upset the 'field' (Mayer, 1989; Ragin, 1991) and needs to be examined in more detail to assess to what extent comparative politics is still a viable and distinctive field within political science. An important theme that runs through the contributions to this book will be therefore: What is the present state of affairs in this respect and which directions appear most promising?

1.3   New Directions in Comparative Politics

With some exaggeration one may put forward the thesis that a new approach is emerging within comparative politics concerning the development of a synthesis between the 'rational choice' approach and the so-called 'new institutionalism' (Olson, 1982; Keman/Lehner, 1984; March/Olsen, 1989; Czada/Windhoff-Héritier, 1991). This new direction in comparative politics, however, calls for a careful evaluation and must be properly discussed in the light of past experiences with other theoretical approaches.

This development has obvious consequences for comparative politics as a distinctive (sub-)discipline of political science in terms of both theorizing and methodology. On the one hand it signifies a shift from inductive to deductive theory-building, on the other it implies that the level of analysis concerns in principle an intersection of micro-macro levels of observation. However, given this synthesis, the examination of political processes should be primarily be on the meso-level (North, 1990; Olsen, 1991). For it is on the level of (corporate) actors and the organizational features of society where the political (inter)action takes place. Given the developments in comparative politics this 'new' trend implies, to put it succinctly, a movement away from political sociology towards political economy, from cross-national analysis to inter-temporal and across-the-board investigations of theory-guided topics on the level of actors and institutions (see: Schmidt, 1987; Budge/Keman, 1990; Scharpf, 1991).

The contributions to this book are intended to set the stage for a proper discussion of these themes. In particular the enhancement of study and research on political processes in terms of *politics, polity, and policy* will be focussed upon (see: Schmidt, 1991; Keman, 1992a). For this 'triad' is among the most essential topics of political science and is in serious need of a more elaborate and encompassing approach. This may be founded, on the one hand, by transcending sheer descriptive types of analysis and, on the other hand, by investigating the political process in a more (rigorous) theoretical manner.

2.   *Overview of the book*

The volume is divided into three parts in which the three themes outlined above will be discussed. In Part I, the focus is on the 'state of the art' as well as on recent developments in comparative politics. In the second Part attention is drawn to the viability of 'rational choice' theory and the 'new institutionalist' approach in order to assess their usefulness for comparative politics. Finally, in Part III, in which the practice of comparative research is under review, the relation between 'theory and method' will figure prominently.

Part I: *Comparative Politics and Political Science*

The first part contains a treatise by Hans **Daalder** on 'The Development of the Study of Comparative Politics'(Chapter 1). The author gives us a bird's eye view of the history of the sub-discipline, in other words the 'roots' of comparative politics. He correlates (international) political history with the changes in focus and themes that have dominated this field of political science. In the early postwar period this meant a search for the conditions under which democracy could flourish as it had been the case in the Anglo-Saxon world. In the course of events it appeared that comparative politics became more or less 'Americanized'. However, later on a change of direction can be observed in theory and method. Broad and sweeping analyses were replaced by detailed analyses of specific questions. In addition, more explicit attention was paid to normative implications (versus empiricism) as well as a more to configurative designs (versus reductionism). Daalder not only shows how comparative politics has changed, but also to what extent this has induced new perspectives, which have contributed to divergent approaches within comparative politics.

In Chapter 2 Hans **Keman** delves into the difficult question whether or not comparative politics can be considered as a distinctive approach within political science. There are a number of conflicting views that seemingly are mutually exclusive: case-study approaches versus variable-related designs; cross-sectional and longitudinal research; synchronic versus diachronic analyses; qualitative and quantitative interpretations and so on. Most of these contradistinctions, Keman argues, are by and large false ones and even misleading. For comparative research rather involves a continuing effort to learn on the basis of theoretically well-defined concepts of its core subject, i.e. the "political", when to compare, why to compare and how to compare. Comparative politics should be considered therefore as an approach within Political Science.

Part I is concluded by Cees van der **Eijk**. In Chapter 3 the focus of attention is on a central feature of representative government, namely on the electoral process, and how to compare this. In a way the argument of the preceding chapters is elaborated. Basically van der Eijk contends that the communalities in political behavior outweigh the cross-national differences. This is an important conclusion, both theoretically and methodologically, for it means that it is possible to analyze the effects and consequences of elections that are hitherto often explained either by nation-specific factors or by the institutional features of an electoral system.

Part II: *Institutions, Actors and Rationality*

In Part II Ian **Budge** takes issue in Chapter 4 with the over-simplified economic approaches that attempt to explain democratic politics. His main point is that economic approaches rely too heavily on very narrow assumptions, and on this basis develop rather sweeping and not testable conclusions about the problems of collective action in relation to the possibility of democracy. Instead Budge proposes to take both the contents (e.g. ideology or issues) and institutions (the 'rules of the game') of democratic politics as a point of reference and to develop from there models that use rational choice as a means of generating hypotheses about political actors that can be put to a test rather than explaining democracy in a purely deductive a priori manner.

Roland **Czada** elaborates in Chapter 5 the theme taken up by Budge in terms of 'rational choice' guided actions of political and societal actors and the existing institutional arrangements. His argument is that rational choice is essentially 'bounded rationality'. Hence political action is much more based on choices that seem to be the best available ones instead of maximizing. At the same time he points out, quite correctly, that institutional arrangements are a product of history and culture, and should not always be considered either as facilitating or as arresting for political action with respect to decision-making.

In chapter 6 Dietmar **Braun** presents a comparative theory of the dynamics of policy-implementation in relation to features of 'political control'. His contribution shows that it is possible to develop theoretical questions about the relation between state agency and societal actors and relate these to empirical analysis by means of a so-called 'intra-systemic' perspective. The principal-agency argument demonstrates that there exists a *via media* between arguing on both the micro and macro-level and this may very well be a new avenue for the study of comparative politics.

Part III: *Comparative Political Research*

First of all, Adrienne **Windhoff-Héritier** demonstrates in Chapter 7 that the institutional features of a society by and large influence the way policy-making for a society is organized (i.e. the 'polity'). This has an impact on the substance of the policy-making process itself, and in addition appears to be decisive for the inclusion and exclusion of political and societal actors participating in the process of policy-formation within the modern democratic state. Policy networks have developed as a result of the institutionalization of democratic decision-making. This approach, Windhoff-Héritier claims, is an appropriate instrument for comparative research in analyzing empirically to what extent the relation between democratic decision-making and policy performance is indeed influenced by the institutionalized behavior of policy actors. Finally she examines the feasibility of applying these theoretical views to empirical comparative research in more detail.

Hans Keman explores in Chapter 8 the relation between political action, institutionalized behavior and public policy performance. Departing from existing explanations of the 'politics of economic management' in capitalist democracies, he attempts to enhance these views. To that end a more quantitative comparative approach is utilized. He concludes that extant explanations often lack a comprehensive research design and use arguments that are only in part accounting for the role of politics. His cross-national and intertemporal analysis shows not only the possibilities to relate theoretical questions to empirical research, but also how the role of 'politics' can be meaningfully analyzed by studying the institutionalized behavior of political and societal actors in relation to the decision-making process concerning public policy formation.

In the final chapter Jan-Erik Lane and Svante Ersson present a cross-national analysis of the role of the modern state by examining to what extent state intervention with respect to the quality of life of its citizens indeed promotes social welfare and economic well-being. The question at hand is in principle a normative one: to what extent do 'rulers' adhere to the 'public contract' between them and the 'ruled'? They evaluate this by referring explicitly to the key values of liberal democracy: liberty, equality and fraternity. Their conclusion is that only a few of the states examined perform accordingly, and that this occurs mainly in comparatively wealthy and democratic societies. At the same time they observe that this normative 'triad' of the liberal ideology is interrelated, if the conditions are favorable. This contribution demonstrates how to combine empirical comparative analysis with important normative questions in political science.

PART I: *Comparative Politics and Political Science*

PART I Contemporary Political Science

1 The Development of the Study of Comparative Politics

Hans Daalder

'Comparative politics' existed long before it became a recognized subfield of the modern discipline of political science. A century or so ago, a knowledge of the variety of political systems formed part of the normal education of *literati* in different disciplines, such as law and philosophy, history and letters. There were classic writers on problems of modern government in different countries such as Mill, Bagehot, Bluntschli, Radbruch, Redslob, Duguit or Bryce. Their treatises contained many comparisons, over time as well between different societies. One might go back further in history. Political theory abounds with comparative discourse on both contrasts and commonalities in political life, as even a superficial survey of the writings of Aristotle and Polybius, of Dante and Machiavelli, of Bodin and Locke, of Montesquieu and De Tocqueville, not to speak of the authors of *The Federalist Papers*, immediately shows. Man has speculated comparatively on problems of government and society in both prescriptive and descriptive terms since times immemorial. If we nevertheless insist that modern comparative politics is somehow different, this is for three not unrelated reasons: first, modern comparative politics deals consciously with a political world which has changed drastically from the universe known to the great writers of the past; second, it has become the special terrain of a recognized subfield of contemporary political science; and third, as such it shares in both paradigmatic shifts and new developments in research techniques in that discipline.

1.1 The Learned Tradition

Several characteristics marked the understanding of government in Europe and the United States as it had developed by the beginning of this century[1].

First, there was a strong normative overtone in discussions on government. Normative approaches were traditionally strong in fields like law, philosophy or theology in which problems of government were discussed at the time. Different ideological traditions, whether Conservative, Catholic or Protestant, Liberal, Radical or Socialist, inevitably had their impact on political discourse. So had more specific traditions of political theory which nourished debates on crucial themes like sovereignty, community, authority, liberty, constitutionalism, rule of law, democracy and so forth.

Second, discussions of government often reflected particular conceptions of history. In the hands of some, this might lead to the elaboration of 'historical laws', often couched in terms of different 'stages' through which societies would develop. 'Diachronic' comparisons thus came naturally. Models of social change often showed a clear evolutionary or even teleological bias.

Third, there was generally a strong emphasis on political institutions, which were thought to be not only the results of past political strife, but also factors which could control present and future political developments.

Fourth, 'comparative' politics generally assumed specific country perspectives. Thus, in Britain 'cross-channel' dialogues easily developed into a contrast between (stable) British 'cabinet government' and (unstable) French 'gouvernement d'assemblée' (or for that matter British 'rule of law' versus French 'droit administratif'). Cross-Atlantic debates resulted into the conflicting typologies of a 'parliamentary' versus a 'presidential' system of government. Perennial debates in France on the merits, or lack of merits, of the French revolution strongly colored political discussions on problems of constitutionalism and popular sovereignty. Debates in what was to become Germany had a powerful impact on the analysis of state and nation, of the exercise of power, of 'organicist' versus 'liberal' modes of social and economic development, and of

---

[1] For a full and sophisticated treatment, see the introductory chapter by Eckstein in: Eckstein/Apter, 1963

the comparative role of bureaucracies - subjects which were to become the concerns of future social science also outside German borders. Comparisons of European countries with the United States underscored the early nature of American democracy and stressed the importance of voluntary groups in a free society, but the United States could also be held up as a negative yardstick for alleged abuses, for its spoils system, the role of lobbies or a yellow press, or more generally the dangers of 'mass society'.

Typically, smaller European countries tended to be neglected in the reasoning of learned men outside the borders of the particular country itself. Linguistic frontiers may partly explain this. But probably more important was the assumption, typical of 19th and early 20th century power politics, that small countries hardly mattered. At best they might be of little more than folkloristic interest, at worst they were seen as no more than transient players in a world in which the larger countries determined history.

'Comparative politics' then went generally not much beyond speculation and the study of 'foreign government'. Other states were generally seen as entities all on their own, or at most as possible yardsticks against which to measure developments in one's own society, and then often as negative yardsticks at that.

1.2 The Political Shocks of the 20th Century and the Erosion of Institutional Certainties

All this was to change drastically in the wake of three fundamental 20th century shocks: the breakdown of democracy in Weimar Germany, the rise of totalitarian systems and the turn towards authoritarianism of most of the new states which were established following the demise of European colonialism.

The formally legal *'Machtübernahme'* in Weimar Germany in 1933 shattered democratic hopes and self-confidence. The Weimar constitution had been heralded as the perfect model of democratic constitutionalism. Its fall destroyed the trust in political institutions as sufficient guarantees of democratic rule. Admittedly, some theoreticians attempted to retain 'institutionalist' explanations, singling out 'faulty' institutions such as proportional representation (e.g. Hermens, 1941), the presence of a directly elected President next to a 'normal' but thereby weakened *Kanzler*, or the absence of judicial review, as major factors in the destruction of democratic rule. But generally, institutionalist analyses stood discredited. A growing awareness of the patent discrepancy between the promises of the Soviet constitution of 1936 and the realities of naked power relations in the USSR reinforced this tendency, as were events in France in 1940.

The rise of totalitarian political systems massively changed the perceptions of politics. Their development, in some countries and not in others, raised new problems of comparative enquiry. Earlier beliefs about the 'natural' development of democracy foundered. 'Autocracy' had been a time-honored category of political analysis, and 'absolutism' had been the natural counterpoint of constitutionalism and later of democracy. But totalitarianism seemed to represent an entirely new political phenomenon. Problems of power and leadership, of propaganda and mass publics, of repressive one-party systems and police rule, came to dominate political discussion. Sociological and psychological explanations seemed to offer better insights in the realities of totalitarian rule than traditional political theory or institutional analysis.

The post-1945 world was soon to see also the rise of many new states from what had been colonial dependencies. Such states had generally been equipped with constitutional arrangements, which in most cases proved ineffective to stem developments of authoritarian regimes, whether in the hands of traditional elites, military or bureaucratic governors, or revolutionary party leaders. Such developments further undermined a belief in institutional approaches, and called for alternative modes of analysis.

One effect of the great political shocks of the 20th century was a massive migration of scholars, notably to the United States, but to a lesser extent also the United Kingdom. One needs only list prominent names such as Karl W. Deutsch, Henry W. Ehrmann, Otto Kirchheimer, Paul Lazarsfeld, Karl Loewenstein, Hans Morgenthau, Franz Neumann, Sigmund Neumann, and Joseph Schumpeter, to make clear the importance of this factor for new developments in the study of politics. That field was also to attract the progeny of European refugees who as a typical 'second generation' turned to the analysis of comparative and international politics in great numbers. Exiles from Hitler were followed by migrants from Communist repression, and later still by a growing number of Third World scholars who opted to stay in the First World. A desire for the systematic study of comparative politics came naturally in such circumstances. It heightened concern with the realities of political power, both within and between states. It made for a characteristically ambivalent attitude about democracy: if anything the belief in democratic values became stronger, but expectations about its chances turned more pessimist.

1.3   Academe and a Changing Political Universe

If migrant scholars looked back naturally on developments in continents they had left, the world was changing, and so was the role of the United States in what was rapidly becoming global politics for policy-makers and students of politics alike. Although Europe remained a key area, other parts of the world, including notably the evolving Communist block, Japan and a rapidly growing number of new states, became matters of urgent political and intellectual concern. So did Latin America, long regarded as a backyard of a Monroe doctrine America. Comparative politics saw the number of its possible units of analysis grow beyond recognition. At the same time problems of political stability and legitimacy, of social and economic development, of competing political regimes and ideologies assumed an entirely new importance.

The need to understand this new world could be met in a variety of ways. It underscored the importance of experts on single countries, notably those which became the object of particular policy concern. It increased the relevance of traditional area studies which it released from their (sometimes almost museum-like) preoccupation with the unique features of 'other' civilizations; in the process cultural anthropology became a more central field in contemporary social science. At the same time, older beliefs about inevitable - and presumably static - differences gave way to concerns with political and social change and beyond this: to discussions to what extent such changes could, and should, be engineered.

All this fitted in well with the traditional temper of American academe. The lure of 'science' had traditionally been strong and had expanded much beyond the 'natural sciences' into the social sciences and even the humanities.

So had the assumption that 'science' could and should lead to practical policy results. There was a strong belief that the academic enterprise should center on the elaboration of testable theories. At the same time, the idea of interdisciplinary study stood in high esteem. It was given a strong impetus within some of the great universities (the University of Chicago being a particularly important center). Such interdisciplinarity was moreover reinforced by new agencies, including government research councils, the newly established (American) Social Science Research Council and a growing number of private foundations all becoming increasingly involved in sponsoring 'relevant' research. This in turn facilitated a massive expansion of graduate schools, and fostered collaborative research between senior and junior scholars, the latter being called upon to 'test' particular theories elaborated by the former through detailed empirical research.

All this came to coincide with the development of new research tools, which helped to foster what was soon to become known as the 'behavioral revolution'. Next to library research and field work in a participatory setting, the survey became a powerful research tool[2]. Governments began to develop more and more important statistical data to monitor the effects of new policies. A rapidly growing number of international organizations, whether global (such as the United Nations and its specialized agencies, the World Bank or the International Monetary Fund), or regional (the OECD growing from the efforts of the Marshall Plan, and the European Communities being particularly important), came to collect statistical data on many countries. To the extent that they were presented in standardized form, this facilitated comparative inquiry. More and more efforts also went into the construction of time-series data, necessary for the study of developments over time. This massive growth of quantitative data (initially developed mainly in the context of economic and social policies and used in particular by economists and experts in social policies) also found their way into data handbooks and data archives. The computer revolution was concurrently to facilitate the storage, analysis and access to such data. The efforts of individual scholars first, research sponsoring agencies later, made the pooling and preservation of research data (including the

---

[2] Most notably in the field of electoral research, but also in other comparative analyses, e.g. the influential work of Almond and Verba on political culture, 1963.

products of survey research for secondary analysis) increasingly common practice. All this occurred at a time of a massive expansion of academic enrolment, which increased facilities not only for graduate research, but also for publishing research findings. Both university presses and specialized commercial publishers massively expanded. Journals proliferated. So did professional associations and the number and specialization of workshop and panels at academic conferences.

If both the mass, and the sophistication, of such developments in social science were taking place initially mainly in the United States, they soon became an international reality. Early in the post-1945 period deliberate efforts were made to foster international comparative research. One powerful stimulus came from UNESCO, which established its own International Social Science Research Council, and which provided a powerful stimulus for the establishment of international professional bodies such as the International Political Science Association (IPSA) or the International Sociological Association (ISA). Many national governments expanded their research councils. The idea of international exchange and research cooperation found increasing favor, with the fellowship programs of a number of American Foundations, the Fulbright program, and to a lesser extent agencies like the British Council setting a pattern. In the process English became increasingly the *lingua franca* of modern social science.

1.4   *The New Comparative Politics*

Against this general background of political change on the one hand, a massive expansion of international and national policy-making and research on the other hand, 'comparative politics' developed rapidly. The shift in terminology from the older term of 'comparative government' to 'comparative politics' was symbolic for what was in fact a conscious desire to move away from the traditional concern with political institutions towards a preoccupation with political and social developments generally.

There are some particular landmarks in the development of modern 'comparative politics'. One of these was the Evanston seminar at Northwestern University in 1952 which brought together a group of then younger scholars including Samuel Beer, George Blanksten, Richard Cox, Karl. W. Deutsch, Harry Eckstein, Kenneth Thompson and Robert E. Ward under the chairmanship of Roy Macridis. In a statement, published in the American Political Science Review, they branded the existing study of comparative government as parochial in being mainly concerned with Europe only, as being merely descriptive instead of analytical, as overly concerned with institutions rather than processes, and as insufficiently comparative being wedded above all to case method approaches (Macridis/Cox, 1953). Some of the members of the Evanston group vigorously clashed with stalwart representatives of an older generation, including such luminaries as Carl J. Friedrich, Maurice Duverger, Dolf Sternberger and William A. Robson during a colloquium of IPSA in Florence in 1954 (Heckscher, 1956). Such older practitioners of comparative government were not readily persuaded by the new gospel. They were to note gleefully that the most irascible proponent of the new 'comparative politics', Roy Macridis, was soon to publish work on France and other countries along what seemed after all rather traditional lines. The continuing need to take account of specific country perspectives was also to become apparent in the work of other scholars of the group, who after all became editors and authors of influential textbooks organized on the basis of country studies (covering again mainly the larger countries; e.g. Beer/Ulam, 1958; Macridis/Ward, 1963).

In the meantime, a group of scholars (including some members of the Evanston Seminar) was being formed who as a group would have a lasting influence on the development of comparative politics. Many of them were, or would be, active in what was soon to become known as 'the Committee' (i.e. the Committee on Comparative Politics of the (American) Social Science Research Council). In the second half of the 1950s, this Committee deliberately brought together a number of leading area experts. With Gabriel A. Almond as its highly influential chairman, it set itself to recasting the analysis of comparative politics along mainly structural-functionalist lines. As Almond explicitly stated in the influential volume edited by himself and James S. Coleman, *The Politics of the Developing Areas* (1960), the ambition was to find "a common framework and set of categories to be used in ... area political analysis"; to this end Almond himself engaged in "experiments in the application of sociological and anthropological concepts in the comparison of political systems", irrespective of time or area. This work was eventually to lead to the famous 'crises of political development' model, which sought to analyze political systems in terms of the character and sequence of six major processes: legitimacy, identity, penetration, integration, participation and distribution (see also: Pye, 1965). One manner in which to validate such approaches was to bring together members of the Committee with experts on areas, particular institutions or social processes for a series of books on different aspects of political development, including communications (Pye, 1963), bureaucracies (LaPalombara, 1963), political culture (Pye/Verba, 1965), education (Coleman, 1965), parties (LaPalombara/Weiner, 1966), and (belatedly) state-formation (Tilly, 1975). Two works were intended to cap the approach: a book offered mainly as a textbook (Almond/Powell, 1966), and a co-authored volume on *Crises and Sequences in Political Development* (Binder et al., 1971). Whereas the first seemed to proclaim certainty, the latter revealed considerable self-doubt and disagreement in the Committee. Clearly, its members did not see eye to eye on such fundamental matters as the existence or not of a linear development from tradition to modernity, and the possibility to engineer social change or not.

Of course, such debates were not restricted to members of the Committee. A great many scholars, in different disciplines, tried their hand defining processes of political development and modernization[3]. For all their diversity and disagreement, such writings had in common an attempt to understand processes of social change, conceived as in principle comparable over different areas and time-periods, and tackled with instruments from whatever social science discipline seemed appropriate. Such approaches also led to a reconsideration of past patterns of political and social change in nations already seen as fully or mainly modernized, including the United States itself and Western Europe. Historians were asked to join in such efforts at comparative understanding (see for example: Black, 1968; Grew, 1978; Tilly, 1975;1990).

The impact of these approaches on the discipline was substantial. All manner of Ph.D. candidates swarmed out to study processes of social and political modernization in countries all over the world. They did so with

---

[3] To mention only some of the more prominent ones: Lerner, 1958; Apter, 1965; Organski, 1965; Barrington Moore, 1966; Zolberg, 1966; Rustow, 1967; Huntington, 1968; Eisenstadt in many works, notably Eisenstadt 1973: see also useful readers such as Macridis/Brown, 1961/1986; Eckstein/Apter, 1963; Finkle/Gable, 1968; Eisenstad, 1971.

different interests and intent. Some became thoroughly intrigued with the persistent role of traditional structures and beliefs, making them eager novices in the ranks of area specialists and cultural anthropologists. Others concentrated rather on the other end of the presumed tradition-modernity continuum, identifying largely with the search of economists and experts on public administration for 'development'. Yet others felt more happy with the work of various international organizations which sought to monitor and stimulate social and economic developments with the aid of statistical indicators, regarding the universe of nations, or some particular sample of it, as a laboratory in which to test particular development models.

1.5   Inevitable Reactions

For all its exhilaration the political development boom was to create its own reactions, in rather different ways.

One reaction consisted in the development of counter-models of development which treated the prosperous West not as the prototype of a modern society which others were naturally to attain at some later stage, but as the root cause of an inequitable distribution of the world's goods. Marxist theories of (neo)imperialism held capitalist development responsible for the exploitation of the Third World, and regarded the so-called 'independence' of former colonies as a thin guise for what was in practice 'neo-colonialism'. Notably from the background of Latin America, which had much older independent states than Africa and parts of Asia, developed the various brands of 'dependency' theory which emphasized the co-existence of traditional sectors of society and the economy with modern economic sectors which were in practice little more than the *emporia* of the advanced economies in the USA and Europe. Such models were given a more elaborate treatment in Wallerstein's World System approach, which became in many ways an academic industry of its own.

A second reaction came from those who had difficulty fitting Communist systems into the framework of general development theories. To many such a problem did not seem particularly urgent: the comparative study of Communist societies was to a considerable extent a world on to itself and many were happy to leave it at that. The idea of a possible convergence of systems in the West and the East seemed to most observers bereft of reality, perhaps a matter of speculation for economists, not for those who knew the patent differences in political life from direct physical experience or historical analogy. But developments of Communist states did yet enter the field of general comparative politics for at least two reasons. Communist models might and did serve as example and inspiration for Third World countries, notably in their Chinese and Cuban variety. And in a more theoretical vein, a debate arose on the issue to what degree totalitarian systems were themselves a product of modernity. This point had been strongly argued by Carl J. Friedrich, who saw in that characteristic the fundamental difference between older systems of autocracy and royal absolutism and modern totalitarian systems (Friedrich, 1954; Friedrich/Brzezinski, 1956), but was denied by scholars like Wittfogel who saw many common features between the systems described by him in his 'Oriental Despotism' (1957) and systems of modern totalitarian rule. Nevertheless, whether seen as possible models of modernization, or as alternative expressions of modernity itself, the study of totalitarian systems remained on the whole outside the scope of general comparative politics writing. At least one reason for this was the tendency to equate political modernity with democracy, in systems already existing or as the natural end-product of political development.

A third reaction to the political development literature consisted in the allegation that it rode roughshod over the uniqueness of particular areas or countries. Such was the natural reaction of scholars nurtured in a tradition of 'configurative' studies, whether of a particular local culture, or a particular political system. Such scholars were not comfortable with what they regarded as overly general categories of analysis. They emphasized that the essence of political and social systems lay in the complicated interaction of many variables which could only be disentangled by destroying the uniqueness of the whole. And they tended to deny the possibility of real comparative study given the inability of scholars to really know more than one or two cases sufficiently well.

1.6 Rethinking Europe

For a time Europe became a somewhat ambiguous area in the development of the new comparative politics. The Third World seemed to attract most of the theorizing and field research, as did to a lesser and more specialist sense the development of Communist systems. Europe seemed possibly somewhat old-fashioned, a world of staid democracies about which all was known and where little happened. The very concept of Europe had become somewhat hazy, moreover. The erection of the Iron Curtain had lopped off a number of countries which had formerly formed a natural part of the European universe. If one saw Western Europe as for all practical purposes identical with 'democratic Europe', then certain European countries (including some members of NATO like Greece, or Portugal, not to speak of Spain) presumably did not belong. If democracy were the defining characteristic, why then not study all modern democracies together, thus abandoning the very existence of 'Europe' as a distinct area (a conclusion drawn for example by Lijphart, 1984)?

Whatever such qualms, 'Europe' was soon to figure prominently on the map of comparative politics again, through a variety of circumstances. The persistent concern about 'totalitarianism' naturally made for comparative enquiry into past events: what after all had caused the breakdown of democratic regimes in some countries, and not others (see notably the consciously comparative study of Linz/Stepan, 1978). When much later Greece, Spain and Portugal all returned to democratic rule, the reverse question arose: what were the causes for such transitions from authoritarian rule (see: O'Donnell/Schmitter/Whitehead, 1986; Diamond/Linz/Lipset, 1988). The failure of imposed constitutional regimes in many former colonies raised the issue whether alternative models of democracy might have done better; where was one to find these but in Europe (the British dominions usually being regarded as mere offshoots of a British system)? The general concern with development posed many questions for which the history of different European countries might provide possible answers, whatever the dangers of historical analogies. There was a rich literature on European countries, and access to sources was relatively easy. Europe provided, moreover, a variety of cases vital for comparative analysis with a generalizing intent, provided one really knew the specific cases that made up Europe, and went beyond the exclusive concentration on a few larger countries only.

Much of the history of the development of comparative politics writing in and on Europe can in fact be written in terms of a desire to take account of the political experience of particular countries (for a fuller elaboration of this theme, see Daalder, 1987). As a special subdiscipline, European comparative politics grew largely from the efforts of a new postwar generation of younger scholars who engaged in a massive *trek*, to some extent to the United Kingdom, but particularly to the United States. They found there an exhilarating world of scholarship, with all manner of theoretical speculation and rich empirical research. This was in strong contrast with the paucity of 'modern' social science literature in their own country, and led naturally to a desire to emulate and replicate studies on America with comparable studies at home. At the same time, a confrontation with Anglo-Saxon scholarship also provoked a natural reaction against what were often felt to be too specifically 'British' or 'American' theories, typologies or models, and fostered a desire to develop alternative theories and typologies which were more in line with the understanding of one's own country. At a minimum, more countries should be brought onto the map of European comparative politics, which somewhat ironically required 'translating' their experience into Anglo-American concepts.

Thus, some of the most innovative comparative politics writing by European scholars betrays, on closer analysis, a strong influence of particular country perspectives. This had been irritatingly clear from what purported to be a general study of political parties by Maurice Duverger (1951), which for all the help the author received in data collection from an early IPSA network of European political scientists, was shot through with French perspectives and prejudices. But one can also document the impact of Italian concerns in the much more sophisticated analyses of party systems by Giovanni Sartori (1976). There is the disappointments of a left-socialist German emigre-scholar about postwar developments in Germany and Austria in the work of Otto Kirchheimer (see the collection by: Burin/Shell, 1969), just as Scandinavia provided the undoubted background of the development of a center-periphery model in the rich work of Stein Rokkan (1970). An even clearer example is the deliberate development of the consociationalist model against the background of The Netherlands, Belgium, Austria and Switzerland, to counter the massive impact of what seemed too easy an identification of Anglo-American models of government with democracy *per se*[4].

From the mosaic of such parallel studies a much more sophisticated picture emerged of the diversities of European experience which could be studied both in a diachronic and a synchronic manner, culminating in what is as yet the most satisfactory attempt at understanding the complexities of European political developments contained in Stein Rokkan's so-called 'topological-typological' map, or 'macro-model' of Europe (Rokkan, 1970; Rokkan, 1975; Rokkan/Urwin, 1983; cf. Daalder, 1979).

1.7   Different Research Strategies

Taking developments in the study of 'Europe' as an example, the considerable variety of modes of comparative study becomes readily apparent.

A seeming paradox is provided by the country monograph. To the extent such a monograph is written to elucidate particular political experiences for a more general public, it may offer insights of comparative importance. This is much more true if the monograph seeks to prove, or disprove, specific theoretical propositions first developed with one or more other countries in mind. The most telling example, however, is the consciously theory-based analysis of a single country case (e.g. Eckstein, 1966; Lijphart, 1968b). Moving to a somewhat higher level of abstraction are comparative analyses of two, or a few, particular countries[5]. Most 'comparativists' must confess that their real knowledge of different countries tapers off quickly beyond a rather limited number of cases. One obvious way to overcome such limitations is collaborative research, in which for any given research question experts on different countries

---

[4]   See: Almond, 1956 and contra Lijphart, 1968a and 1968b; Lijphart, 1977; for a review of Lijphart and the parallel work of other writers like Huyse, Lehmbruch and J. Steiner, see Daalder, 1974.

[5]   The value of this strategy had not been lost by members of the Committee on Comparative Politics which sponsored as one of its first projects a comparison of Japan and Turkey, see Ward/Rustow eds, 1964

are asked to join in a common research effort. Much the most frequent books on (European) comparative politics consist of edited volumes of this kind. Such volumes bring much needed information on different countries together and testify to the fruits of cross-fertilization. But most of them suffer the natural defects of group enterprises. The choice of countries is often a function of the availability, or even the reliability, of individual country experts. Even the most rigorous attempt at editorial guidance rarely results in an even quality, let alone genuine comparability, of country chapters. Introductory and concluding chapters very often are of a rather ad hoc and impressionistic nature (but see for impressive examples volumes of a lasting nature, such as Neumann, 1956; Dahl, 1966; Rose, 1974; Budge/Robertson/Hearl, 1987).

This strengthens the case for attempting individual syntheses after all. The difficulty of such an enterprise becomes readily apparent, however, if one seeks for post-war equivalents of the great comparative government treatises of the past (e.g. Friedrich, 1937; 1941; H. Finer, 1932; 1949, not to speak of earlier classics such as Lowell, 1896 or Bryce, 1929). These are very hard to find (e.g. Blondel, 1969; Finer, 1970; for later attempts to analyze 'European politics' see Smith, 1972; 1989; Steiner, 1986; Lane/Errson, 1987; Pelassy, 1992; and the three-author volume of Gallagher, Laver and Mair, 1992), and encounter the obvious problem of an increased number of countries to be treated, with many more empirical research findings of potential relevance to be covered.

Rather than on analysis at the level of countries as a whole, work has tended to focus on particular institutions such as monarchy (e.g. Fusilier, 1960), heads of state (Kaltefleiter, 1970), the formation of cabinets (e.g. Bogdanor, 1983; Pridham, 1986), parliaments (Wheare, 1963; Von Beyme, 1970), electoral systems (Lijphart, 1993), parties in general (Sartori, 1976; Von Beyme, 1985; Panebianco, 1988), particular party families, interest groups, bureaucratic structures, and so on. In studies focusing on particular institutions or groups, there is always real danger of analyses out of political and social context.

Alternatively, there is the massive growth of quantitative 'cross-national studies'. As stated before, both the quantity and the quality of data has increased massively in the last decades, through the efforts of governments, international organizations, the gallant work of those who prepare 'data handbooks'[6]), and organize data archives. Such data invite cross-national studies, in a large number of fields. Thus one need only inspect the guide to journal articles in 'Electoral Studies', not to speak of important collaborative volumes (ranging from Rose, 1974 to Franklin et al., 1992), to see the richness of studies on electoral behavior, and of elections (cf. Bartolini and Mair, 1990). We have important studies on political participation (influenced notably by the works of Verba/Nie/Kim, 1978; and Barnes/Kaase, 1979) and on the impact of changing values (an area dominated by the highly debated analyses of Inglehart, 1977; 1990). The study of cabinet coalitions has offered a fertile a testing-ground of formal theories (for a useful survey and discussion see: Laver/Schofield, 1990). As we shall see presently, the data revolution has also had a great impact on the study of the development and problems of modern welfare states and public policy. Not all such cross-national studies are really comparative, however. Although they draw on data from many countries, they are often directed more to problems of general political sociology or psychology than to a systematic inspection of country variables. 'Contextual' knowledge is often neglected, and with it possibly the essence of comparative politics itself, which in the words of Sidney Verba presupposes that one

> "tries to generalize - using that term loosely - about nations, or to generalize about subnational entities like bureaucracies, parties, armies and interests groups *in ways that use national variation as part of the explanation*"(italics HD; Verba, 1986: 28)

A lack of knowledge of the countries studied has made some such 'cross-national' analyses verge on what Stein Rokkan once dubbed mere 'numerological nonsense'.

---

[6] See for some notable examples covering rather different variables and countries Taylor/Jodice, 1983; Flora, 1983; Mackie/Rose, 1991; Lane/Mackay/Newton, 1991; Katz/Mair, 1992; Woldendorp/Keman/Budge, 1993

1.8   New Approaches

Developments in modern comparative politics, then, were largely the result of a greater knowledge of individual countries on the one hand, and of a true revolution in data collection and analysis techniques on the other. But at the same time, new political problems appeared on the political agenda, which resulted in something like a paradigmatic shift. If comparative politics had concentrated thus far mainly on problems of regime change, political institutions, and what in systems theory one calls 'input' structures, a new concern developed with problems of public policy and political 'output'. Various factors contributed to this development.

One cause was the (renewed?) 'left' revolution in social science in the 1960s and 1970s, which faced the question why 'capitalist' systems endured, once-confident prophesies to the contrary notwithstanding. This led to a new concern with the role of the state which seemed somewhat forgotten in otherwise rival approaches of systems theory and economic determinism[7]. A parallel debate arose on the extent to which political parties - notably Socialist ones (see Castles, 1978; Schmidt, 1982; Scharpf, 1992; Keman, 1988; 1990) - did affect government policies or not. A major element in the discussion became the degree to which states differed in their dependence on external economic forces (e.g. Katzenstein, 1985), which could only be solved by comparative inquiry. Even when such studies related to European countries only, the obvious relevance of international economic structures and events brought scholars closer to those who had long been preoccupied with world economic realities (e.g. the proponents of a World Systems approach mentioned earlier).

A second major factor was the development of 'neo-corporatism'. Originating to some extent from a transposition of an approach found useful in the study of Latin America (e.g. Schmitter, 1974, reprinted in Schmitter/Lehmbruch, 1979), it won great acclaim in attempts to explain 'Europe', and possible differences within it. By emphasizing the close interaction between public and

---

[7] In that light the famous title of Evans, Rueschemeyer and Skocpol, 'Bringing the State Back In' (1985) would seem to testify as much to a new vision of those who had been strangely blind, as to the real record of political studies they criticized.

private actors, the neo-corporatist approach seemed successfully to bridge input and output structures, and to present a more realistic picture of power relations and policy-making than either those who had spoken uncritically of 'the' state, or those who had embraced a naive 'pluralism', had been able to provide. Neo-corporatism became in Schmitter's words 'something like a growth industry'. But the gap between 'general' theory and empirical validation remained substantial, to the detriment of the value of the approach as a tool for general comparative analyses as distinct from the study of specific policy areas.

A third major contribution came from those who set out to analyze the development of the welfare state in comparative terms. On the one hand, this work fitted in well with the concerns of older development theorists: one should note the link between state expansion, economic policies and processes of political development which had characterized the work of German *Kathedersozialisten* and *Nationaloekonomen*; (re)distribution had been one of the paramount concerns of the Committee on Comparative Politics; and the leading empirical scholar in this field, Peter Flora (1974; 1975; Flora/Heidenheimer, 1981: Flora, 1986 and following years) saw his work as filling a gap Rokkan's macro-model of Europe. On the other hand, comparative work on the welfare state was to encounter what was soon to become the major debate on its 'fiscal crisis', and on possible limits of state intervention more generally (Lehner et al., 1987; Keman et al., 1987; Lana/Ersson, 1990). The label 'political economy' was to cover a wide variety of concerns, ranging from rational choice paradigms based on individualist self-interest, to studies of specific policy areas, competing models of general economic and monetary & fiscal policy, and renewed debates on political legitimacy. The full weight of such new approaches on the study of comparative politics is discussed by other contributors in this volume.

1.9   The Great New Challenges

But such challenges would seem to pale before the momentous changes taking place in what had been thought of as the Communist world, and the attendant shifts in contemporary international relations. In addition, the progress of European integration, however halting, is affecting the very basis of independent states as the unit of analysis on which so much of comparative politics has rested.

The long-standing assumption of a natural division of labor between the study of international relations engaged in analyzing the interaction of states, and comparative politics concerned with the study of processes within states, always rested on somewhat dubious ground. It left unclear what scholars were to handle the formation of (new) states; it glossed over the great importance of domestic political processes on the making of foreign policies; it belittled what became known in the international relations literature as 'transnational' politics; and it postulated a degree of political independence for 'sovereign' states which never completely fitted the realities of an interdependent world (as advocates of a World System approach, dependency theorists and other political economy theorists had long maintained).

The division of the world in rival blocs had arguably permitted a certain separation of international relations and comparative politics. The assumption that existing states within a bloc remained distinct units of analysis seemed tenable in a world of relatively stable alliances (the necessary *ceteris paribus* qualification being as easily forgotten as it was given). The much more fluid international scene of to-day makes such an assumption rather more questionable.

At the same time, developments within the European Community increasingly undermine the role of member states as independent units, even though international modes of decision-making remain juxtaposed to supranational ones. Powers of decision in vital matters are either shared or transferred to organs 'beyond the nation-state', while at the same time states also lose formal or effective powers to regional or local units. The 'national' power to control citizens, groups and enterprises becomes more dubious in a world of increased mobility and communication, affecting the status of individual 'states' as realistic units for comparative analysis.

But the greatest, if generally unexpected, challenge to comparative politics comes from events in Central and Eastern Europe. We mentioned earlier that the study of Communist states had become mainly the concern of a specialist group of scholars. Experts on Communism have largely lost their 'subject', although they have retained their knowledge of language and area. Scholars who were mainly concerned with the study of the development and the working of democracies, on the other hand, stand before an entirely new universe. Their concern had generally been with the comparative treatment of *existing* democratic states, which is a far cry from the *making* of new democracies in societies which have not known democratic rule for two political generations or more. For all the words spoken by pundits at symposia, in newspaper columns or journal articles, the extent to which proven knowledge exists is unclear.

The future of democracy presupposes at a minimum the creation of new institutions, but the brunt of comparative politics teaching since Weimar has tended to discount the independent effect of political institutions. Seemingly abstract debates on the merits of presidential, semi-presidential or parliamentary systems of government, on unicameral or bicameral legislatures, on electoral systems and their effect on the politicization of cleavages and the formation of party systems, on the proper role of judicial bodies, become suddenly matters of crucial importance again. But they must function in areas with all the remnants of a totalitarian past, rival claims for political control and citizenship, possibly severe disagreements on the nature of the political unit itself - and all this amidst economic ruin and change. It is as if all major issues in the study of comparative politics are chaotically thrown together: the formation of states, the working of institutions, the rivalry of parties and groups, competing ideologies, the provision of state services and their limits, issues of economic interdependence, international power politics, and what not. Against this, one must ruefully acknowledge that basic political phenomena such as civil war, terror, ethnic conflict or the shattering effects of ideological strife, have traditionally tended to fall in the interstices of the study of international relations, comparative politics and political theory, rather than forming their core.

Comparative politics, then, stands before its greatest challenge yet. Never before were so many fundamental questions raised at one and the same time. In all honesty one should acknowledge that it provides few definite answers.

2 Comparative Politics: A Distinctive Approach to Political Science?

Hans Keman

There have been several attempts to delineate the boundaries of comparative politics, yet there is little agreement at present on its distinctiveness. Essentially, one could argue that there exist four different ways of defining comparative politics: firstly, those who distinguish it from other approaches to political science by referring to certain concepts employed which can only be properly understood by means of comparative analysis; secondly, those who take as a point of departure the central features of the political process which can be analyzed for all political systems; thirdly, there are those who maintain that politics can only be understood by employing a macro-scopical perspective; fourthly, and finally, there are many who define comparative politics by means of its method: i.e. the art of comparing, and who justify this by referring to the famous quote of Kipling: what know they of England, who only England know!

Although the last way of delineating comparative politics is purely methodological, it is the most prevalent one and not the worst way to define this field. However, I do not wholly concur with this view, for it would mean that the domain of a discipline is defined by its method, rather than by either its *core subject*, i.e. the study of politics, which is then, of course, still in want of a definition itself, or by its *mode of explanation* that is supposed to advance our knowledge of the core subject. In this chapter our concern will be therefore to demonstrate what comparative politics can add to political science by means of its *use of attributes of macro-social units in explanatory statements* (Ragin, 1987: 5). This calls for an elaboration of the core subject in terms of an identifiable object of study and how this relates to various levels of analysis. In addition, a second concern will be to develop a meta-theoretical approach that is capable of *explaining or interpreting* multi-level variations of the subject under review (the so-called micro-macro linkage). A final concern is a resultant of the preceding ones, and involves scrutinizing existing logics of comparative inquiry to account for the observed variation by means of *testing empirical hypotheses*, thereby either corroborating or falsifying them (Lijphart, 1975: 159).

All these concerns are in itself worthy of serious discussion and deliberation, yet the main issue at hand is that comparative politics, as a field within political science, lacks coherence in terms of a set of theoretical references and related logics of inquiry. In short this chapter is not only an attempt to delineate comparative politics as a separate field, but most of all must be seen as an *argument* to relate theory and method of this approach of political science in order to gain a viable and feasible approach to explain political processes.

In order to clarify my point of view, I shall first elaborate some of the existing definitions of just what comparative politics is (section 1). In addition I shall argue in section 2 that comparativists should focus on the political process rather than on the context of 'politics' In the sections 3 and 4, I shall delve into the matter whether or not comparative politics can be characterized by a 'core subject' of its own, and if so, whether or not it can be distinguished by a theory? In section 5, I enter into the most disputed domain of comparative politics, i.e. the comparative method and its implications for a 'proper' research design. In section 6, I shall tie together the different arguments regarding views on comparative politics as a more or less distinctive field within political science. The central argument will be that a coherent framework of theoretical references and a corresponding logic of inquiry is required. If it is not possible to do this, comparative politics will still remain a valuable asset to political science, yet any claim of being a distinctive approach should then be put to rest.

2.1 Delineating the Field of Comparative Politics: Definitions and Justifications

Comparative politics has grown out of the wish to know more about one's own political system by comparing it with others. In particular, it was previously believed that knowledge about the institutional framework of politics would not only help to understand the peculiar rites of one's own polity, but would also enable one to draw conclusions about its merits and disadvantages. However, this approach was dominated by the idea that supplying comparable information on the structure and working of a political system in toto would be sufficient to further knowledge about the political process and that the analysis should therefore remain of a descriptive nature based on facts. For example, James Bryce (1929) stated his task as a comparativist as follows:

> "What I desire is, not to impress upon my readers views of my own, but to supply them with facts, and (so far as I can) with explanations of facts, on which they can reflect and from which they can draw their own conclusions" (p. IX).

This institutional and empiricist approach ("it is facts that are needed: Facts, facts, facts. When facts are supplied, each of us can try to reason from them", Bryce, 1929: 13) lost its appeal after the Second World War when a more analytical perspective was introduced (Blondel, 1981: 173-178). A good example of this change is offered by Roy Macridis (1955), who argues strongly favor of a more 'scientific' approach to politics in general and considers the comparative approach as the most promising, if not revolutionary way to go:

> "Comparative analysis is an integral part of the study of politics. The comparative study suggests immediately the laboratory of a scientist. It provides us with the opportunity to discuss specific phenomena in the light of different historical and social backgrounds. It suggests variables of a rather complex order that can be dissociated from the cultural background and studied comparatively. (.....)The comparative study of politics is beginning only now to enter a new stage which reflects in essence the progressive systematic orientation in the study of politics. It is beginning to assume a central role in empirically oriented study" (Macridis, 1955: 1 & 3)

In sum, Macridis believed that comparative politics as a distinctive field within political science, as he saw it, would be able to bridge the growing cleavage between political theory and the empirically based study of politics. This so-called 'revolution' of political science did not materialize and became a "stalled revolution" (Mayer, 1989: 20) being reduced to a 'movement' and not a distinctive field, or sub-discipline within political science. Almond contended that comparative politics has indeed revolutionized political science, but that this development should be considered as a stage in the development of political science. He concludes:

> "It is difficult to see therefore, that comparative politics has a long-run future as a sub-discipline of political science. Rather, it would appear that, like the political behavior movement which preceded it, its promises lies in enriching the discipline of political science as a whole" (Almond, 1968: 336).

Almond's 'developmental' explanation, of course, would mean an integration of the comparative movement into political science. His view is not wholly shared by all of his contemporaries such as Macridis, Rokkan, Daalder and Verba (compare: Daalder, 1986). Although they are critical with respect to the development of comparative politics as a distinctive field within Political Science, they instead stress the fact that the 'stalled revolution' might be seen as the paradoxical result of the growth of comparative research. Thus, instead of a 'paradigmatic' development there has been a 'pluralistic' one. Verba therefore concludes his views on "where have we been, where are we going?" as follows:

> "For the future, one can expect to see more of the same in the comparative politics field. It will remain fragmented and appear disorganized. (....)My guess, nonetheless is, that the discipline will maintain its heterogeneity of styles and theories and that most of its practitioners will continue to view that as healthy."
> (Verba, 1989: 36)

I do not concur with this view, for such a liberal approach to a sub-discipline ultimately evades the question what distinguishes it from other fields within political science. Furthermore, it avoids the important question of what it has to offer to a student of politics in his, or her, quest for understanding *and* explaining the politica process in a society. It is remarkable to note that those who assess the 'state of the art' in comparative politics choose either to view it in an evolutionary way, or to see it as a pluralistic development.

For example, Holt and Turner represent the evolutionary, not to say a 'positivist', view. In the early seventies they stressed the pre-paradigmatic situation and sought a solution in 'scientism' in order to move beyond heuristic schemata (Holt/Turner, 1970: 70). Hence the future of comparative politics depended, according to them (and many others; e.g. Mayer, 1972; Lasswell, 1968; Merritt/Rokkan, 1966), by and large on the development of a proper methodology and genuinely comparable datacollections. There is nothing wrong with such an empirical analytical approach, but one wonders to what extent this 'solution' is in fact different from Lord Bryce's optimistic view that factual description would render deeper knowledge about the nature of politics.

The 'later' Macridis does indeed not share this way of thinking any more. Reappraising his own optimism of the 1950ies in 1986 led him to a rather ambivalent position. On the one hand, he maintains that "Comparative politics is emerging as the most comprehensive and theoretical branch of political science" (p.49), and on the other hand, he suggests that the search for a grand theory should indeed be abandoned and political scientists should rely entirely on the development of subfields or specializations (p. 21). Hence heterogeneity and compartmentalization suddenly becomes a positive development, for:

> "clustering, as opposed to the search for grand theory, has given to the field a new vitality, and may ultimately pave the way to the development of some unifying models and priorities" (Macridis, 1986: 22).

These lines of reasoning to justify comparative politics as a distinctive approach are not appear fruitful, nor do they help to develop a description of this field within political science. Such reasoning only leads to a situation, which Wiarda (1986) has described as follows:

> "Indeed, the field itself seems presently so fragmented and dispersed as to raise the question in some minds of whether comparative politics can still properly be called a field at all" (Wiarda, 1986: 5).

Clearly the lack of a general theoretical framework and the continuing debate on both the method and the principal concepts to be used is most disturbing. This is not necessarily a consequence of using different approaches within comparative politics, or of employing a wide variety of concepts alone (see for this: Sartori, 1970). However, such a pluralistic attitude precisely produces a situation that most protagonist of this field with to avoid. For this 'live-and-let-live' attitude implies an abandonment of the search for a more coherent approach to comparative politics and, in fact, robs it from any substantial meaning and theoretical rigor. It will only lead to sacrificing substance to method, or to raising only those questions that can be empirically answered, but do not relate to the critical problems of mankind (also: Mayer, 1989: 21; Castles, 1987: 222). It is also unproductive to focus on partial problems within the field, such as choosing the correct method, selecting the right concepts, and finding the proper data. However, do not let me be misunderstood, it is not my aim to suggest an alternative 'grand theory' or an overarching 'concept' of politics, that would save the day for the comparative approach and retaliate its critics. Nor do I think that by solving the methodological issues comparative politics will become a 'paradigm' of political science. Instead, I propose the following guidelines to define comparative politics as an *separate field within political science*:

1. describe the *core* subject of comparative politics. In other words to question how do we recognize a comparativist, what distinguishes him or her?
2. develop a view on which *theoretical* concepts can 'travel' comparatively as well as possess a unifying capacity for explaining political processes?
3. discuss the logic of the *comparative method* as a means to a goal, rather than as an end in itself. In other words, which method fits the (research) questions asked by a political comparativist best?

This is, of course, a rather ambitious agenda, but if we do not at least attempt to investigate the possibilities of new directions in comparative politics to journey toward a more or less integrated and distinctive field within political science, we had better leave the field as a separate approach. Yet, I wish to uphold the original motives and intentions of comparativists to develop this approach to political science to enhance its rigor and claim as a discipline. Whatever the today's skepticism of the erstwhile protagonists may be, it is worthwhile to investigate the possibilities of comparative politics thoroughly. Let us therefore now turn to the first point on the agenda: the description of the field.

2.2   Comparatively Researching the Political Process

Comparative political research is generally defined in two ways: either on the basis of its supposed core subject, which is almost always defined at the level of political system (Kalleberg, 1966; Wallerstein, 1974; Almond/Powell, 1978), or by means of descriptive features that claim to enhance knowledge about politics as a process (e.g.: Apter/Andrain, 1972; Roberts, 1978; Dogan/Pelassy, 1990). These descriptions are generally considered to differentiate comparative politics from other fields within political science. Although it is a useful starting point, it is not sufficient. Some authors are more specific in their description and add to this general point of departure that comparative politics concerns nations and their political systems (Wiarda, 1986), or the study of geographic areas. Finally, some authors deliver a more or less exhaustive definition in which "the comparative study of political phenomena against the background of cultural, sociological and economic features of different societies" is the focus of comparative politics (Macridis, 1986; Berg-Schlosser et al., 1987).

All these descriptions may be useful up to a point, but they do not help to mark off the field and require greater specification. Comparative Politics must be defined in terms of its theoretical design and its research strategy on the basis of a *goal-oriented* point of reference, i.e. what exactly is to be explained. A way of accomplishing this is to argue for a more refined concept of 'politics' and develop concepts that 'travel' and can thus be related to the political process in various societies. In addition, a set of rules must be developed that direct the research strategy, aiming at explanations rather than at a complete description of political phenomena by comparing them across systems, through time, or cross-nationally. At this point most comparativists stop elaborating their approach and start investigating, often however, without realizing that theory and method are interdependent modes of explanation.

In contrast, comparative politics should be seen as an approach that aims at explaining the political process in a society by means of a (meta-) theoretical framework of reference and where explanations are validated by comparing units of analysis (see also: Roberts, 1978; Ragin, 1987; Przeworski, 1987; Castles, 1989). The goal of comparative politics is to explain those 'puzzles' which cannot be studied without comparing and are derived from logical reasoning. Hence, no comparative research without an extensive theoretical argument underlying it, nor without a methodologically adequate research design to undertake it.

In most discussions of comparative politics, it appears to me, that both theoretical and methodological aspects are divorced, or - at least - treated separately. For example, Ragin (1987) and Przeworski (1987) emphasize predominantly the methodological aspects of the art of comparison as a 'logic of inquiry', which is often underdeveloped or incompletely elaborated. At the same time these authors argue their case by means of examples that are seemingly picked at random. Worse even, it seems that some of the examples are selected to demonstrate the tenability of their view. Theoretical progress and explanatory value appears then to emanate from their 'logic'(see: Przeworski, 1987: 45ff; Ragin, 1987: 125ff). Yet, the comparative analysis of the political process must be founded *a priori* in theory and then related to the best fitting 'logic of inquiry'[1].

Another example of such a separation of theory and method can be found in the study of electoral behavior. This vital part of the political process can be explained fairly well on the basis of deductive reasoning. To validate its micro-level founded hypotheses a comparative research design is not necessary. It can be done, but it is only genuinely comparative, if the explanatory concepts are analyzed by examining the variation in the political properties on both the micro- and macro-level. Electoral behavior or party behavior that is explained by means of the working of electoral systems, features of a party system, or the existing rules of government formation are in need of a comparative anlysis (see, for example, Lijphart, 1984; Sartori, 1976; von Beyme, 1985; Bogdanor/Butler, 1983; Budge/Keman, 1990). However, studies which focus on intra-systemic variation or micro-level variation are, notwithstanding their quality *per se* and

---

[1] It should be noted that the work of Adam Przeworski, when focussing on a 'core subject' is not guilty of the charges made here; e.g. Przeworski, 1985; Przeworski/Sprague, 1986. It remains a remarkable feature, however, that his and Ragin's methodological work appears to be divorced from actual empirical analysis. Ragin's replication of Rokkan's mapping of nation-building in Europe, or his case-related ideas on intra-national developments (Ragin, 1991) are hardly convincing in relating theory and method.

usefulness as sources of information, not genuinely comparative in nature (see, for example, Blondel, 1985; Henig, 1979).

This conclusion seems to hold for other types of cross-national research too: since the seventies the study of 'electoral volatility' in Western Europe gained momentum, when it appeared that the division of party systems and the structure of voting patterns was less stabilized than originally assumed (Crewe/Denver, 1985; Daalder/Mair, 1984). It is interesting to note (with the help of hindsight) that most analyses were, in fact, based on country-based analytical descriptions with little comparative information. What was lacking was a truly comparative set of theoretical references concerning - in this case - the *explicandum* i.e. 'political stability' that at the same time is consciously linked to a comparable set of operational terms (see: Bartolini/Mair, 1990: 35-46).

The same observation can be made with respect to the study of government formation. On the one hand, there are collections of country-studies (more often than not, I hasten to add, developed on a shared list of elements present in each case description; e.g. Pridham, 1986) that stress the idiosyncratic nature of a country's political process, rather than the communality of the development under review. On the other hand, a development can be observed with respect to the politics of coalition-building in which an underlying theoretical argument has been developed that directs the research, where countries are not the principal focus, but a collection of comparable cases that show variation concerning what is to be explained (e.g. Laver/Schofield, 1990; Budge/Keman, 1990). Other examples could be mentioned to support this point regarding the relation between theory and method in comparative politics (such as the comparative research into the relation between 'politics & policy'; see: Castles, 1989; Schmidt, 1991; Keman/Lehner, 1984; Chapter 7 & 8 in this book). Yet, the principal message is that much of the research that is labeled as comparative, either lacks theoretical foundation, or is based on a research design that is not comparative.

In fact, what one often sees, as Sigelman and Gadbois (1983) have found for the United States, is that the majority of studies published as being comparative are single nation studies. Even if this criterion is relaxed (i.e. case-studies with a comparative focus) the non-comparative studies are one-third of the total reviewed. The same applies to textbooks and courses on comparative politics. Mayer (1983) concludes that nearly half of these are basically country-focussed presentations without a clear overarching theme or comparative focus. Again, however useful and interesting these studies, textbooks and courses actually may be, they are not genuinely representing comparative politics nor, for that matter, enhancing it as a distinctive field within political science. What is needed, therefore, is to examine the possibility of developing a theoretical perspective of the 'core subject' of comparative politics.

2.3   Modes of Explanation in Comparative Politics: Topics and Approaches

The 'history' of the theoretical development has by and large already been told in Chapter 1 and can be characterized by the development from 'grand theories' spilling over in central topics and related concepts which gradually evolved in more or less separate approaches (see also: Nohlen, 1983: 1077-1079; Wiarda, 1986: Chapter 1; Macridis, 1986; Berg-Schlosser et al., 1987). What is remarkable is that in most contributions the core subject under review is either taken for granted, or assumed to be self-evident (e.g. Blondel, 1981). 'Politics' is what governments do (or do not do), the actions of politicians and (their) parties, the institutions that make up a political system and also the process of policy-formation. Yet, little is said about what the nature of politics is, apart from referring to it as an inevitably 'contested notion' (Cf. Connolly, 1983).

I shall not endeavor to put forward here a neatly packaged definition of politics, but rather attempt to show that it is possible to circumscribe it in terms of reference that enables us to distinguish 'politics' from other phenomena in society. I feel this to be necessary, since many of the theories that have been used in comparative politics have failed to recognize that without a coherent circumscription of its core subject, i.e. the 'Political', explanations have tended to become de-politicized. Hence, the theory was not using politics as an explicandum, but as what had to be explained by other non-political features. This development can be amply illustrated by means of the 'grand theories' which were in essence cultural, or functional explanations of political behavior, or conversely remained 'economistic' in nature.

It is not relevant for our discourse to repeat here the criticisms on these socio-cultural inclined 'grand' theories of comparative politics. Our aim is rather to demonstrate that the developments in this field led to a kind of theoretical 'escapism' by an attempt to explain politics by means of *non*-political features of a society and to create an almost ideal-typical concept of political behavior: the concept of the 'proper' citizen, who would enhance the (value-related) concept of the 'best' political system, namely sustaining the working of democracy. Such an approach, however, will often not lead to a theory about the political process, but rather will offer an explanation about its socio-cultural preconditions. Hence my point here is not whether the theory or methodology is correct or not, but rather that this approach is missing the important point of explaining what the political process itself is about (see: Blondel, 1981; Roberts, 1978; Keman, 1992a).

In the same mold is, albeit from another angle, the 'economistic' approach (see for this distinction: Barry, 1970). The 'rational choice' school is less guilty of 'escapism' and confusing research designs. Yet, in this approach the main problem is the extent to which the concept of rationality is narrowly defined or not (see: the Chapters 4 & 5 in this book; for an excellent overview consult: Renwick Monroe, 1991), the degree to which the topic under review is essentially still formulated in terms of individual behavior (i.e. on the microlevel of observation), and thirdly, whether or not these theories are - implicitly or explicitly - equating the 'logic' of the market with the 'logic' of the political arena. These criticisms point to a central problem of this approach in terms of theory and research: an 'economistic' concept of rationality suffers from an ecological bias (both on the level of formulating hypotheses and of measuring beyond the level of individual behavior; Dogan/Rokkan, 1966), on the one hand, and from the fact that there is more to politics than can be explained by economic rationality alone, on the other. However, it must be noted that protagonists of the rational choice-approach have attempted to solve this problem. Both the 'public choice' literature (e.g. Mueller, 1989; van den Doel/van Velthoven, 1989) and the development of the so-called 'positive political economy' (e.g. Laver, 1986; Alt/Shepsle, 1990) elaborate the political process *per se* by means of the institutions that direct the scope of rational behavior of the participants and the consequences in terms of interdependent relations (Scharpf, 1987; North, 1990; Chapter 7 in this book). Notwithstanding the fact that these developments are promising, it is not yet clear to what extent this type of explanation will eventually lead to a genuine definition of the political process as a core subject of investigation in comparative politics.

In sum: whatever the merits of these approaches are as potential explanations of politics, they do not tell us much about the nature of politics, and therefore are not really theories of the political process, but are instead possible explanations about political phenomena and (series of) political events. How then should we proceed from here if socio-cultural and socio-economic properties are to be considered merely relevant as *contextual* variables in explaining variations of politics, but not always adding knowledge about the 'political' itself?

Generally speaking comparativists have proceeded from this point either in the direction of focusing on central concepts, or they have resorted to a 'scientific' mode of explanation by applying the canons of empirical-analytical methodology (including high-powered statistical techniques) to political topics.

The first approach, for example, concentrated on various topics like democracy, political regimes, parliaments, revolutions, welfare states, war & peace, etc. (see for an extensive list of such topics, including the literature: Berg-Schlosser et al., 1987: 271-304). The 'scientific' approach did not differ from the first in this respect, but concentrated much more on the question whether or not hypotheses could be corroborated by available, quantifiable data. Again, this certainly added to the body of knowledge of political situations, events and societal development, but hardly answered the question what politics was all about and how politics itself may have an impact on societal developments. In other words: it appears that we know a lot about politics in the real world, and due to comparative research how different its complexion can be, but at the same time we know preciously little about its nature and the extent to which it is an *independent* explanatory factor.

An example of this latter issue is a debate within comparative politics on the question whether or not 'Politics Does Matter' (see: Castles, 1982: 4-15; von Beyme, 1985: 334-359; Keman, 1988: 71-75; Gallagher et al, 1991: 236ff). It has been one of the first attempts to re-install the 'political' (here: parties and governments) in comparative politics as a variable influencing societal developments. On the one hand, the debate focussed on a topical relation, i.e. democratic decision-making and public policy-formation; on the other hand, it searched for the method to prove right from wrong. Both the theoretical conceptualization and the correct comparative method were at issue. Regardless of the result of this debate, it demonstrated that seemingly endless debates were possible on concepts itself, the way of analyzing it and the data and techniques used and so on. At the end of the day it appeared, dependent on the countries studied, the time-period under review, the level of measurement and the operationalizations employed, that all contenders were sometimes right and sometimes wrong (see also: Castles, 1987; 1989; Keman, 1990). Undoubtedly, this debate within the realm of comparative public policy analysis has helped to further our knowledge of political processes and the usage of the comparative methods. However, it also shows that without a clear view of what the core subject actually is, both the methods used and the data collected cannot really enhance our knowledge of 'politics' as such. Moreover, it does not help us to define and describe comparative politics as a distinctive approach within political science.

2.4 The Political as the Core Subject of Comparative Politics

The 'political' in a society can be described on the basis of three dimensions: politics, polity and policy (Schmidt, 1991; Keman, 1992a). Politics is then what I would like to call the *political process*. On this level actors (mostly aggregates of individuals organized in parties, movements, or groups) interact with each other when they have conflicting interests or views regarding societal issues that cannot be solved by themselves (i.e. deficiency of self-regulation). The process of solving those problems which make actors clash, is more often than not visible through the *institutions* that have emerged in order to facilitate conflict resolution. Institutions help to develop coalescence and to achieve a consensus among conflicting actors through compromising alternative preferences. These institutions manifest themselves in the rules of the game in a society. This is what is meant with the 'polity'. To put it more formally, rules are humanly devised constraints that shape political interaction. Institutions are here considered to be both formal, like for instance in a constitution, and can be enforced, and informal, i.e. they evolve over time and are respected as a code of conduct by most actors involved[2].

The necessity to solve deepseated societal conflicts and thus the need for effective 'rules' which enable a political consensus among contestants can be understood as follows: firstly, rules reduce uncertainty among the actors involved, hence they can act strategically (see Chapter 5 in this book); secondly, they provide room for exchange and compromises for those problems that are aptly circumscribed by Ostrom (1990) as "common pool requirements". The options chosen or decided upon for political action to solve the problem (in whatever form, i.e. this also includes non-decisions and non-actions) is what we shall call *policy formation*. This process is equivalent to what others would call 'state-intervention' or the 'authoritative allocation of values in a society'. The actions of the state or the allocating agency are in this conceptualization of the 'political' viewed as relatively independent from societal interests (Skocpol, 1985: 45). That is to say: political action, i.e. the relation between politics and policy-making, requires a degree of autonomy in order to be feasible and effective. If this is not the case then the political process is merely 'ritual' and indeed simply a reflection of societal features and developments. In short, a theory of the political process must assume that there exists a mutual and interdependent relation between politics and society, and that its organization is to a large extent independent from society. The issue at hand is then to investigate to what extent and in what way this process can be observed and affects social and economic developments.

It should be kept in mind, that the triad of "politics-polity-policy" in itself is *not* a theory of the political process. It is instead a *heuristic* device to delineate the 'political' from the 'non-political'. This description of the 'political', however, makes it possible to elaborate on the core subject of compa-

---

[2] It should be noted that both the informal and the formal 'rules of the game' depend on the fact whether or not they are enforcable, i.e. whereas the 'Rule of Law' in a liberal democracy is in most instances accepted and adhered to, this is less self-evident with the informal rules. Here the efficacy depends on the fact whether or not the actors involved in the 'game' are able to sanction each other for non-cooperation, defection or non-compliance; see also: Laver, 1981; Axelrod, 1984; Scharpf, 1987; Ostrom, 1990; Keman, 1992a.

rative politics. That is to say that all those processes that can be defined by means of these three dimensions are worthy of our attention as long as the analysis requires comparison in order to explain the process. The next step therefore is to specify the *unit of analysis* for comparative purposes.

This is a more complex undertaking than it appears since, as Ragin (1987: 7-9) and Przeworski (1987: 2-4) correctly point out, the unit of analysis is not by definition the same as the properties under review, but may also indicate the theoretical categories that direct the research question at the same time. The term 'unit of analysis' can have two meanings therefore: on the one hand it signifies an elaboration of the theoretical argument, on the other hand it concerns the translation of the theory in properties to be observed empirically.

A number of comparative researchers have drawn attention to this confusing way of using the term 'unit of analysis', which easily leads to equating description with explanation. However, it is quite important to know exactly what is under discussion, if we wish to validate theoretical statements by means of empirical knowledge. Przeworski and Teune propose a distinction between 'levels of observation' and 'levels of analysis' (1970: 50), whereas Ragin introduces the terms 'observational unit' and 'explanatory unit' (Ragin, 1987: 8-9). Both these distinctions between respectively empirical knowledge and theoretical statements appear useful, but I still find them confusing.

Levels or units of observation and analysis may either appear to correspond, as is the case with, for example, studies of political parties and party systems, or in fact do not intersect (e.g. with respect to theories of the world system, where the explanatory variable, the system, by definition equals the observational units, i.e. the nation-states). However, in both these examples, both units are, in one way or another, supposed to be conceptually interlinked. Whatever name one gives it, it does not solve the problem at hand. The comparative analysis of the 'political' always involves a multi-level type of argument. Hence, it involves the observations of comparable parts that are considered to be an analytical whole. Of course, both Ragin and Przeworski realize this also, but instead of specifying the core subject of comparative politics, they resort to a methodological refinement as a solution. I therefore propose to consider the unit of analysis to encompass every topic that can be formulated in terms of the heuristic triad of politics, polity and policy. The unit of observation is then simply the operationalization of the 'triad' in comparative perspective, making them belong to the field of comparative politics. That is, if the question under review can only be explained in terms of *macro*-scopical properties which vary from one system to another.

To give a concrete example: the study of the development of the welfare state is not, by definition, a subject of comparative political research. In my view, it becomes a comparative topic only, if an attempt is made to explain this development by means of macro-political properties such as conflicting interests between economic classes. These conflicts are, depending on the existing features of the liberal democratic state, fought out and subsequently may result in a patterned variation of public policy-formation at the system-level of the state. Hence the core subject is not the welfare state, but instead the extent to which politics, polity and policy can be identified as properties of the political process. This being the case, the extent to which elements of this process are relevant, is explaining the *political* development of the welfare state.

Alternatively, if one focusses on 'classes' it is not their existence *per se* that matters, but their degree of political action which may, for instance, explain the emergence, or the change of political institutions (e.g. the rule of universal suffrage, or the role of trade unions in the decision-making process). In the latter case, i.e. institutional change, the 'political' is regarded as *consequential*, whereas in the first example, i.e. the development of the welfare state the 'political' is *explanatory*. In both examples the unit of analysis is expressed in terms of macro-scopical properties related to the political process, and measured or observed across systems or across time within a system at a level that is representing a coherent political unit. Politics, polity, and policy are thus in my view a set of theoretical references as well as an empirical point of reference, which form together the core subject of comparative politics.

Although here the core subject of comparative politics has been specified in relation to the 'political' in a society, it does not imply that we have a theory too. This implies that an appropriate (meta-)theoretical approach should be related to the macro-scopical properties, which represent the features of politics, polity and policy. This means, in my view, that approaches which are basically formulated on the *micro*-level are less likely to be useful to explain political processes (like, for instance, economistic explanations of government formation; see: Lijphart, 1984: 46-66). The same applies to 'grand theories' that depart from one overarching concept (like, for instance, political development;

see: Mayer, 1989: 64-74; Lane/Ersson, 1990: 90-126), or theories that are in fact based on socio-economic or socio-cultural features (see: Rokkan, 1970; Dogan/Pelassy, 1990: 3-44). The problem is namely that these *macro*-societal approaches cannot separate the political from the non-political in their explanation of events, situations or developments.

Rather than looking for broad concepts or micro-based theories it appears to me that a theoretical approach in comparative politics should be focusing on the interaction between political actors and institutions, in which way this interaction influences a system's capacity to perform in accordance with the needs and demands of a society. A viable trajectory to follow is the political economy of institutionalized behavior of interdependent actors in relation to the political actions which are, in turn, molded by the political organization of the state in a society (see: Laver, 1986; Krasner, 1988; North, 1990; Scharpf, 1987; 1991; Strom, 1990; Alt/Shepsle, 1990; Budge/Keman, 1990; Ostrom, 1990; Czada/Windhoff-Héritier, 1991; Grafstein, 1991; Schmidt, 1991; Olsen, 1991; Keman, 1992a). What these authors have in common, is the idea that actor-related behavior (i.e. 'politics') must be understood within the context of political institutions (i.e. 'polity'). In addition, that the variation of the policy performance of a political system can to a large extent be accounted for by examining the patterned interaction between the working of institutions and the related room for manoeuver of political actors.

Hence the *theory-guided* question of comparative politics is to what extent the 'political', the core subject of comparative politics, can indeed account for, and is shaped by the political actions in one system compared to another. It is this process and the attempts to explain it by systematic comparison that distinguishes comparative politics from other fields in political science and it at the same time makes it a field within political science. Which brings us to the next question this essay seeks to answer: how and when to compare in a methodologically sound fashion?

2.5 *The Meaning and Use of the Comparative Method*

There is little dispute about the comparative method being the most distinctive feature of comparative politics. Yet, at the same time there has been a continuing debate about what, when, why and how to compare (e.g. Lijphart, 1975; Roberts, 1978; Dogan/Pelassy, 1990; Rueschemeyer et al., 1991). There is no need here to go into the comparative method as such (see: Przeworski/Teune, 1970; Merrit/Rokkan, 1966; Mayer, 1972). In view of the theoretical perspective developed in the previous section, I would instead like to focus on the extant methodological controversies which this debate provoked.

What to compare? Rather than focusing on 'macro-social', 'societal' or 'contextual' entities, it should now be clear that I propose to study the 'political' in a society. This further implies that the conceptualization of 'politics, polity and policy' as a comparative tool is the major methodological concern. The social and economic configuration of a society, or situation is not the primary goal or meaning of comparison, instead capturing the *specifica differentia* of the 'political' across situations and across time will have my concern.

By taking this point seriously, there are a number of implications for the controversies on the comparative method. It concerns questions like:

- whether or not *political science per se is comparative by nature* (e.g. Almond, 1966; Lasswell, 1968; Przeworski/Teune, 1970; Lewis er al., 1978; Mayer, 1989).
- whether or not the *substance*, i.e. the relationship between theory and reality, *defines the correct approach* in terms of case-studies, cross-sectional analysis, variable-oriented (often equated with statistics) research designs (e.g. Lijphart, 1971; 1975; Przeworski, 1987; Ragin, 1987).
- whether or not comparisons are only meaningful by applying the *longitudinal* dimension and *confine the number of relevant cases* to analyze (e.g. O'Donnel, 1979; Castles, 1989; Bartolini, 1991; Rueschemeyer et al., 1991).
- whether or not *causal explanation* is achieved by means of empirical-statistical corroboration (Ragin, 1987; Lijphart, 1975; Holt/Turner, 1970; Smelser, 1976).

The first issue is more or less reminiscent of the transition from the 'behavioral' dominance in political science and its attempt to achieve 'scientific' status (Mayer, 1972). The comparative method was considered to be the ideal platform, if executed on the basis of statistical techniques of data-collection, variable construction and causal modelling, to reach this status (e.g. Holt/Turner, 1970).

This position strongly coincided with the search for a 'grand theory' of politics. Apart from the fact that for various reasons 'scienticism' in the social sciences has lost its appeal, it simply induced a situation in which we lost track of what the substance, i.e. the 'political', is (Mayer, 1989: 56-57). Francis Castles (1987) has succinctly pointed out that "the major incongruity is not a matter of theory not fitting the facts, but of the facts fitting too many theories" (p.198).

Thus, even if one knew *what* to compare, the refined techniques cannot really help us in deciding what is right or wrong, since what we often lack is a adequate theoretical perspective that is consciously elaborated in proper conceptualizations of the 'political'.

The latter point, i.e. the relation between conceptualization and operationalization (Sartori, 1970; Lijphart, 1975; Scheuch, 1980; Przeworski, 1987) has been taken up since the early 1970s. Even if one thinks one knows what to compare, the question remains of how to translate it into proper terms for empirical research.

As I pointed out in the preceding section the use of the term 'unit of analysis' is confusing, moreover I concluded that this issue cannot and should not be solved by means of a methodological point of view alone, but instead ought to be primarily formulated in terms of the core subject of comparative politics. However, this task remains unresolved by the definition of the core subject of the 'political'. It essentially means that one has to chose, on the basis of a topical research question that is formulated in terms of the 'political', the correct research design (see for this: Robertson, 1978; Schmidt, 1987; Keman, 1988; Rueschemeyer et al., 1991). The question *what* to compare leads to the matter of *how* to compare.

Generally speaking, the 'logic' of comparative research goes back to the famous predicament of John Stuart Mill (1806-1873) which has led to the equally well-known distinction between the 'most similar' and the 'most different systems' design for comparing (Przeworski/Teune, 1970: 32). Most comparativists agree on this distinction, but differ on the question of whether or not the research design should be based on as many similar cases as possible, or upon a small number of dissimilar cases. The first approach leads easily to the so-called 'Galtons problem' (Lijphart, 1975: 171), that is to say: few cases, many variables, which make it difficult to arrive at conclusions of a causal nature. This is ultimately the result of 'diffusion' (i.e. processes of historical learning), which leads to spurious relationships, or to 'overdetermination' (i.e. even if cases are, to a large degree, similar, the remaining differences will be large due to the use of concepts that are too broadly operationalized) and in turn this situation will affect the relation between apparently independent variables and the dependent phenomenon (Przeworski/Teune, 1970: 34; Przeworski, 1987: 38-39). As far as I can see, there is, as of yet, no proper solution to this problem. It is by and large due to the dynamic nature of social reality, which cannot be captured by means of controlled experiments.

This problem, inherent to the substance of social sciences, is thus also an inevitable problem of comparative research of the 'political'. Rather than abandoning empirical research aimed at explanatory results altogether (like, for example, MacIntyre, 1971 concludes). Instead I suggest to take into account the limitations and constraints of the comparative method and to attempt to develop a research design that is suitable for the research question under review (see also: Ragin, 1987: 9-10).

Four issues with regard to method are to be observed when a research design is developed. Firstly, the context of what is compared; secondly, the role of 'time' with respect to the problem under scrutiny; thirdly, the level of inquiry, i.e. the micro-macro link; and fourthly, the number of cases involved. These issues are equally important and decisions made upon them will have a great impact on the plausibility, validity and quality of the outcomes of a comparative research project.

Contextual variables are those variables that make up the environment of the core subject, i.e. of the 'political'. A 'most similar' design is intended to reduce them to the barest possible minimum by means of selecting cases (or: systems) that are by and large identical, except for the relations between variables under review that represent the research question, i.e. what is to be explained. The debate on 'Does Politics Matter' which I referred to, or the analysis of the development of welfare states that I mentioned, are both examples of how important the choice of cases is in relation to the analytical conclusions based on them. For instance, comparing non-democratic regimes with democratic ones, or 'young' democratic systems with long established ones could lead to conclusions of whether or not parties do play a role in political decision-making. However, such a comparison would not render information ragarding about the question to what extent political parties in parliamentary democracies do matter with respect to policy formation in general, or whether party differences are relevant for the development of welfare statism (Castles, 1982; von Beyme, 1985; Schmidt, 1987; Keman, 1990).

Moreover, the number of variables not controlled for in such a research design would be immense and would thus engender Galton's problem. Obviously, this is an erroneous path to take, although it is worth noting it has been suggested that the problem could be by-passed by using functional equivalents, i.e. assuming that particular actors and institutions in one system are identical to certain phenomena in an other system. For instance the role of 'leaders' in the Third World and 'traditional' modes of decision-making could be compared with the ways party elites and concomitant bargaining take place in a parliamentary democracy (Dogan/Pelassy, 1990: 37-43). However, given the already existing problems of comparing on the basis of similarity I do not consider this a sound trajectory to follow. The number of contextual variables must be low in the eventuality of a research question that is akin to the most similar approach, and even in a most different design the number of 'contextual' variables should not be excessive, otherwise one would end up with conclusions that everything is indeed different and all situations are peculiar by definition. It is the enduring paradox of Scylla and Charybdis, and there is no easy solution.

Much comparative research is characterized by a *time*-dimension. This poses a number of problems which are related to the consequentality of time itself, the number of cases that can be studied and finally, the measurement of time in terms of variation (Grew, 1978: Flora, 1974; Bartolini, 1992). Bartolini notes that, surprisingly enough, the historical method is rarely disputed by social scientists. However, there exists a large body of literature within historiography that discusses the complexities of temporal variance and its explanatory value (Romein, 1971; Braudel, 1977; Althusser, 1983; Burke, 1978) and has revolved around the so-called 'Annales' school. Like the pervasive discussion within social science on levels of measurement, i.e. the micro-meso-macro linkages, the 'Annales' (and Braudel in particular) attempted to differentiate 'time' by distinguishing three levels of diachronic development: the long term (macro), the cyclical movement (meso), and the occurrence of events (micro). The long term development structures the other levels and makes it possible to relate events to cycles and, according to Braudel, events can be understood in their proper historical context. In this way, it was claimed, objects of study, such as the political development of a society, can be compared as if they were synchronical. Yet, a problem remains that one is implicitly assuming that the structuration of time is a result of a few, universal factors (for instance, the impact of processes of 'modernization'). Hence, time remains uni-dimensionally defined and is therefore potentially an overdetermining factor.

The alternative route, which is often advocated, is to incorporate time in the research-design by means of a case study design (Abrams, 1982; Tilly, 1984; Skocpol, 1985; Ragin, 1991). Apart from the problem of the time dimension in relation to consequentality, another problem is contained in the conceptualization of the 'political': are we looking at the same phenomenon through time or at functional equivalents? In other words: is the *development* of a political process captured over time, or does it concern the cross-time *variation* in a political phenomenon[3]?

As Bartolini correctly points out, there is no fundamental (or logical) difference between using a synchronical or a diachronical research-design. In both cases the comparativist has to grapple with the fact of whether or not the observed variation is part and parcel of both the independent and dependent variables. Hence, the so-called qualitative comparative case approach (Ragin, 1991; O'Donnel, 1979) which claims to be superior to the quantitative comparative spatial approach is wrong-footed, as long as its proponents do not supply us with a logical argument that the time dimension can only be applied in a comparative analysis based on case studies.

Again, I would instead suggest to reach a decision on the use of time in a research-design on the basis of the research-question. If one investigates, for instance, economic policy-making in OECD-countries, one may make use of a *periodization* which represents a similar incident or event in all the cases under review (see Chapter 8 in this book). If one wishes to analyze the development

---

[3] Barrington Moore (1966) is an example of a study of the development of democracy over time, whereas the analysis of revolutions by Skocpol (1979) concerns a cross-time research design. Barrington Moore's research is in search of the consequentiality of a political process. Conversely Theda Skocpol focusses on the patterned variation in the occurence of a similar political phenomenon. Both authors ask the same research question, namely how to account for a political process, but use a different research design regarding the time dimension.

of 'welfare statism' one could decide to use *time-series* analysis, whether or not it concerns one or more countries. A final example of choosing a research design may be the study of processes of democratization of a society. To do this on the basis of a single case-study is very well justified and useful (e.g. Daalder, 1966; Rokkan, 1966), but a comparative investigation of this process diachronically can be equally justified and useful (e.g. Lipset, 1963; Rueschemeyer et al., 1991). All these examples demonstrate that time can be explicitly taken into account with respect to the research-design. However, the choice in what way this is done has more to do with the research question than with a specific approach of including time into comparative research.

Contrary to the time dimension, as has been pointed out here, the problems with spatial analysis have been discussed at great length. Spatial analysis has to do with the level of measurement in relation to the selection of cases under review. Lijphart (1971) in his seminal article, distinguishes three types of spatial analysis, namely: statistically based, case-oriented, and the comparable case approach (see also: Ragin, 1987; Rueschemeyer et al., 1991). Ragin, in particular, overstates the differences between the various methodological approaches. He develops a dichotomy that is separates the 'case-oriented' from the 'variable-related' research design. The first approach would enable the comparativist to analyze the 'political' more comprehensively than would be possible by means of a 'few variables, many cases' approach. The latter method is, in Ragin's view, inferior to the 'comparable case' approach because the relationships observed are bound to be biased or 'overdetermined' as a result of empirical indicators which are either too generally constructed or measured at a highly aggregated level. Hence conclusions based on (quantitative) broad comparative analyses are often only seemingly (statistically) robust and the causal interpretations not always as valid as is pretended they are (see also: Robertson, 1978; Przeworski, 1987).

However valuable these insights may be and how important a reflection on these issues is, it concerns an argument, which is a false one. In my view behind these arguments there is essentially a difference in epistimological tradition and even in 'belief systems' or paradigmata. The differences between research designs is often exaggerated and often not based on logical arguments. It is quality (i.e. historical knowledge) versus quantity (i.e. analytical empiricism), holistic explanations versus parsimonious modelling, interpreting patterned diversity (e.g. on the basis of a 'most different' design) versus judging patterned variation (by means of a 'most similar' design), detailed knowledge of the cases versus theoretical knowledge from relations and so on (Ragin, 1987: Ch. 2 and 3). Yet, is there really such a difference between the two approaches that warrants such strong views on the rights and wrongs of either approach? It is obvious, that I do not think this to be the case nor that it is necessary (see also: Rueschemeyer et al., 1991: 27ff on this point). Elsewhere I have attempted to clarify this point about applying the logic of comparison to a research question as a means to develop a theory within the field of comparative politics:

> "to construct a theory at all one has to simplify and generalize, rather than describe. There is no point in constructing a general explanation clogged up with minutiae of time and place. The purpose of a theory is to catch and specify general tendencies, even at the cost of not fitting *all* cases (hence one can check it only statistically, and it is no disproof to cite one or two counter-examples). The theory should, however, fit the majority of cases at least in a general way, and provide a sensible and above all an applicable starting-point for discussion of any particular situation, even one which in the end it turns out not to explain -- here it can at any rate serve as the basis of a special analysis which shows which (presumably unique or idiosyncratic) factors prevent it from fitting.
> A general theory of this kind serves the historian by providing him with an entry point and starting-ideas. These, we would argue, he always brings to the case anyway; with a validated theory he knows they are reasonably founded and has a context within which he can make comparisons with greater confidence. As we suggested at the outset, there is no inherent conflict between historical analysis and general theory. Each can, indeed must, be informed by the other and supplement the other's efforts. Theory is therefore a *necessary* simplification and generalization of particular motives and influences, not simply a restatement of them, though complete loss of contact with historical reality will render it too abstract and ultimately irrelevant."(Budge/Keman, 1990: 194)

2.6 Comparative Politics as a Distinctive Approach in Political Science

The main argument throughout this essay has been that the purpose of applying the comparative method in political science is to identify regularities regarding the relationship between societal and political actors, the accompanying processes of institutionalization of political life, and the societal change that emerged simultaneouly. In addition the logic of comparison is seen as the 'royal way' to establish theoretical and empirically refutable propositions that explain these regularities in terms of causality.

To this end, comparative politics as a distinctive approach selects and compares the 'political' in a variety of different situations. *Comparative* analysis is considered to provide a greater opportunity to analyze a greater variety of political behavior and institutions, within and among political systems. Assuming, one knows what to compare and foremost why, the proper research design can be developed to allow for an analysis that accounts in a plausible way for the research question. Thus, it is not a matter of discovering a particular method that can be considered as quasi-paradigmatic for comparative politics.

There are a number of options open to the comparative researcher. In the process of selecting the correct research design one should be aware of the caveats and pitfalls of the several approaches that are in existence. Instead, comparative political science may be defined by the use of a particular core subject, i.e. the triad of *politics-polity-policy*, which involves understanding of:

- firstly, how concepts are derived from the 'political' in relation to the research question posed;
- secondly, how these concepts can be made to "travel" from one system (understood here in relation to the unit of analysis) to another;
- thirdly, how a set of units of observation can be developed within which systems may be compared and classified;
- finally, how and when one compares similar and dissimilar systems, synchronically and/or diachronically; and how and when case-studies may contribute to more general theoretical knowledge.

The understanding of these 'rules' is vitally important for every student of comparative politics and distinguishes it from other fields within political science. They characterize the distinctiveness of comparative politics. In the following table the main distinguishing features, which have been discussed in this chapter, of comparative politics as a *distinctive* field are summarized (see for this also: Nohlen, 1983: 1083):

Core Subject: the *political*	*Level of Observation*	*Time Dimension*	*N. of Cases*	*Contextual Variables*
1. Politics, Polity & Policy	Political System & Society	Synchronical Diachronical	Many Few	Heterogeneous Homogeneous
2. Politics & Polity	Intra-System	Synchronical Diachronical	Many Few	Homogeneous Homogeneous
3. Polity & Policy	Inter-System	Synchronical Periodical	Many Fewer	Heterogeneous Homogeneous
4. Politics	World System	Diachronical	One	Heterogeneous

Of course, other classifications are also possible, but the main point is that a student of comparative politics learns how to develop his or her research design by systematically assessing which options are available on the basis of the research question under review. Such a research design must then be conceptualized in terms of the 'political' that is competent not only answering the specific question under review, but also enhances our (meta-)theoretical understanding of the political process, the 'core subject', for instance in 'rational institutionalist' terms.

Examples of comparative research which can be categorized within this framework are the cross-national analysis of political performance (core subject #1) throughout the world by Powell (1982), the comparative analysis of the politics of government formation (core subject #2), the development of the welfare state (core subject #3), and the 'world system' approach (core subject #4). In all these instances important choices were made to connect the research question with a research design. Budge and Keman, for instance, consciously choose to explain the process of government formation in terms of actors (i.e. political parties) in relation to their room for manoeuver due to existing modes of institutionalized behavior (the 'rules of the game'). The level of observation is 'intra-system' oriented and to increase the number of meaningful cases within a 'most similarity' strategy of comparison (i.e. reducing the contextual variables) are assumed to be homogenous). The diachronical perspective is preferred here to a case based strategy or a mere country based comparative approach. Two arguments justify this decision: firstly, not countries are the units of analysis but parties and governments, and the time dimension is considered to be constant; secondly, given the 'rational institutionalist' point of departure as a mode of explanation and the wish to validate the research question empirically, as much cases as possible had to be collected as units of observation.

It is vitally important that an understanding of these "rules" for doing systematically comparative research forms an essential part of learning and training not only in comparative politics in particular, but also in political science in general. Ultimately this is one of the reasons why a grounding in comparative politics is so essential to a wider political science education. Political science in general, which has been accurately defined as "an academic discipline which seeks to systematically describe, analyze and explain the operations of government institutions and overtly political organizations" must necessarily include comparative politics, if only by virtue of its explanatory intent. Indeed, perhaps the only single circumstance in which a general political scientist is not also at least implicitly a comparative political scientist is when he, or she remains consistently and exclusively concerned with his, or her own national system. However, even then, any attempt to explain one's own system *entirely* without reference to either the experience of other systems or across time (explicit comparison) or to those theories which have been derived from the experience of other systems (implicit comparison) is almost always doomed to failure.

But if we are to know other countries, and, through this, to begin to understand how politics works, then it is essential that we promote an understanding of how to do comparative political analysis, and of how to become "conscious" comparativist. And this, more than anything else, requires us to include comparative politics, and the comparative method, as core elements of a more general political science program. Without such an approach, we will end up by training our students simply to interpret the national experience for the benefit of a more comparatively inclined foreign audience, instead of developing systematic explanations of the political process.

3. Comparative Studies of Elections and Political Science

Cees van der Eijk

Elections are one of the most familiar political phenomena all over the world. Owing to their clear structure, their regularity, their observable nature, their normative and alleged empirical importance they are also among the most frequently studied phenomena in empirical political science. Little wonder that they offer a fertile area for comparative studies. Yet the area of comparative studies of elections is hardly integrated. Distinct sub-areas exist in relative isolation from one another, each addressing different substantive questions.

This essay attempts to approach the field of comparative electoral studies from the perspective of political science. How can studies of elections contribute to political science? This discussion is followed by a summary of findings and interpretations from recent studies on electoral change in Western countries which is intended as an illustration of how studies of elections help increase understanding of politics. Finally, a brief agenda of future research is comparative studies of elections is discussed.

3.1 *Election Studies and Political Science*

A brief survey of the literature suffices to show that studies of elections, irrespective of whether or not they are comparative in character, focus on apparently quite different phenomena. Frequently they are classified in a few, rather broad categories.

On the empirical side, one can find for instance studies on *election rules and procedures*. This area is characterized by keywords such as electoral systems, suffrage and enfranchisement, electoral (and sometimes constitutional) law, the administration of electoral law, the history of electoral procedures, registration, electoral reform, electoral fraud, electoral formulae, electoral bias, electoral recall, redistribution (the British term) or reapportionment (the American equivalent), thresholds, indirect elections, electoral colleges, political finance, etc.

A quite different area of study is that of *election results and their aggregate distributions*. This is an area of macro-analysis, where relevant terms include electoral geography, electoral cleavages, normal vote analyses, electoral change, constituencies, (again) redistribution and reapportionment, electoral sociology, popularity functions, electoral cycles, etc.

A third large part of the literature is concerned with *voter behavior*. Characteristic terms in this area of micro-analysis are, amongst others, electoral participation, party choice, party identification, issue preferences, candidate evaluations, political ideologies, (non)rational choice, as well as all kinds of attitudinal referents such as competence, apathy, efficacy, alienation, (post)materialism, etc.

Yet another area focusses on the agents who compete for votes, and the way in which they do so: *candidates, parties and their campaigns*. The relevant vocabulary of this area includes: recruitment, selection and nomination, election campaigns, political financing, political communication and mass media, propaganda, primaries, canvassing.

In addition to empirically oriented literature, there is a vast body of work which is primarily normative or conceptual in nature. Implicitly or explicitly, much of this work centers around the relationship between *elections and democracy*. Some of this work is very general in nature, some of it centers around the (mathematical) (im)possibility of voting procedures being proof against manipulation, and some is specifically directed towards the pros and cons of different electoral systems. Still different bodies of literature, which may be empirical as well as normative in character, deal with phenomena such as referenda, plebiscites, initiatives and recall.

In addition to the topics mentioned above, a multitude of additional subjects can be found in the literature of electoral studies, as well as additional and alternative ways of categorizing them. In view of this diversity, one might wonder whether it makes sense at all to speak about *the* field of electoral studies. After all, what do have studies in common which deal with, for example, the determinants of turnout in American elections (Wolfinger/Rosenstone, 1980), funding of political parties in Britain, (Ewing, 1987), constitutional design and elections (Powell, 1989), the impact of issues on party choice in the European elections of 1989 (Kuechler, 1991), and similarities between voters and their representatives in the Netherlands (Thomassen, 1976)? At times one could also wonder about the relevance to political science of a large number of the sometimes esoteric topics researched. Why should political scientists concern themselves in great detail with phenomena which at first sight seem to belong to the realm of (social) psychology, or law, or sociology, or history? Already in 1967 it was, correctly, observed that

> "work in the field is now a recognized sub-discipline within political science. Limited consideration, however, is given to the relevance of voting and elections for the political system as a whole" (Rose/Mossawir, 1967: 173).

The relevance of this observation has hardly diminished since then.

The contribution and relevance of electoral research to political science is difficult to assess from a categorization of the real-world topics addressed in such studies. As is the case in other disciplines as well, research into specific phenomena is relevant only because it contributes (or is assumed to contribute) to solving larger 'puzzles', the relevance of which is more obvious. The more developed a field of scientific inquiry becomes, the larger the number of seemingly esoteric details and sub-specializations. One can view these only in their proper place by stepping back into more general perspectives. In this case this means first of all to appraise the proper place of studies of elections in the discipline of political science.

From the perspective of political science the rationale for electoral studies is to determine what impact elections have on politics. Slightly more elaborated, this involves the task to elucidate -empirically as well as normatively- the *impact of the institution of regular elections on the character of the political system and the course of political processes*. Two elements of this description deserve clarification: character and course.

The term character is used in this context to denote how democratic a political system is, or how just it is, or equitable, open, efficient, stable, peaceful, etc. It refers to characterizations of the state of the political system, which are generally of a normative or moral kind. The meaning of such terms is never self-evident or uncontested, but can be appraised by analyzing the conceptual and theoretical foundations of the context within which they are used (refer to, e.g. Connolly, 1983). Character refers also to the way in which symbols, values, parties, population groups etc. are associated with one another, or, in the jargon of the discipline, to existing alignments in a political system which to a large extent constrain the processes of daily politics.

The course of political processes refers to the dynamics of a political system, the ongoing processes of power-acquisition, agenda formation, decision making, policy implementation, conflict resolution, etc. Character and course are necessarily interrelated. The course of political processes may alter the character of a system, which in turn facilitates or obstructs those processes develop in specific directions.

The rationale for electoral studies presented above presumes that the institution of regular elections does indeed affect character or course of politics. But how justified is this assumption? Is it more than merely a reiteration of one of the central ideological tenets of representative democracies? This chapter is based on the proposition that it is more than just that, at least to the extent that one is willing to make the assumption that character and course of politics are affected by the behavior of the individuals and groups. It is manifest that many people including those who command social and political institutions are convinced of the political relevance of elections and that they act accordingly. Were they not, the large investments would be inexplicable which they make in time, effort, money and other resources to conduct elections, to attempt to influence their outcome and to participate in them.

3.1.1 *Comparative Studies of Elections*

Having established in what the contribution can be of studies of elections to political science, the next question is what sets *comparative* studies of elections apart. For the study of politics, such comparative studies derive their value not from taking electoral behavior and election results as the phenomena whose variation is to be explained by systemic differences, but rather how variations in electoral phenomena (behavior, procedures, outcomes, etc.) affect politics. Furthermore, in the line of the rationale for electoral studies discussed above, comparative studies of elections also analyze the consequences of systemic or contextual differences on the impact which elections have on politics. The 'dependent' variables are thus, just as in the case of not explicitly comparative studies, the character of the political system and the course of political processes.

Systemic or contextual differences may be institutional in character, or political, cultural, social or economic. They should be identifiable as variables, and should not be referred to in terms of proper names of systems, periods, etc. (Przworski/Teune, 1970).

In principle, comparisons can be made across different dimensions. One possibility is, for example, comparison between different administrative or organizational levels of a single system, as when one compares within a single country local, regional and national elections. Alternatively, comparisons may be longitudinal, as when one compares within a single system elections at different times, i.e. elections conducted under different historical, economic, and possibly also different institutional, cultural or political circumstances. A third possibility is comparison between systems. Most frequently this involves national elections in different countries. Although not entirely correct, the last-mentioned case is most frequently referred to as 'comparative'. This chapter concentrates in particular on such cross-national comparative studies.[1]

---

[1] Cross-level and longitudinal comparisons have great value in comparative research. Cross-level comparisons within a single country often show the significance of systemic differences which are overlooked in cross-national comparisons. For example, differences in the autonomy of the political arena for which the elections are conducted have great impact, both on the behavior of actors in the electoral process (voters, parties, media, etc.), and on the systemic consequences of elections , e.g. Reif/Schmitt, 1980; Van der Eijk et al., 1992). Cross-level and longitudinal comparisons have the disadvantage, however, that many interesting systemic characteristics are by and large invariant.

3.1.2 Political Consequences of Elections

The overwhelming majority of publications on elections hardly addresses the question of the impact of elections on politics and often neglects the consequences of systemic differences on this impact. Most of the literature starts from the unspecified assumption that elections matter politically. This assumption is then believed to justify a shift of focus to all kinds of phenomena which may affect elections and which, by virtue of the assumption just made, are therefore also possibly relevant beit in an even less specified way to the study of politics. Instead of studying election results, for example, one focusses on the behavior of voters, or of parties. Sometimes the choice of topics reflects a further regression into antecedent phenomena, for instance when not voter behavior, but factors possibly influencing it become the phenomenon to be explained. Such research may very well make invaluable contributions to the study of politics, but only if its findings can be integrated in a more direct focus on politics. This requires a more integrative perspective which specifies the ways in which elections (or more antecedent events) have political consequences. A number of authors has attempted to make such attempts by classifying the consequences which elections may have for politics (e.g. Rose/Mossawir, 1967; Converse, 1975; King, 1981; Kirkpatrick, 1981; Beck, 1986; Van der Eijk, 1992). Although they do not arrive at identical results, their suggestions are largely overlapping and clearly compatible with one another. The most important classes of political effects they distinguish will be discussed below.[2]

---

[2] When this text speaks of 'the impact of elections on politics', this is not meant to indicate a simple one-way causal process. In most cases, reciprocal causal influences appear to be much more plausible, resulting in a chicken-and-egg relationship between cause and effect. King (1981, p. 294) states this very aptly as follows: "...to discuss the effects of democratic elections on the political systems in which they occur is rather like discussing the effects of skyscrapers on New York or of Judaism on Israel. Each is typically defined in terms of the other....".In spite of this, the assertion of this chapter is that it makes sense to talk about impact (or, as some authors do, of 'function') even when this is part of reciprocal relationships and feedback loops.

a.   official *recognition and legitimation of values* which are inseparably embodied in the electoral process and its institutionalization. In western democratic systems, such values include those of popular participation in politics, political equality, majoritarianism, free expression of political preferences, representation, accountability of power-holders. In spite of their apparent negation by existing electoral practices in authoritarian or totalitarian systems, these values retain even there some of their liberal-democratic and in those contexts subversive meanings. Differences in electoral institutionalization and actual practices generate variation in the extent to which these, and possibly other, values are legitimized.

b.   *allocation of power*. Manifestly, the most direct political consequence of elections is that individuals or groups (parties) are invested with the power of elected positions and offices. Which positions varies between systems. Most common is that legislatures are elected. Less common is the election of executives and still less common that of judiciaries. How important elected offices are is dependent on their relation to other positions of power, such as economic, military, religious, etc. Irrespective of whether or not such relationships are codified in constitutions and positive law, their actual contents can only be assessed by an analysis of the systems under consideration. In those countries where the executive branch is not elected, there is usually a more or less direct link between the composition of government and that of the elected legislative. Depending upon the party system, such a link may be direct (as is, for instance, usually the case in Great Britain) or mediated by a process of coalition formation which is not controlled, but at most circumscribed by electoral verdicts.

Depending upon the manner in which it is institutionalized, the electoral process may also affect the structure of the competition for votes (i.e. the party system) and the composition of (elected) leadership in a political system.

Finally, elections serve as mechanisms for the transformation of other sources of power into political power. Political systems differ in what they encourage, allow or inhibit in this respect. Quite often, limitations are set on the use of financial or economic power in electoral settings. Votes are usually supposed not to be (directly) for sale. Yet, where poverty is rampant and economic inequality is large such practices are exceedingly frequent, which has made cynical observers remark that elections are one of the few effective mechanisms for redistributing wealth. In a less direct way, economic resources may electorally be transformed into political power by financing campaigns etc. In a similar way, religious power, government power, military power, etc. can under certain circumstances be transformed into political power by electoral means.

c. *legitimation of the political community, the regime and officeholders.* Particularly in the age of general elections, where substantially the entire adult population has the right to vote, elections define political communities. Often these definitions are uncontested, elections then reinforce them by default. In some cases, however, elections may undermine the legitimacy of the political community as formally defined, for instance when segments of a population boycott elections, or when election results induce secessions. Obviously, it is not the election *per-se* that undermines legitimacy, but rather the manifestation of such disagreement which elections permit.

Whereas the legitimacy of the political community is often uncontested, that of officials is more frequently subject to dispute. One of the important functions of elections is to bestow legitimacy on officeholders. Often, the legitimizing effects of elections for officeholders are thought to be so inevitable that they can even be obtained by fraudulent practices. Indications are, however, that this is an oversimplification at the very least, and that the strength of whatever legitimizing effects elections may have depends on a number of characteristics of the electoral process. One can think in this regard of, amongst others, the freedom and fairness of the election, the breadth of choices offered, how directly the occupation of certain offices is tied to an election result, disproportionality between election results and distribution of seats, etc.

Legitimacy of regimes may be reinforced or undermined by election results. Reinforcement may be the default, at least to the extent that elections withheld popular support for anti-regime forces while being free and fair and open for such forces to compete. When these conditions are not fulfilled, the regime legitimacy accruing from elections may be very low indeed, as the experience of Eastern Europe since 1989 has demonstrated.

As Easton (1965) already suggested, legitimacy for the political community, regime and officeholders may be distinct, yet interrelated. This is particularly the case for community and regime, where the borderline between them may be hard to draw, as the cases of Canada and Belgium illustrate.

d.   *control over, influence on and legitimacy of policy.* Control over policy is rarely exerted by way of the electoral process. Referenda are of course an exception, as are the very rare cases where the entire electoral contest is dominated by a single clearly defined and discriminating issue. Influence on policy formation may be a more common phenomenon. It may involve that voters base their choice on the difference between parties' or candidates ideologies or values in the expectation that these will guide policy choices on future issues. A different possibility is that parties anticipate (some) voters' preferences in the expectation of acquiring (or retaining) their support. Legitimacy of (government) policy is usually the consequence of the legitimacy of those who enact it, at least to the extent that the policies concerned fall within the normal scope of power of officeholders. Legitimacy of policy may be undermined to the extent that it violates explicit pre-election promises.

In most cases, prudence should be exercised in attributing influence over policy to voter choice. Careful analysis on the level of voter perceptions, motivations, and actual behavior is required before the an electoral majority for a party or coalition is interpreted as popular support for its platform (Klingemann et al., 1993).

e.   *expressing and integrating conflicting interests in a society.* As Lipset and Rokkan (1967: 4-5) pointed out "the establishment of regular channels for the expression of conflicting interests ...helped to stabilize the structure of a great number of nation states". Obviously, the institution of regular, free and competitive elections is one of the most important of such channels. It allows the formation of groups or parties which represent the expression of diverse sides of social conflicts, and it provides a framework for the acquisition of shares of power within a larger system. and therefore a stake in that larger system, at least
As long as this larger system may contribute to the furthering of the various conflicting interests, elections promote their gaining an interest in the larger system itself, thus performing an important integrative social and political function.

f.   *communication between elites and non-elites.* The perspective of elections offering a mechanism for ordinary citizens to collectively exert control, or at least influence, over the behavior of governing elites may be overly naive. Political leaders and elites can, and do influence the electoral process by shaping the agenda of public discussion, by their participation in public debate, by influencing reality through the process of governing, etc. When taking this into account, the electoral process shows itself as a channel of communication between elites and ordinary citizens. To the extent that it operates effectively, it transmits messages from a population to its political leaders. These involve support, disaffection, preferences, etc. It also transmits information from elites to the masses which they govern: information, explication, persuasive messages, and so on, all in the context of elections and election campaigns. This channel of communication can be said to be effective to the extent that the flows of information carried by it are intelligible for both sides. This aspect will be discussed separately below.

Elections are, of course, not the only channel of communication between masses and elites. People may use petitions, demonstrations, lobbies, all kinds of activities to convey their opinions and preferences to their governors. Likewise, elites may in all different forms attempt to inform, persuade, cajole, bribe or mislead populations. Yet, the unique character of the electoral process is that it is the only of such channels of communication which embodies the democratic principle of political equality, and that its effects on leadership composition are unequivocal.

3.2. Electoral Change and the Decline of Cleavage Voting

This section summarizes an important and voluminous tradition of (comparative) research on elections which is focussed upon the explanation of party choice. As will be apparent, such research is of particular importance because it helps to illuminate central aspects of the character of a political system: the nature of the long-standing conflicts in a society, their relation to political parties and social groups, their importance as anchors or orientation and choice of individual voters. With this focus, it contributes also to understanding other political consequences of elections, such as the bases upon which electoral power is acquired, the grounds of legitimation of political communities, regimes, and officeholders, the kinds of policy areas in which representation, control and influence is important, and the terms in which elites and non-elites can communicate with one another.

On the basis of a comparative analysis of West European countries, Lipset and Rokkan concluded in 1967 that

> "... the contemporary party systems reflected, with but few exceptions, the cleavage structures of the 1920s. (...) the party alternative, and in remarkably many cases the party organizations, are older than the majorities of national electorates" (p.169).

They characterized this state of affairs as 'frozen party systems', a term referring not only to party systems in a narrow sense, but also to the relation between political parties and electorates. In other words, the party systems of the 1960s not only reflected the cleavage structure of the 1920s, but also that of the 1960s, and this cleavage structure itself, with its consequences for voters' behavior and election results, was equally frozen. This implicit conclusion was empirically tested by Rose and Urwin (1970), who were indeed able to demonstrate that during a period of rapidly changing circumstances the electoral support for most relevant parties had been remarkable stable. Rapid economic growth, the emergence of welfare arrangements and decolonization in the period 1945-1969 had evidently had little impact on election results in Western countries during this period.

Just about at the time that Lipset and Rokkan and Rose and Urwin published their results, the situation started to change. Many countries experienced dramatic increases in electoral change. New parties sprang up, old ones were often in disarray, the erstwhile predictability appeared to have vanished. The changes appeared to be different in different countries. They did not set in at the same time, they affected different parties, they took different forms. In the Netherlands the most striking was the stark decline of christian-democratic parties in the 1967-1972 period. In Denmark, 1973 showed a sudden fall in the electoral support of the four traditional parties from 84 to 58 percent of the vote, and a doubling of the number of parties in the national parliament from five to ten. In Britain the Labour Party split in 1982, resulting in such unprecedented electoral support for a third party (an alliance of Liberals and the split-off Social Democrats) that the traditional two-party dominance in

British politics almost lost its self-evident character. Yet other countries showed their own timing and manifestations of electoral changes which contributed to the demise of the perspective of frozen party systems. What had happened? How was this to be explained?

The dominant mode of analyzing and explaining electoral behavior and election outcomes was by means of the kind of social cleavages Lipset and Rokkan had referred to. These included the cleavage between classes, between urban and rural interests, between different kinds of religious interests, and between these and secular ones as exemplified in the modern state, between cultural, ethnic and linguistic segments of a population. The most relevant of these cleavages had, according to Lipset and Rokkan, resulted in the formation of parties in the late 19th and early 20th century which represented the interests of populations groups which were demarcated by cleavage distinctions. The extension of the suffrage in this period offered the possibility for political parties to establish their own cleavage-based clientele, to build their organizations and to become part of the political system. When universal suffrage was attained, new parties could only establish an existence at the expense of the already existing ones, which usually proved too difficult. At the same time, the existing parties tried to convince their respective clienteles of the continuing relevance of cleavage distinctions, and of the need to safeguard the interests of the various segments of the population by cleavage-based parties. Such processes account for the stability referred to by Lipset and Rokkan and by Rose and Urwin.

The success of the cleavage perspective for the period until the late 1960s accounts for various attempts to rescue it as an analytic approach for the period thereafter. First of all, the cleavage perspective did not predict only stability. When demographic, social and economic developments alter the size of cleavage-based groups in a population, it was to be expected that the parties deriving their support from those groups would be affected accordingly. This line of explanation ran, however, in unsurmountable problems. One problem involved timing. Why would all kinds of contextual developments, which were already under way for decades, all of sudden impact on the size of clienteles? How to reconcile abrupt electoral changes with very gradual and slowly evolving social and economic changes? Even worse, electoral changes were often not uni-directional in their effects, whereas the contextual developments which alter the size of cleavage-based groups are. A second kind of attempt to rescue cleavage based approaches was to attempt to adapt the definition of the cleavage structure which was supposed to underlie the electoral support of parties. This has most frequently been attempted with respect to the class cleavage. The simple distinction between labour class and middle class, which might have been adequate for the early 20th century, was not so any more later. A 'new middle-class' was often proclaimed to have emerged, which would constitute the electoral basis for new parties, or, in their absence, for electoral volatility. Here too, however, empirical evidence was hard to reconcile with this notion. Apart from the problem of how to sensibly define new class distinctions, newly defined groups did not behave as expected, or were hard to distinguish in their behavior from others. A third way to rescue the idea of cleavage politics is to hypothesize new cleavages, which earlier were of no or less relevance. The newly politicized issue of women's rights, the different interests associated with public versus private employment, or with public versus private consumption, or with materialist versus post-materialist concerns have all at one time or another been hypothesized as new cleavage dimensions which could account for electoral change and volatility. None of these, however, has had much empirical success in explaining electoral behavior and election outcomes (see for this: Dalton et al., 1984;Franklin et al., 1992).

The conclusion of diminished relevance of the cleavage perspective was drawn in a number of non-comparative studies in the 1980s. Van der Eijk and Niemöller (1985: 367) referred to it as "the political emancipation of individual citizens who can now choose, rather than be predestined by social position". Franklin (1985: 175-9) termed it "the post-collectivist era", and Rose and McAllister (1985) alluded to it in the title of their book *Voters begin to choose*. All refer to a new situation in which voters' position in terms of socio-demographic cleavages had lost its former stronghold on their individual behavior. Even where such rather general interpretations were given to electoral changes, the specific national contexts of studies generated quite different interpretations of the origins of these changes. In the Netherlands, for example, much emphasis was given to processes of secularization which undermined the potency of religious cleavage divisions, in Britain it was the declining importance of class. Only recently did a large-scale comparative investigation of patterns of electoral change in Western countries demonstrate that similar patterns of diminishing relevance of cleavage voting exist or are under way in many political systems, even in countries where they were not yet identified before, and in systems where (aggregate) electoral change so far had been quite small. Franklin, Mackie and Valen, who directed this study (1992), concluded that a more general process of change exists than what has been detected earlier in separate country studies.

The declining importance of social cleavages for electoral choice was demonstrated for a large number of countries, some of which had shown not very much turbulence in election outcomes, and each of which has to be characterized by a separate set of traditionally relevant cleavage distinctions. A simultaneous longitudinal (1960s-1970s-1980s) and cross-national comparison documented a strongly diminished capability of cleavages to explain voting behavior in Norway, Denmark, Sweden, Belgium, the Netherlands, France, Britain, Australia, New Zealand and Ireland. In the United States and Canada, not much of a decline could be found, but there impact of cleavages on voter behavior was already very low in the 1960s, allowing for only small downward changes. The only two exceptions to the general pattern are Italy and Germany, where the impact of cleavage positions on voting had remained the same since the 1960s, or had even increased somewhat. At any single point, a comparison between these various counties would not have been very illuminating. In the 1960s they varied considerably in the strength of cleavage voting, which was very strong in some countries, intermediate in most of the rest, and weak only in a few. The time at which this strength declined, the rate of decline, and the remaining strength in the 1970s and 1980s do all vary. Only comparison over a longer time-span than a few years or even a single decade allowed the common pattern of decline to show itself clearly.

Franklin et al. (1992) suggest that the observed loss of capacity of social cleavages to determine voter behavior in many countries is part of a long-term process which antedates and follows the window of observation provided by longitudinal comparisons over a period of two to three decades. Exactly when this process starts differs from country to country, causing quite different 'views' at any specific point in time. This suggestion implies on the one hand that all of the systems under study (western democracies with competitive elections) experience a stage in which voter choice is strongly determined by social cleavages, whatever those may be in each specific country. On the other hand it implies that this electoral importance of cleavages will eventually disappear largely. This perspective is not only based on extrapolation of documented changes so as to encompass periods prior to and after the actual observations, but follows also from a careful breakdown of results according to generations. In virtually all countries studied, party choice of younger generations is less strongly determined by cleavages than that of older ones. Consequently, the extrapolation of over-all changes in cleavage impact is in agreement with the consequences of a simple and inescapable process of generational replacement prior to and after the actual period studied. Yet the question remains what the nature, origins and implications are of this suggested general process.

3.2.1 Origins and Implications of Declining Cleavage Voting

The decline of cleavage voting which had apparently occurred in many western countries, or which is still under way, cannot adequately be understood in terms of country-specific factors, such as secularization, decline of class voting, etc. Such interpretations are not necessarily incorrect, but cannot account for the commonality of the process in different systems. The common denominator is a decline in the relevance of traditional social groups (on whatever basis these may be constituted) as anchors for voters and political systems. In a discussion of the origins of this process Van der Eijk/Franklin et al. (1992: 420) state that

> "In the most general terms, the decline of socially structured voting can be explained in the same way as the decay of many other empirical structures, in terms of the fact that none of the countries we have studied constitute closed systems. Therefore, their structures may well have contained the seeds of their own decay. Leakages and contamination might be seen as being 'bound' to bring about an eventual decline in cleavage politics."

This general principle is illustrated in four different ways, each of which contributes to the decay of an erstwhile cohesive structure of alignments between social conflicts, the social groups and their interests which are defined by these conflicts, and political parties.

First of all, social structure itself has changed in quantitative terms. Some cleavage defined groups grew in size, others diminished. Such slowly occurring changes have their origins in demographic, social and economic developments in the past century. They may gradually cause a change in the character of entire societies as erstwhile dominant groups are replaced by others. This in turn undermines the strength of linkages of voters to a party system based on increasingly more outdated cleavages.

Second, social structure has changed in qualitative terms, rendering party systems based on cleavages of many decades ago increasingly less relevant for increasing numbers of voters. New occupational groups, new modes of acquiring income, new patterns of residence, changed systems of transport and communication all create new interests and conflicts which are not easily expressed, let alone represented by parties defined in terms of cleavages at the beginning of the century.

Third, the coherence that previously existed between central and reinforcing characteristics of particular social groups has reduced. The once existing reinforcement given to for example occupational class by education, income, housing type, health care, etc. has disappeared, to no small measure as the consequence of state interventions in the course of the century, and in particular of the creation of welfare arrangements. This lack of coherence puts increasing numbers of people under frequent cross-pressures. In such a situation, people may seemingly retain for a long time linkages with established cleavage parties, but these will increasingly rest upon inertia and be subject to sudden change.

Fourth, generational replacement is an evident factor preventing the closedness which a cleavage structure would require in order not to be subject to decay. It can be argued that parental transmission of attitudes and values can only be entirely successful if they are not reinforced by personal experiences felt by succeeding generations. Unless this is the case, successive generations will have increasingly less reason to re-transmit their inherited identity. Consequently, the strength of identifications with cleavage-defined groups will gradually be reduced, unless successive generations will personally experience the conflicts which gave rise to these cleavages in the first place.

The first three of these causes of decay of cleavage structures relate to a diminishing capacity of the old structure to accommodate newly emerging conflicts, interests and problems. The fourth specifies a condition which must be fulfilled for the first three to be consequential: if important old conflicts have not been resolved new ones are unlikely to achieve prominence. To the extent that Western countries managed to find political solutions for the conflicts, social problems and unfulfilled aspirations which were the foundation of the cleavage structures in the beginning of the century, these cleavages ran out of steam and simultaneously allowed new conflicts and interests to gain prominence, which further undermined the bases of the traditional cleavages. Evidently, this process has run its course in many Western countries, leaving in the course of the 1960s the traditional cleavage-based party systems seemingly intact, but without much resistance against whatever challenge. Little wonder that wherever such challenges occurred, serious electoral change resulted.

It must be emphasized that the decay of cleavage structures is not portrayed as the inescapable result of the mere passage of time. Earlier, the condition has been formulated that the important conflicts which gave rise to the cleavage structure in the first place must be resolved for this outcome to occur. Northern Ireland is a clear example of what happens when this condition is not met. In the course of the 20th century, economic and social developments in Northern Ireland have not been very different from most of the rest of the United Kingdom. Yet, group identifications, cleavage structures and the traditional conflicts underlying them are as much in place, if not stronger, than at earlier moments in the century. The inability to adequately resolve the conflict between Protestants and Catholics in Northern Ireland resulted in a continuous barrage of personal and intense experiences for all generations which reinforced the saliency of the conflict and of personal identifications with either of the two sides. Regarded from this perspective, the decline of cleavage voting which was observed in elsewhere was the consequence of the successful resolution by political systems of deep-seated conflicts of social interests. These countries succeeded in politicizing their major and most divisive conflicts in the form of cleavage-based political parties. This not only allowed the expression of group-based conflicts of interest, it also helped to resolve them by integrating them into a single national political system: "the establishment of regular channels for the expression of conflicting interests ... helped to stabilize the structure of a great number of nation states" (Lipset and Rokkan, 1967:4-5). Obviously, the institution of regular, free and competitive elections is one of the most important of such channels. The crucial difference between Northern Ireland and many other countries is the degree to which all conflicting groups in a society can express their interests legitimately and effectively, and the extent to which minorities are safeguarded against oppression by majorities. The decline of cleavage voting in many countries can be regarded as an indicator of the resolution of conflicts, as the audit of decades of successful democratic government.

3.3. The Agenda for Comparative Studies of Elections

Many, if not most studies of elections are not comparative in character. They may contribute to comparative research by providing empirical information for comparative analysts. Yet, in a number of ways the national character of many studies is also an obstacle. As Van der Eijk and Schmitt (1991: 260) remarked:

> "..the national peculiarities and resulting incomparabilities of election studies in various Western countries have repeatedly curtailed the scope and plagued the execution of efforts to arrive at a comparative and more general understanding of the electoral process and its place in the operation of democratic political systems. The situation is somewhat of a paradox: while the field of electoral research is among the oldest, and certainly most developed areas of empirical social research, it has not generated the kind of large-scale cross-national survey projects which have been so successful in the development of other areas of comparative mass political behavior".

Important items on the agenda for future comparative studies of elections have been listed elsewhere by van der Eijk, Franklin et al. (1992: 427). Their major suggestions are the following:

1. research into the circumstances and processes which either promote or discourage the emergence, development or maintenance of systems of orientations that may serve to constrain both party and voter behavior after the decline of cleavage politics has run its course. Obviously, when cleavage-based interests lose their power to structure behavior of parties and voters, something else most take its place for elections to retain a meaningful communicative function in the interaction between elites and non-elites. Relatively stable orientations may develop on the basis of values, ideologies or personalities, but

it is equally possible that for some period of time party systems and voters lose their 'moorings' and will drift in whatever direction they are propelled by unpredictable events. Research by, amongst others, Granberg and Holmberg (1988) suggests that it is of great importance to what extent political parties, other relevant elites and media offer the voters (and one another) a 'model' of political coherence. This, in turn, seems to depend on the structure of political parties where individual politicians' careers are made or broken. Parties which control to some extent the careers of politicians (as is the case in most European party systems) offer more opportunity in this respect than the much less-homogeneous American political parties which have little influence on the careers of individual political entrepreneurs.

2. research into the genesis of whatever relatively stable political orientations voters may hold. The cleavage perspective on politics suggests that relevant orientations were more ascribed than acquired, and that they had their origins in parental transmission, supported by homogeneous social settings and contexts. This suggestion does not hold good anymore once cleavages lose most of their erstwhile impact on voters. So, by what kind of processes do people acquire the stable orientations which they often evidently have (e.g. Van der Eijk/Niemöller, 1992).

3. one of the consequences of the decline of cleavage-based voting is the increase in electoral competition between parties. What once were 'natural' reservoirs of support for parties have ceased to be so. This is even so in the presence of stable ideological or value orientations which guide voters in their party choice. Obviously, the degree and structure of electoral competition is an important determinant of what earlier was referred to as the course of politics. To the extent that the structure of such competition is relatively stable, it may also be considered as one of the indicators of the character of a political system, much in the way in which stable alignments have been used to that avail. Promising lines of research which lend themselves easily for cross-national research have been pioneered by Van der Eijk and Niemöller (1984), and have been applied for the countries of the European Community by Van der Eijk and Oppenhuis (1991).

4. a final urgent priority for comparative studies of elections is the organization of truly cross-national comparative studies of voters, parties and their interactions. For parties' behavior in electoral settings an important line

of research has been initiated by the Manifesto Research Group (Budge et al, 1987). For organizing comparative voter studies, the institution of direct elections to the European Parliament, conducted simultaneously in all member-states of the Community, has been an invaluable and powerful stimulus. In 1989 this yielded the first large-scale and truly comparative study directed primarily at voter behavior. Results from comparative analyses on the basis of this study can be found in Schmitt and Mannheimer (1991) and Van der Eijk and Franklin (forthcoming).

To conclude: electoral studies are an important part of comparative research into the relations between 'politics - polity - policy'. However, traditional electoral research tended to remain country-based, stressing intra-systemic features rather than inter-system characteristics. Analyzing the comparative impact of elections on politics requires a research design that focusses on the common denominator of the electoral process: the functional equivalence of the institutions and the related behavior of the political and societal actors that shape the process.

PART II: *Institutions, Actors and Rationality*

4 Rational Choice as Comparative Theory: Beyond Economic Self Interest

Ian Budge

During the last twenty years 'rational choice' approaches have become the dominant paradigm in political science. Their focus on problems of collective choice and collective action which exist independently of a country's specific history or of its institutional peculiarities make them an attractive framework for any comparative research which does not want to get bogged down in descriptive detail. The argument of this paper is however that the current identification of 'rational choice' approaches with purely economic-style theorizing is a mistake and ultimately a dead-end. Rational choices include economic ones but also many other modes of decision-making.

Economic-style theories in comparative politics which assume costless maximization of self interest under perfect information are:

1) too narrow a conception of rational choice to be useful at general levels of discussion;

2) not the only basis for specific models of national decision-making either.

An example of an alternative 'rational choice' approach to comparative voting and party competition is given in the course of the paper. This provides a basis for comparative theorizing which avoids the excessive narrowness and dogmatism characteristic of existing economic models, on the one hand, while not lapsing either into country-by-country descriptions or history as so much comparative research currently does.

4.1 Economic Theories of Comparative Politics

It is no exaggeration to say that the major and most stimulating theories of comparative politics are now 'economic' both in the basis and form. Such theories cover the major institutionalized actors of modern democracies - parties, interest-groups, governments and bureaucracies - as well as relations between states. A short listing and description of the main ones gives an insight into their characteristic style and methods of reasoning:

a) Interest groups

The big work here is Mancur Olson's *The Rise and Decline of Nations* (1982). Rise and Decline in Olson's sense is a country's relative economic success as measured by growth rates of GDP. Decline is explained primarily by the tendency of various groups in the population, mainly producers and trades unions, to organize themselves and put pressure in governments to maintain their prices (in the case of unions, wages and restrictive practices) and smother competition. The longer a country has been industrialized and democratically organized the more this will happen. Only a radical restructuring of the polity and the economy, such as foreign occupation or internal revolution, will clear out the restrictive practices which hamper growth. Hence Britain, where both have been lacking, constitutes for Olson the emblematic case of decline, with Germany and Japan exactly the opposite.

Many criticisms can be made of Olson's theories (e.g. de Vris et al, 1983). Here we are concerned with its methodological aspects. The blocking tactics of interest groups are a specific aspect of the general problem of collective action within economic models. Given that they assume that all behavior is self-centered there is an immediate problem as to how selfish individuals can generate collective action to provide public goods such as roads, security or economic growth (Olson, 1965). The answer, generally, is that they cannot, even though all would benefit from them in the long run. Only state coercion or (more rarely) positive inducements can produce optimal collective outcomes (e.g. by means of corporatist arrangements). Thus the models produce what many political doctrines have sought on the past - a justification for the existence of a coercive state.

One other methodological aspect of Olson's model of decline is interesting here - that is the interaction between the abstract model and national history. The model identifies the big variable-interest group formation and collusion over time - and makes the prediction that where this is strongest economic decline will be most evident. Theory thus functions without reference to history, making predictions in the abstract. Specific national history can then be fed into it however, to specify the country(ies) most likely to have interest group collusion, and to see if in fact this is associated with low economic growth. But the sequence is model-history rather than history-model. This insistence on well-specified, deductive approach is a strength of economic models. Some however are better specified than others are we shall see.

b) Parties

An Economic Theory of Democracy was set out by Anthony Downs in 1957. Although often discussed in specific national contexts it is clearly a comparative theory of party and voter behavior. A Left-Right continuum is assumed to be central to voting decisions electors are all located at some point on this, and will vote for the party closest to their own position. Parties composed of politicians who simply want to gain office, and have no policy views of their own thus have an inducement to move closer than their rivals to the largest concentrations of electors. A unimodal distribution of electors will give rise to a two party system in which the parties, moving as close as possible to the position of the median elector. will become only just distinguishable:

Figure 4.1

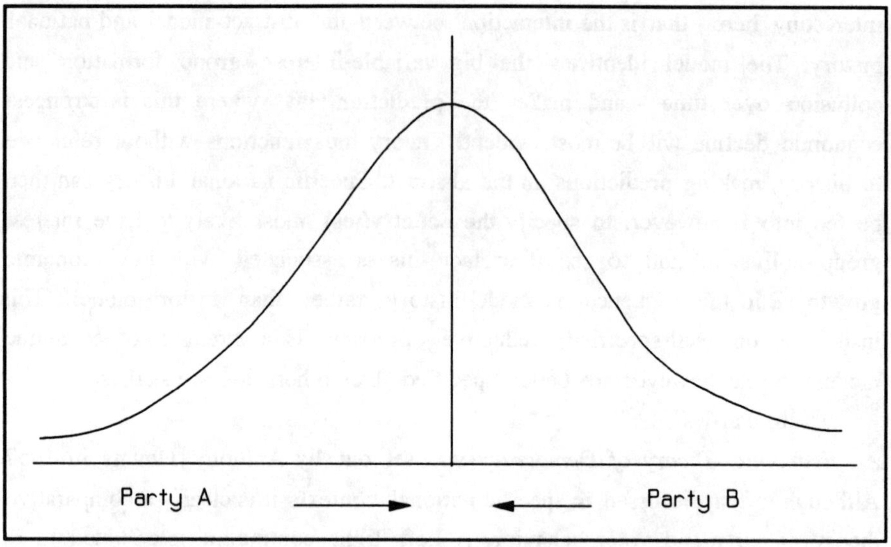
Party A
Party B

A multi-modal distribution will produce several parties, each sitting on a mode (since they cannot hope to gain more by moving off):

Figure 4.2

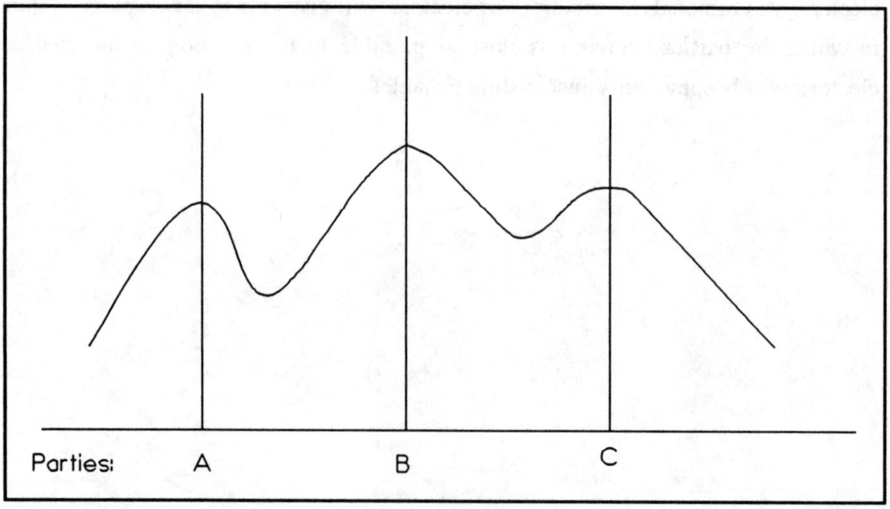
Parties:
A
B
C

This last situation is compatible with Lipset and Rokkan's (1967) developmental theory of the evolution of European party systems. Various groups excluded by the 19th century franchise generated political and social demands which were advocated by political entrepreneurs seeking advantage. As these core groups still make characteristic demands, the parties remain very much in their own segment of the ideological sphere. Here again we have a case in which the *a priori* economic model covers, but is not derived from, historical evidence, and puts the historical experiences of various countries into a wider theoretical context.

c) Governments

Riker's minimal winning coalition (MWC) formulation is well-known (Riker, 1962). Assuming that parties are concerned only with office, government coalitions will include only a bare majority of parties (enough to prevent the government being overthrown) - but no more than this otherwise the parties will have to share the spoils of office further.

Only about 35 to 40% of post-war European coalition governments are minimal winning in nature. As a result policy has been brought in to explain coalition-formation, either along the lines of the parties closest on the policy favoring the government, or some kind of clustering around the median voter. Most coalition governments which form do conform to one or other of these models: the problem is that many which do *not* form also conform to them (Budge/Keman, 1990). Most work on coalitions explicitly or implicitly uses one of these frameworks nevertheless because it needs to draw upon more general accounts to interpret specific details of actual coalition-formations.

d) Bureaucracies

The best known theory here is probably Niskanen's (1971) model of bureaucratic over-supply. In conformity with the generally self-centered assumptions of the other 'economic' models, Niskanen assumes that bureaucrats and their agencies are anxious for personal aggrandizement and growth. Hence they will seek to expand their services and clients at every conceivable opportunity, leading to problems of over-supply, sub-optimal allocation of resources and inefficiency wherever bureaucracies are the major mode of provision for a society (see for a critic: Dunleavy, 1991: 162-164).

e) Inter-State Relations

Realist theory assumes that state are unitary, self-interested actors interested primarily in the power relationships. Weak states will be taken advantage of by stronger states. Norms, rules and moral obligations mask underlying realities, based ultimately on force (Morgenthau, 1948; Keohane, 1984).

4.2 Common Characteristics of Economic Theories in Politics

The theories listed in the last section are in various states of development. In particular realist theory in international relations is notoriously hard to pin down in precise terms. In attributing all inter-state behavior to self-interest it runs the risk of tautology and forfeits on the whole the chance to make precise predictions. It must be said however that some of the other models described above are reasonable well-specified and do give rise to predictions which, in principal at least, can be upheld or refuted against historical and other evidence.

This, plus the fact that the theories as mentioned cover most of the main democratic institutions in a clearly generalizable way, gives them a strong claim on the attention of analysts of comparative politics. The different models cover different aspects of political life but their strong similarities also give them a close relationship with each other - as much at least as the different elements of economic theory have in their own field. These similarities are:

a) the self centered, not to say self-interested motivations of the actors in the models. While in principle actors might be motivated by altruism or concern for others within the models, in their actual working our actors pursue narrowly specified goals with great single-mindedness (Mansbridge, 1990).

b) the assumption of perfect information on all aspects of life related to the working of the model. Thus, members of Olson's distributive interest coalitions have no difficulty in identifying and linking together with their fellows. Downs' parties know what electors' preferences are, just as electors know where parties stand. Niskanen's bureaucrats know perfectly where their prospects for power or aggrandizement lie, and so on.

c) methodological individualism. No matter what collectivity is involved in the real world - party, bureaucratic agency, state - they are all treated as super individuals, with one set of goals and outlook. Internal factionalism is ignored.

4.2.1 Problems of Collective Action

Given these assumptions, it is no wonder that a common preoccupation of economic models, when applied to politics, is the problem of co-ordination. How does one get precisely calculating, self-interested individuals to co-operate for the collective good? Indeed, given such rampant self interest, is there really anything that could be described as the common good or public interest? Are collective decisions not simply a victory of the strong, or of successful coalitions over the weak?

It is in their shared doubts about the validity and legitimacy of collective action and provision that the various models outlined above converge to form an almost unified theory of comparative politics. Given the self interested action posited in the models, their theories of politics and of democracy are adversarial (Mansbridge, 1983): only a strong and fairly arbitrary state can ensure determinate outcomes (cf. Hobbes, 1951). Here concerns come out particularly in two areas: free riders and the provision of public goods, on the one hand and voting cycles on the other.

a) Public Goods

Olson's (1965) theory of collective action and collective goods rests on the idea that in a large number of potential beneficiaries each person will calculate, selfishly, that his individual contribution will have little effect on overall provision, but he will maximize his personal benefit by not co-operating. If the good is provided he will gain, as by definition no-one can be excluded from enjoying a public good (clean air, for example). If it is not provided at least he has minimized costs. This 'free-rider' problem, linked to the (non-) supply of public goods, clearly rests on the assumption of selfish action by individuals. It can be overcome only by offering individuals inducements to act collectively or by coercing them into doing so - the most common alternatives. Where these do not exist most individuals will refrain from action (e.g. from voting, within Downs' *Economic Theory of Democracy*).

b) Voting Cycles

An even more devastating critique of the possibilities of collective action which develops out of these simplified *a priori* models applied to collective political choices, is the problem of voting cycles. The power of the critique lies in the fact that, if a seemingly reasonable set of *a priori* conditions are laid down for voting, individuals acting in accordance with them can quite often generate public choices which are unstable, in the sense that any alternatives chosen can be beaten by another alternative. Under these circumstances the actual public decision is arbitrary, since under slightly different condition (say a difference sequence of voting or alternatives) another decision might have been taken. Democratic procedures thus appear inherently incapable of guaranteeing true majority decisions. McLean's (1991: 506) summary of the dilemma is admirably succinct:

> "a rational individual who prefers A to B to C must prefer A to C ...it is always possible that majority rule is intransitive. In the simplest case, if voter 1 prefers A to B and B to C, voter 2 prefers B to C and C to A, and voter 3 prefers C to A and A to B, there is a majority for A over B, a majority for B over C and a majority for C over A. Transitive individual preferences lead to an intransitive social ordering, otherwise known as a cycle".

The cyclical model predicts arbitrariness and instability of public choices in the normal course of democratic politics, including arbitrary choices of governments and instability of coalition agreements.

4.2.2 Economic Theories: A Reconsideration

The question we now ask is whether the building of a theory of rational comparative politics on rational choice lines inevitably leads to a concern with problems of collective action and to such pessimistic conclusions? Or have these more to do with the specific characteristics of the economic models we have outlined, which we do not necessarily have to accept as part of the price to paid for comparative theorizing? The question is a central one for students of comparative politics because the economic theories outlined above *are* the most extensive and well constructed, and empirically tested in the field. So they and their conclusions have to be taken very seriously if we are to build comparative theory at all.

The following sections of the paper argue that there are alternative forms of rational choice theory which can be applied to comparative politics and which do not give rise to the pessimistic conclusions about democracy which we have just discussed. To make this case is necessary to go back to first principles and reconsider what it is that we mean by 'rational choice'. Is it more than acting selfishly to maximize gains and reduce costs? We go on to consider how introducing realistic assumptions about scarce and costly information modifies many conclusions of the economic models, and in particular shows that voting cycles are unlikely to occur in most real situations. We conclude that rational choice theories are indeed the major way in which a truly comparative political science can be advanced, but that rational choice itself is a much broader and more internally diverse concept than economic theories give it credit for.

4.3   Definitions of Rational Choice

Rationality is such a key term in modern society, implying so many positive attributes, that its use cannot be confined to narrow economic contexts. In particular, it has moral connotations: to recognize someone as rational is to recognize that his/her choices are considered ones worthy, *prima facie*, of respect. It is rather alarming that an economic approach writes off so much behavior (going out to vote for example) as non-rational or irrational (Barry, 1970). This is a particular example of the assumption that rationality only takes one form: a precisely calculated type of utility maximization, undertaken with perfect information and at no cost. This is the prevalent assumption in economics and is generalized to politics in the economic approaches. Socrates, Christ, and Regulus going to duty and death in Carthage, do not seem utility - maximizers in the economic sense. Are outstanding moral actions then irrational ones?

There are really two problems involved here. For general purposes, above all for moral assessments, we have to regard most people as rational in the overwhelming majority of their actions. To seek to impose definitions which exclude many of these choices is to manipulate the definition for particular purposes. To claim that only behavior is rational which conforms to the canons of classical economics is certainly to do this, whether consciously or unconsciously, 'economic imperialism' of a high order.

However diverse the grounds on which they base decisions, we have to accept that the vast majority almost all the time make rational choices in a broad sense, even if many of these are not utility - maximizing ones. Are we to conclude that everyone who acts from a sense of duty or obligation is irrational? (Renwick Monroe et al., 1990). Either we do (a step even the most hardened philosophical utilitarian would shrink from) or we expand economic concepts of utility maximization to include such considerations. This move however, renders them tautological, (anything one does is utility-maximization) and this prevents them providing useful explanations of behavior, which in their original narrower (and potentially falsifiable) form they certainly can do.

These considerations point to the importance of developing a broad, all-embracing definition of rational choice which will not allow partisans of a particular approach to claim rationality only for themselves: and of distinguishing sharply between this and the various specific models, which develop the concept of rational choice in particular ways, so that they can yield predictions about behavior and be checked against evidence to see whether they are valid. Proceeding this way saves us from the philosophical thickets into which economic approaches have perhaps unwittingly blundered; and clears the way for real empirical assessments of their validity.

A general near-tautological definition of a rational choice, which seems suitable, is that rational choice is one that can be defended by reasoned argument. This formulation is potentially circular. However, it is not fundamentally so, as we can appeal to external criteria. A reasoned argument is one that is not clearly self-contradictory in a logical sense and does not deny obvious facts at a level appropriate to them.

Precisely because it covers most peoples' behavior most of the time, such a definition is indeed almost tautological and not directly useful for empirical explanation. Its strength is to provide a broad context within which we can develop more specific models of rational choice for explanatory purposes, to describe and possibly predict the reasoning process of particular groups of people in particular situations.

It is also useful for reminding us that such models do not codify the only possibilities for rational behavior. On the contrary, they deliberately exclude many of them in order to be more informative in a Popperian sense: that is, to predict that only narrowly specified kinds of choices will be made so that, if it works, the model tells us quite precisely how the individuals to which it applies will react in the given situations.

The great strength of economic theories in comparative politics is that they do narrow down the possibilities a great deal and give us relatively precise specifications of how people are hypothesized to decide in given situations; and what the social consequences of this will be. This very fact prevents them from covering all possible types of rational behavior. They only embody a particular type of choice - that is, costless calculated utility maximization with perfect information. Obviously, this excludes other forms of behavior which have a perfect *a priori* claim to be regarded as 'rational', in the broad sense.

It follows from this that alternative 'rational choice' models can be created, in comparative politics, which hypothesize that decisions are made differently and with different consequences from the mainstream economic models. An obvious way to do this is by varying the range of goals which actors can pursue, the costs they incur, and the uncertainty they experience. As a result different specific models will generate different predictions. What appear as paradoxes of collective action in the perspectives of economic models will not appear so in ones based on other conceptions of rational choice. I discuss this below. The main point here however is that below the general level there are many different models of particular kinds of rational choice, depending on what assumptions are made about it. In short, there is not just one model type which serves at the same time as a unique description and evaluative criterion for all kinds of choice.

4.4   *Evaluating Specific Economic Models of Rational Choice*

With this point established we can turn to see how well the narrowly economic models perform empirically in explaining variations in comparative party and governmental behavior relative to possible alternatives. The ability of theories to match and explain actual behavior should be for comparativists a major reason for accepting or rejecting the claims of a particular explanation to have empirical validity.

Such an evaluation is however complicated in the case of economic models by the traditions of theory-building inherited from economics. These tend to evade the complications of the real world by building a highly simplified model along the lines of costless utility-maximizing with perfect information discussed above. It is recognized that this is over-simplified: however, the justification runs, we must first of all get this model right, then we can complicate it suitably later on by making special assumptions, for example for imperfect information. Very often however, the process stops here as attention gets directed either to mathematical elaborations based on the original assumptions; or to interesting problems and paradoxes generated by the model itself. By dint of so much attention the model gets accepted as a legitimate description of the real world without any real validation.

When we go beyond the surface plausibility of the various economic models we have discussed we can see that they have had very mixed success in explaining comparative variations in political behavior. For example, Olson's theory fails to explain the generally slow economic growth of the English-speaking nations as a whole, most of which are 'new', and among which Britain is not a laggard (Castles, 1991). Downs' *Economic Theory of Democracy* is riddled with inconsistencies and party movement is better explained by a saliency theory of party competition (see below) rather than his confrontational one (Budge/Farlie, 1977). Minimum winning theory has very limited success in explaining the government coalitions that actually form, as do policy closeness and median voter models (Budge/Laver, 1992). There is little systematic evidence for Niskanen's ideas about bureaucratic expansionism as compared to that of big business (McLean, 1991: 505), while 'realism' in international relations is almost impossible to test.

With regard to the Arrow model of voting cycles and instability of collective decisions and coalition governments, a paradoxical finding is that democratic governments seem in fact to be reasonably stable, nor are their decisions under constant challenge as arbitrary or inconsistent. Were the theory being genuinely put to the test, this failure to observe predicted consequences might be taken as evidence that it does not really describe the workings of democracy. The tendency in economic-style reasoning however, it to take the models as more real that the evidence, so notions such as 'structure-induced equilibrium' have been introduced to show how its prediction of instability is compatible with observed stability (McLean, 1991: 509-510).

4.5   *An Alternative Rational Choice Model:*
       The Saliency Theory of Party Competition

Despite the shortcomings of economic theories they are the best that we have in the field of comparative politics, so in developing alternative models we should try to build on their strengths while eliminating their weaknesses.

One alternative developed from Down's model by Robertson (1976) and Budge et al., (1987) is the saliency theory of voting and party competition. As noted above Downs assumed that parties competing for votes arrayed themselves by means of policy pronouncements on a range of alternatives along a left-right continuum, seeking to be situated as close as possible to major concentrations of electors. Electors signal their preference by voting for the party whose place on the continuum comes closest to their own. In the election, the party closest to the greater numbers of electors gets the most votes, which then gives it a prominent or (if it got a majority) unique role in the formation of the government. It thus has a mandate to carry through the policies which attracted its votes.

Downs' model requires that policy flexibility or mobility to move left or right as anticipated electoral parties have the advantages are perceived. Downs also assumes that the parties are able in principle (depending on the electoral distribution) to place themselves at any point on the continuum. They can do this because leaders are themselves indifferent as to policies, being motivated exclusively by desire for office. Hence they will alter party policy and their position on the left-right continuum so as to attract most votes. Of course, this will only work if the electors believe that parties will do in government what they promise in elections, so the parties also have good, if selfish motives for carrying through the mandate.

A difficulty in Downs' model comes in specifying how parties move in relation to each other. Specifically can they 'leapfrog' each others' positions so as to get ever closer to the major concentration of electors? This might lead to continual movement and confusion as parties jostled each other to get ever closer to the median voter. Downs, therefore, at one point in his argument bans 'leapfrogging' by parties. But this prohibition may enable one of the parties to station itself between the major electoral concentration(s) and its rivals, thus invariably winning as the others would be unable to get any closer to the potential votes.

Besides the logical inconsistency in regard to leapfrogging, Downs' arguments also lacks a broader kind of plausibility. If politicians are ideologically indifferent to policy but relentlessly keen on office, why do those in losing parties not join the winning party, especially given that the Downsian model has a short time perspective, centering on the current election and government? If carried to extremes this argument would predict new parties at each election, as losers pulled out of their old ones and the governing party(ies) split in the run-up to the election, with leaders jockeying for new, favorable, unique electoral positions.

Clearly this does not happen - presumably because, whatever their desire for office, leaders are also attached to their party's enduring ideological stance. Robertson (1976) points out that this alone would preclude their free movement along a policy continuum, since at a certain point they would feel the strain of ideological compromise.

There is, however, another reason why parties cannot move freely from end to end. If they did so they would endanger essential and inedible associations with particular policies and issues - whether because of ideology, previous history, actions in government, association with certain support groups, or a mixture of all these factors. In other words, even if parties wanted to repudiate their past for short term current advantage, they could not easily do so and they might not be believed if they tried. Previous actions cast doubt on present promises when the two are not consistent.

This is exactly the point where saliency theory comes in. Past and present promises must be largely consistent to be believed. In spatial terms this means that parties' ability to move along the type of continuum postulated by Downs is severely limited. In particular, parties will not be able or willing to leapfrog: Labor cannot rationally pretend to be Conservatives or Communists to be Christian Democrats (not even US Republicans to be Democrats nationally). Parties would lose support if they tried this and would not be believed anyway. Taken to extremes this constraint might mean that parties would each have only one position that can be taken on the spatial continuum and thus must wait for electors to do the moving.

This conclusion of partisan rigidity, however, does not necessarily follow. Parties will be wary of repudiating previous position outright, to be sure. But there is much less to prevent them selectively emphasizing or de-emphasizing items from their political inventory. We can conceive movement along the spatial continuum as constituted by emphases or de-emphases of traditional issues, along with some picking up of new issues. Contrasted with a process of dichotomous affirmation or denunciation of policy positions, the process of relative and shifting emphasis and de-emphasis allows parties to push themselves into the middle from their particular end. But they will always stick to their own 'side' of the center, and they rarely or never leapfrog.

There are other important consequences of this revision of party competition theory - of substituting different emphases on issue priorities for competition between polices on the same issue. Parties have a motivation to move to the center if they need extra votes. There is no need, as in Downs' model, for a majority of electors to be near the middle to the parties to be 'centrist'. Indeed, it is likely that most electors will be piled up firmly within each party's own zone and will constitute committed party supporters. Relatively few votes might be necessary to increase a strategic plurality or to win an election. Each party has to seek those few marginal but crucial votes at their party's political boundaries.

The political caveat and the empirical variable is, of course, whether or not the parties think they need the extra votes. If they do not think they will gain - that they will be bound to win or lose or that the constitution of the next government is predetermined in some way - they will tend to re-emphasize their own characteristic issues. They will seek to stave off internal criticism if they are bound to lose. They will try to satisfy ideological preferences if they are bound to gain. Uncertainty, combined with competition, therefore, makes parties moderate. The absence of either heightens immoderation (Strom, 1990).

Quite apart from the theoretical difficulties salience theory overcomes within Downs' spatial model, there is considerable empirical evidence to the assertion that parties compete by emphasizing or de-emphasizing characteristic issues. Party documents such as election programmes carefully avoid taking definite positions or making definite statements of what the party will do when in government that differ from the promises of rival parties. References to other parties and candidates as a whole, let alone discussion of their issue-positions, takes up an average of only ten percent of the document. Pledges to take specific actions are made only in peripheral areas of policy (Budge et al., 1987). Mostly the documents present the party's views of the history of a certain problem's development and characteristics, while also explaining its importance and priority. What is specifically to be done about it is omitted or minimized.

So much for party behavior. How do electors react to the parties' differential emphasis on policies? It seem that they select the limited number of issues they are worried about and vote for the party which 'owns' most of these (Budge/Farlie, 1983: 26 & 150). In other words they will employ a simplified decision rule to decide, giving each party a score of one for each of 'their' issues which are of concern to them and voting for the party with the highest score (Kelley/Mirer, 1974).

4.6 *Re-evaluating Problems of Collective Action in the Saliency Context*

Predictions from saliency theory about parties' electoral success given the prominence of certain issues in election campaigns, and about leaders' reactions to prospects of close electoral competition or defeat, have been upheld in a comparative context (Budge/Farlie, 1977: 428-31; 1983: 57-115). The theory thus has better empirical support than any rival 'economic' theory. Implicitly therefore the conception of 'rational choice' which it incorporates has more validity that any rival 'economic' model. In this section we evaluate the differences between 'Saliency' and 'economic' ideas, and then go on to show how this alternative conception of rational choice solves or evades the problems of collective action so central to economic models.

As saliency theory develops out of the Downs model, they are not entirely different of course (both are individualistic, in basis). The two points of contrast are:

a) saliency theory assumes that politicians have ideological as well as selfish office-seeking motivations. They will not say or do anything to serve their immediate advantage which totally repudiates their ideological position. What comes uppermost in a particular situation depends on circumstances but ideological motivations are never entirely absent. Similarly electors can either vote selfishly or altruistically within the model: it does not preclude either possibility.

b) saliency theory allows for imperfect information and simplified decision rules which cope with that. In particular, issues are separated out from each other, and a score given to each party, and then they are aggregated to produce a final decision as to which party to vote for.

Such a procedure eliminates the possibility of cyclical instability in voting. The theory of voting cycles (Arrow, 1951) assumes that political decisions are naturally taken in a multi-dimensional issue space because 'rational' actors will always want to assess the results of inter-connected decisions simultaneously (McLean, 1989: 124-125). In spaces of three or more dimensions no equilibrium point exists and there will always be an alternative preferred by a majority to that adopted, so cycles are endemic (and probable also in two-dimensional spaces).

This critique can however be turned round immediately if we recognize that the assumptions of perfect information and costless calculation, on which the cyclical model rests, are themselves highly implausible in the political context, and certainly in the contexts of mass electorates. In particular, the implications of one issue (or set of related issues) for other(s) is not known. They are not really known to experts or politicians, still less to electors. Far from it being 'natural' for politicians and electors to consider all issues together, therefore, in the real world this is often impossible and the 'natural' mode of decision-making is to take one issue at a time. Thus, one considers whether one wants more or less welfare as a question on its own merits, separately from the questions of whether one wants more or less taxation. The fact that many electors want more welfare and less taxes is often used as an example of their inconsistency (McLean, 1989: 109). However, as the case of the Thatcher administration and many other governments shows, welfare spending can easily be increased while taxes are reduced - the two can be reconciled by cutting other areas like defence; or by increasing economic activity so lower taxes produce more money; or through inflation. The actual possibilities are many and inconsistency is in the eye of the analyst rather than in the real world. Still less are welfare decisions linked to law and order, social reform, transport, defence or other substantive issues.

The separation of one issue from another is important theoretically because deciding on a one by one basis and then aggregating, is a type of decision-taking which avoids voting cycles. In effect electors deciding this way are making a series of decisions each on one dimension of a policy space. Now, a well known mathematical result with regard to voting cycles is that when alternatives and voters are ranged along a single dimension (say left-right) and voters have single peaked preference schedules (i.e. they always prefer closer alternatives to those further away), the alternatives preferred by the median voter will be the stable majority preference. An important generalization of this result is that decisions stably reflect majority preference if made on a series of separable issues. For example, parties are judged on left-right issues and the winner chosen, then on religious issues and a winner chosen, and so on, and the winner over most dimensions is elected (Ordeshook, 1986: 250). Voting cycles are thus one of the collective action problems artificially generated by economic models which an alternative - still rational choice - model can deal with.

What about free riders and the problems of providing public goods? Immediately we pose the question we can see that the problem emerges only in a theoretical setting where:

a) standing institutional mechanisms for registering and implementing a collective decision, such as political parties, are lacking. Parties exist in part to articulate solutions to public problems and to carry through mandates for action given by their voters. Comparative research in ten countries shows that they do this (Klingemann, Hofferbert, Budge et al., forthcoming).

b) free riding emerges as a problem where all actors are typified as self interested. If there is even a possibility that action may be altruistic or ideologically inspired, the reasoning breaks down. Saliency theory leaves the possibility of altruism open and explicitly allows for ideological motivations: hence public goods provision is not a problem.

4.7 Widening Rational Choice Theory Beyond Economics to Apply to Comparative Politics

To restate the often repeated assertion of the paper: rational choice theory is much wider than economic style theorizing and more relevant in its other forms to comparative politics. Economic model-building has been a useful stage in advancing the rigor and truly comparative nature of theory in the field. But it has also invented problems of collective action which on the basis of alternative analyses do not seem to exist.

Insofar as the cyclical instability of voting procedures and free riding are also normative critiques of democracy as arbitrary and necessarily coercive, their refutation serves to show that current trends towards greater democracy in the world are not invalidated by inherent defects in its procedures. Comparative research can build on these insights to construct genuine theories which at the same time are less narrow and dogmatic than economic ones have turned out to be - but no less 'rational' for all that.

5 Institutional Difference, Concepts of Actors, and the Rationality of Politics

Roland Czada

> "Because man is the meaning-seeking animal, he gravitates to loci (or institutions) where meaning is likely to be found or created" (from: Alan Sica, 1988: 264)

The rational choice approach of decision-making and strategic interaction is intended to apply everywhere and at any time. The meaning and solutions of, for instance, a prisoner's dilemma game or the public goods-problem do not vary across countries (Ostrom, 1990). Being pure theoretical constructs, they are independent from the bounds of time and culture. So far, the rational choice paradigm follows a natural science model of explanation. It assumes man to be a logically calculating animal.

If all men chose rationally the comparative method would loose its significance, for decision-making processes would be explained by a general algorithm of perfectly calculated choices. Cross-national differences would then be due to the free parameters of this algorithm, e.g. actors' preferences, available means etc. They could be explained in every case without cross-national comparisons. Yet it seems that the rational choice paradigm actuates major advances in the field of comparative politics, rather than eradicating this approach within political science.

The question is therefore whether the field of comparative politics could profit from the rational choice approach without being sacrificed to it. In this Chapter I shall demonstrate that the functional and cognitive limitations of rationality are an important source of cross-national variation, and that, with some theoretical modifications, the rational choice paradigm can enhance our understanding and use of the comparative method in political science. I shall elaborate upon these points, starting with a critique of the rational choice approach.

5.1   Political Choice: Calculation with Infinite Solutions

Rational choice is a function of the strength and direction of an actor's preferences, available means and individual assumptions on the cause-end-effect relationships of action. From this perspective, cross-national or intertemporal variations of politics and policies can be seen to be caused by differences in the preferences, means and causal concepts of political actors. For example, during the 1970s the British Government tried to win the trade union's support by proposing a social contract in order to combat inflation. The government failed, because the unions preferred high wages and lacked the organizational means to control their membership. In addition, considering associational and governmental control deficits most of the union leaders did not really believe that wage restraint would cause less inflation and more employment. In contrast, the highly organized German unions preferred not only high wages, but also co-determination, and they believed firmly in the concept of Keynesianism. During several years they were able to lower the wage-demands of their members in return for co-determination and expansionist economic policies (Scharpf, 1987).

Politics is a process based on relations of conflict and consensus among interdependent individuals and corporate actors. Therefore, political choices are always concerned with interaction (Keman, 1992a). Treating unions as rational corporate actors, their own interests, organizational means and policy-concepts will not fully determine their choices. Since overall policy-outcomes also depend on the choices of their counter-actors, unions must calculate the interests, means and policy-concepts of employer associations and governments; and this again includes an assumption about how these other actors would estimate the interests, means and policy-concepts of the unions which they themselves are also trying to calculate at the same time. In this way, every next step of calculation increases the time-horizon and number of possible solutions of a choice-problem. Actors, in attempting to calculate their decisions, meet with cognitive and functional limits of rationality quite quickly, because of their interdependent relations.

Whereas preferences can be treated as exogenously given, and available means are relatively easy to calculate, the idea of how a certain choice effects the realization of a desired end appears to be highly speculative, because it depends not only on the adequateness of a policy-concept but also on how other actors will react to one's own action. This not only causes an "exploding complexity of simultaneous optimization" (Scharpf 1991: 278), but can also result in a circular argument as far as reciprocal assumptions of the choice calculations of co-actors are concerned.

The attempt to choose perfectly rationally would leave an actor with endless calculations to perform. Beyond a certain level, this would be highly inefficient because of the inevitable rising costs of decision-making. This, however, theoretically means that human action is incalculable. Nevertheless actors do want to give their choices specific meaning. This is a procedure of rational (self-)interpretation. Actors do also assume that there is a meaning in the choices of other actors and, hence, interpret these choices accordingly. This interpretation depends on, and adds new elements to, their own world views or 'cognitive maps' (Axelrod, 1976). This causes a significant research problem for the analysis of actors in comparative politics.

Whereas structural relations between actors can be objectively measured, and functional correlations between variables can be made across different units of analysis, actions have to be interpreted in their specific contexts. It is impossible, for instance, to explain the motives of a Finnish president dealing with a party in parliament in comparison to the American political system and the notion of political rationality that it carries. Strictly speaking, researchers have opted for the "policy-maps" (Schneider 1988: 82) of actors and for the institutional framework of action. In his research on chemical control policies in a transnational policy-network, Schneider (1988) investigated the views of all relevant actors on the 'problem' at hand. He found that conflicting parties can share views on the nature of the problem; although they differ with regard to their various interests, policy goals, means, and institutional incentives.

The rationality of political actors is a subjectively disclosed and apprehended quality of action and thought (Goodwin, 1976: 10ff.), although it is molded by social membership and institutional incentives. If attempts to calculate choices turn out to be nothing more than speculations on an uncertain future, actors can rely on their intuition or they can develop, learn, or adhere to collective world views. The latter is, of course, a cultural-institutionalist approach to the problem of rationality which is opposed to economic explanations based on the assumption of pure wealth maximizing actors (see Chapter 4 in this book). These actors should stop calculating their choices only to save information costs. Thus, economic man would calculate how long it pays to calculate. This, however, is not very convincing, because one cannot rationally decide where to stop the search for information. As long as every future search can possibly add decisive new clues about how to decide more rationally, it is necessarily a more or less nonrational decision to stop searching (Elster, 1986). Hence, rational choices can lead to a vicious circle of reasoning without a final result other than making a subjective decision in the end.

To sum up the principle argument on the status of rationality in politics and social life: problems with information and interactional dilemmas between conflicting parties result in uncertainty and ambiguity. Ego's action becomes meaningless, if he or she lacks any reliable knowledge about its consequences in terms of alter's reaction. Due to these obstacles, institutions have emerged as loci where meaning is likely to be found or created (Sica, 1988: 264). From this perspective, institutions are a prerequisite of rational, meaningful action. There is, and cannot be, any rationality without them. For instance, in some Indian tribes it is rational to give away all of one's belongings in order to win social status. The 'potlatch' as the procedure is called, makes entirely rational what Europeans would undoubtedly call irrational. Thus, the rationality of an action has something to do with the meaning which institutions attribute to that action, be it through informal cultural features or by means of formal organizational rules. This is particularly important for cross-national comparisons, because otherwise we might possibly call the deliberate choice, of, say, an Italian union leader, irrational, on the grounds of, say, the Dutch industrial relations system.

Institutions determine the rules of the game and, thus, furnish the conditions of the choices of individuals as well as of corporate actors under those rules. Institutions constrain choices and make actions more predictable. They routinize action and enhance the opportunities of actors for consequential, strategic interaction. Political institutions give rights and impose duties on individual and corporate actors. Simultaneously, they must be regarded as arenas for conflict, political leadership, ideology and goal-setting (Strom, 1990; Keman, 1992a). As a structural framework for strategic choices, institutions serve as opportunity structures rather than as frictionless decision-making machines.

5.2   *Cognitive Concepts and Strategic Choices*

Institutions determine the capacity of political actors to act and interact with each other. Thus, they do not fully determine political action, but instead leave room for strategic choices. Therefore, a singular knowledge of institutional rules is insufficient to analyze, explain or forecast political behavior. Political goals and actors' ideas on cause-end-effect relationships are equally important. For instance, if political parties or labor unions believe in Keynesianism they will promote deficit spending and high wage policies in order to overcome mass unemployment. In such cases, institutions are to be seen as enabling or restricting certain policies (Scharpf, 1987; Braun, 1989). Policy-concepts may be rational in themselves, but can cause unforeseen, non-rational effects depending on institutional environments. Moreover, policy-concepts may appear to be rather parochial, at least this depends on the perspective of an actual observer. His or her primary task is, however, not to judge the rationality of concepts in themselves. Political scientists should leave this to economists and should instead concentrate on policy-concepts as determinants for political choices. This includes research on the relation between concept-building and institutions, as well as on the relation between institutions and the realization of concepts.

So far we have distinguished the conceptual policy-rationality, based for instance on the Keynesian theory, from the political rationality of actors seeking to promote certain ends in institutional settings. Comparative policy analysis has to scrutinize political institutions and policy-concepts (Keman, 1984; Schmidt,

1987). They both influence political actors' choices. It makes a difference, for instance, whether or not a central bank chooses to support high wage demands and governmental deficit spending by an expansionary monetary policy. This choice depends on the institutional autonomy of a central bank, its political goals, and its adherence to the causal assumptions of the Keynesian concept. One could say that the room for choice and strategic interaction is determined by an actor's institutional position, political goals and cognitive concept of action (Dean, 1984).

Institutions, goals of an actor and concepts of action influence each other. This makes it methodologically difficult to use them as explanatory variables in comparative research designs. Scharpf (1987) and Schmidt (1987) suggest that it is the will and skill of politicians that determines political success. In this respect we could say that political skill is the ability to construct and use political concepts that fit a given institutional opportunity structure. Thus, institutions determine the extent to which concepts are in fact rational, i.e. they can help to realize certain goals in practice. Rational political actors must combine theoretical concepts with practical constellations of interest intermediation, power-dependencies, scarce means and so forth.

Political actors can have a multitude of goals and concepts, which are meaningless in regard to the rational choice paradigm. In fact, there is non-rationality in politics in the sense of actions not comprehending causality in attempts to secure ends. Another type of non-rationality consists of a defiance of rational procedure. In this case actors use causal concepts to realize their goals, but they do so without considering the institutions which can be supportive or hostile to the concepts. To apply a political strategy of polarization in a consociational democracy, as the Dutch labor party did during the 1980s, would be a case in point (Braun, 1989). If this was due to a lack of institutional knowledge, it however provides us with a rational explanation of nonrational behavior. Thus, the existence of non-rationality does not necessarily mark the limits of a rational choice approach of explanation in political science.

Political actors can pursue joint interests and share cognitive concepts. In this case, consensus about policies will be high and the actors easily coordinated. Integrative institutions as, for example, corporatist arrangements do also support consensual policies. The more actors, interests and concepts that are present in a decision-making process, the less likely it becomes that coordination is feasible as a decision-making style. Politics then approaches a market-like pluralist process. Policy outcomes become unforeseen aggregate effects of choices of single actors. They emerge from the interplay and intersection of more or less isolated political actions. The rationalities of a particular actor's choice loose significance if their overall consequences cannot be calculated, but follow from the configurative rationality of a whole social system instead. In this case, institutions become rather important, not for the explanation of particular strategic choices on the micro-level of action, but of the formation of public choices. Many political institutions have not been designed to influence individual choices, but instead to translate the wills of individual actors into collectively binding decisions to be executed by a corporate actor, be it the state, interest associations or any other corporate body. Electoral systems would be a particular case in point. Such systems are explicitly designed not to predetermine the result of elections. All modern institutions of democracy, public administration, and the rule of law are intended to register and aggregate rather than to determine individual choices (Czada/Lehmbruch, 1990).

The rational choice paradigm embraces both, the logic of interaction between a few actors and the logic of public choices, i.e. the transitory coupling of atomized actors or the joint action of groups and organizations. The first is dealt with by game theory, the second by approaches relating to the public goods problem (Arrow, 1951; Downs, 1957; Olson, 1965; see also Chapter 4 in this book). In the next section, I will focus on the empirical complexity of political interaction and I shall discuss some systemic, macro-political aspects of choice in relation to comparative politics.

5.3   *New Challenges in Comparative Politics*

The study of comparative politics is today confronted with more and more differentiated structures of governance. In most of the liberal democratic countries, majoritarian national governments are just one source of legitimate authority (Lijphart, 1984). Sub-national governments, supra-national regimes and governmental bodies, national and international associations, big multinational firms can be seen more or less interwoven policy-makers determining overall policy outcomes. This complexity makes policy-analysis rather difficult (see also Chapter 7 in this book).

In areas where the nation-state becomes increasingly replaced by supra-national authorities, the institutional framework of politics still includes national and sub-national elements. In fact, new political institutions often cross old-established borderlines of territory or functional domains. For instance, nuclear melt-downs at Three Mile Island in 1979 and Chernobyl in 1986 caused farreaching reforms of the institutions and measures of nuclear safety regulations. Among others, a private institution, the 'World Association of Nuclear Operators' was established in 1987, 130 firms operating nuclear plants in 29 countries participated. If one compares the politics of nuclear regulation cross-nationally, one has to investigate the role of such an international actor. At the same time, German sub-national state governments led by Social Democrats and the Green Party tried to use nuclear safety regulations to phase out of nuclear energy, whereas the national government defended the established policy-concept. In sum, a complex multi-level network of actors with moveable borderlines and without a clear center of decision-making is emerging. Political choices have become embedded into a bargaining system, which cannot be deliberately changed by any one of the participating actors (Czada, 1992), but is in itself a bargained system.

The move towards supra-national and sub-national arenas of decision-making, certainly does not reduce institutional varieties. On the contrary, the number of institutional arenas increases. The history of politics is a history of institutional differentiation moving towards more and more specialized, and at the same time interwoven, organizational units of decision-making. This challenges the discipline of comparative politics in several respects:

- The nation-state cannot be regarded as the exclusive unit of inquiry anymore.
- Formal institutions such as law and government and their organizational attributes are not sufficient to explain institutional choices.
- Descriptions of constellations of interest representation and of transaction networks of political actors must be complemented by an explanation of dynamic processes of the so-called 'logic' of interdependent choices.

Below, I shall demonstrate how these points relate to the conceptual history of comparative politics. In addition, two approaches will be introduced, which seem particularly promising in regard to an institutional explanation of policy-making:

1. The notion of moveable boundaries between units of action and overlapping memberships of actors in bargaining networks, as well as interdependencies between institutional domains, should add new perspectives to comparative analysis. Such a perspective is by and large compatible with the network approach, discussed by Adrienne Windhoff-Héritier in Chapter 7 in this book.
2. Cultural norms of behavior play an important role in explaining cross-national variations in policy-making. Even in international bodies with unitary organizational structures and procedural rules, members of different nationalities behave differently in identical situations (Hofstede, 1980). For instance, American nuclear inspectors have applied identical regulatory standards as those of their German colleagues for a completely different task (Czada, 1992), and it is doubtful that this is only an outcome of different organizational structures (Kelman, 1981). Often the norms of behavior embrace the centuries of historical experience, which political or social communities have endured. Hence, it requires historical knowledge to explain and understand actual developments. This is an old theme mastered by the classicists of comparative analysis - for example, de Tocqueville, Weber, Lipset and Rokkan.

5.4 The Antiformalist Revolution and its Consequences

The formal principles of government and public policy-making are in most cases laid down in constitutions and administrative law. So far, the process of government has been influenced by legal rules, which vary considerably across countries. Constitutions give rights to individuals, they constitute individual freedom and regulate how individuals can legally participate in public affairs. Conversely, public administrations could be called the 'operating state', executing decisions made according to constitutional rules. Political scientists have for some time studied those formal mechanisms under the heading of 'Comparative Government' (Finer, 1970). After the Second World War, an alternative antiformalist approach came to the fore. It focussed on social facts of interest intermediation and political regulation. From this perspective, the process of government is driven by interest groups trying to influence public policy without being directly involved in governing. The so-called pluralist movement "was a sociological revolt against legal formalism: group interaction constituted the reality of political life, operating behind the formal legal-institutional disguises of society and the state" (Almond, 1983: 173). A bulk of interest group studies appeared covering many countries on all continents. Suzanne Berger (1981: 18) alleged, for instance, that in "formulating social demands and channeling them into the political process" interest groups gave definition to the varieties of political processes and its outcomes in different countries.

Whereas former studies of comparative government could rely on normative theories of law, the separation of powers, representative government or of legal bureaucracy, the antiformalist movement was essentially empirical in its approach. The historical richness of, for example, the works of Truman, Beer, Ehrmann, Latham, Leiserson is still impressive, but leaves behind a sort of discontent as far as the development of theory is concerned (see also Chapter 2 in this book). This feeling of discontent has been expressed by Mancur Olson quite strongly in his book on the 'Logic of Collective Action' published in 1965. He claimed that the pluralist 'group school' started from wrong assumptions in regard to the associability of individuals and resulting mechanisms of group action.

Olson's argument is that sharing an interest will not automatically lead to collective action in favor of its achievement. From a rational choice perspective, the marginal contribution of an individual to a lobby group would hardly increase its chances of success. Furthermore, it is not feasible to exclude non-members from the consumption of public goods, and certain overall policy outcomes, which result from pressure politics. Therefore rational individuals tend to avoid becoming due-paying members in interest associations. They instead prefer a free ride on the actions of others. Such behavior is less likely, if not impossible, in smaller groups. The mutuality and social control amongst their members favor individual involvement. Most small groups often pursue specific goods whose consumption is exclusive. Hence, it is easier to organize as well as to manage small narrow interests groups. In contrast, large groups are difficult to organize due to the free rider problem. Once established, they tend to be internally divided and therefore hampered in their attempts to represent interests in a coherent manner.

The pluralist 'group school' did not consider that interest politics is molded by individual choices, which are in turn channelled by organizations and interorganizational networks. The latter translate individual choices into public ones according to the rules that are laid down in national institutions of interest intermediation. In this way, cross-national variations can be attributed to certain patterns of cultural choice and to incentive structures developed in national institutional settings. The institutionalist and rational choice perspectives clash with the pluralist approach. Essentially, the latter approach subscribed to a functionalist view of politics. "It presented the notion of multifunctionality as a property of all political structures" (Almond 1983: 180). Regardless of their structural characteristics, competing groups were seen as demanding and supporting public policies in a functionally equivalent manner. Thus, even under authoritarian regimes and in developing countries, informal groups and various forms of pluralist pressure politics appeared to drive the political process (Linz/Stepan, 1978). Up to the early seventies, cross-national comparisons were dominated by this more or less ethnocentric view, which treated political systems as a variety of the American pressure group lobbying. Implicit to this analysis was a functionalistic optimism, which attributed policy outcomes to the beneficial consequences of the pluralist process.

It was not until the challenge of 'corporatism' in the mid-seventies that institutional characteristics of national systems of interest-intermediation came to the fore. Such systems have now been defined as organized, hierarchically structured and more or less biased with respect to different wants in a society, i.e. interests are not equally represented in the system. In several countries associations not only represent their members to governments, but also the government to their members. Thus the corporatist 'school' puts interest groups into an intermediary position between the government and individual citizens (Streeck, 1984). The pluralist emphasis on pressure and influence was replaced by the idea of interest groups being involved in governing (Katzenstein, 1985). Thus, associations were considered to be a specific form of governance besides markets, states, communities or clans and firms (Streeck/Schmitter, 1988).

Both the corporatist school of interest intermediation and Olson's logic of collective action seriously undermined the pluralist explanation of politics. But in a way, the corporatist view was even less consistent with Olson's theoretical findings than the pluralist one (Olson, 1986). Why should one pay for membership of an association that occasionally represents the government against ones own individual interests? Nevertheless, interest associations in Sweden, Austria, Switzerland, the Netherlands and Germany often act as quasi-governmental bodies regulating certain aspects of public life. Their incorporation into politics is part of a historically inherited institutional structure that cannot be deliberately changed by individual actors (Van Waarden, 1992). From a universal rational choice perspective, it seems that they are entrapped by institutions forcing them into membership relations against their own individual interests. However, an instutionalist-cum-rational choice perspective suggests specific cultural expectations of how to account for such pattern of interdependency. Such an explanation focusses on decision-making styles like confrontation, bargaining, problem solving (Scharpf, 1991) which are being produced and stabilized by processes of political socialization; a case of social learning within institutions which is determined by institutional content or spirit, rather than by institutional structures.

To illustrate this point, the problem resembles the question of whether the roman-catholic church survived so successfully during more than a millennium because of their hierarchical organization, or because of the spiritual orientation and loyalty of their members. The same problem applies to the comparative analysis of labor movements and trade-union organizations. To concentrate on organizational properties, as researchers do on corporatism (e.g. Schmitter, 1981), ignores such problems. If it is true that culturally inherited orientations may substitute the effects of formal organizations in controlling the opportunism of actors and directing their transactional choices (North, 1981), then comparative research has to deal with the complex interrelation of socialized actors and historically grown institutions.

It is difficult to explain the emergence and stability of corporatist systems as a result of individual rational choices. Methodological individualism, as expressed in rational choice theories, appears to be incompatible with an institutionalist explanation of politics. Institutional macro-structures clash with individual micro-motives (see also Chapter 6 in this book). From the viewpoint of normative and functionalist theories this is not surprising at all, because institutions should serve as barriers for opportunism. Institutions are meant to give meaning to a specific action and thereby are meant to reduce the possibility of alternative paths of action. They constrain individual choices. However, in some countries the institutions of interest intermediation constrain such choices more than in other countries. There exists considerable cross-national variation in associational density and the degree of organizational regulation of capitalism, which cannot be explained by functional necessity. Economies can be governed predominantly by corporate 'clans' as is the case in Japan (Ouchi, 1981), by voluntary associations as in Switzerland (Farago, 1987), or by bureaucrats as in France (Dogan, 1988; Zysman, 1984). These forms of governance are, however, not in constant flux. Their key feature is a pervasive stability. Therefore we should examine patterns of political action within institutional systems from a comparative perspective. This would allow us to understand the stability, causal links and operating mechanisms of governance and interest intermediation in various countries, however different they may look superficially.

5.5   Rationality, Culture, and Patterns of Interaction

Both comparative politics and policy analysis are intended to explain difference. Researchers examine variations and investigate how they come about. As has been demonstrated above, the rational choice approach holds some resolute assumptions about the sources of variation across countries.

To assume that the political process is based on rational choices on the micro-level of societies leaves three possible explanations of the cross-national variations of that process. Firstly, as preferences, means and cognitive concepts of political actors differ, the process and outcomes of policy-making will also vary. Differences will exist between nations, if preferences, means and concepts of actors are linked to social and cultural environments. Secondly, the rationality of choices is shaped or even determined by institutions. Differences between nations would then simply reflect differences in their institutional design. Thirdly, differences between nations can follow from specific, culturally defined understandings of rationality. In this case, even identical preferences, means, cause-end effect concepts and institutions could produce different choices. These possible sources of variation do not necessarily exclude each other.

Critics of the rational choice paradigm have always emphasized the cultural roots of the concept (Hirschman, 1977; 1982; March/Olsen, 1989; Douglas, 1986). The notion of a sovereign individual is the historical product of rationalized societies. In this view, rational choices require a specific cognitive base that has to be learned. Historical learning leads to the assumption that the shaping of rationalization differs across nations.

Cultures vary in the extent to which action is expected to be carried by individual actors. This approach points to a normative framework of rules and obligations which is external to individuality. It determines the actor's understanding of what to do in any given situation. According to this approach, cognitive concepts of how politics works, plays an important part in the explanation of cross-national differences of political action. If, for instance, actors believe that a freely elected national parliament is only an arena for discussion, but which hardly ever functions as a decision-making arena, as has been held true for long by left wing and right wing politicians in Germany, dictatorship appears to be just another form of normalcy. The Weimar constitution, at its time the most modern one constructed by notable experts of law, history and the social sciences (Bolaffi, 1989; Luthardt, 1990), did obviously not provide the democratic institutions appropriate for political and administrative actors who had been socialized and used to an authoritarian monarchy; especially since this was an early developed welfare state and, thus, enjoyed a somewhat legitimate status. To establish a highly proportional system of parliamentary representation, and supplement this with elements of direct democracy, was probably a wrong incentive structure for most German political actors at that time. Otto Kirchheimer (1932) said the constitution limped ahead of its time. Others asserted that it set up a democracy without democrats.

This makes clear, what is meant by cultural attitudes of actors: these are group specific orientations which can exist independent of institutions, particularly in times of institutional chance or break-down. We then experience a cultural lag between the cognitive orientations of actors bound to past institutions and to the newly established institutional incentive structures. Such lags, of course, mark the limits of institutional reform. The argument, however, is not be understood to say that there is a somewhat genetically inherited spiritual orientation of nationalities, clans, families or any other groupings. Instead, subjective orientations being individually internalized although collectively shared images of reality do not necessarily cope with changing institutional environments without ruptures. This has been empirically shown in numerous developmental programs throughout the Third World (Prechtel/Harland 1986). One can currently observe this, by examining the way in which West German institutions are being transferred to the former East German territory. It is said that the Berlin wall was much easier to remove than the wall in the brain, which blocks the unification-process more than any other aspect.

In contrast to the view of new institutional economics (e.g. Williamson, 1975; North, 1981), the cognitive aspect is important, not just because it influences individual calculations, but even more so because preferences and the perception of a situation are already shaped by culture. For example, social equality is highly valued in the Scandinavian countries, whereas Americans prefer individual achievement (Lipset, 1963). Hence, the "rationalities and irrationalities of the nordic welfare state" (Andersen, 1988) can certainly be understood as a result of cultural attitudes; and the same is true for American politics. Hofstede (1981) found that "uncertainty avoidance" varies along national cultures. So one can assume that cultural belonging determine one's choices, particularly when high risks are involved. This leads to another factor in the explanation of cross-national variations of policy-making.

The rational choice paradigm is based on the assumption that actors have perfect information and are able to make decisions that maximize some concrete ends. It is a common-place idea, since Herbert Simon's research on organizational decision-making showed that actors search for satisfying instead of optimal solutions because of informational restrictions (Simon, 1957). On the one hand, this adds to a cultural-institutional explanation, since cultural rules and organizational routines reduce the uncertainty and ambiguity of individual choices. On the other hand, the concept of bounded rationality leaves room for random walks in decision-making. If the consequences of a choice cannot be calculated because of poor factual knowledge and ambiguities about preferences, then problems and solutions become not only more complex but to some extent reciprocal or circular. Actors may start from existing solutions and apply them to unknown problems. They may alter or even discover their motives by acting. In this way, decisions can emerge from the random matching of solutions and problems. The 'garbage can model' (Cohen/March/Olsen, 1972) of organizational decision-making suggests that in the face of new problems, when actors are highly uncertain, a recombination of existing solutions will often occur. Randomness comes in, because:

> "the model assumes that problems, solutions, decision-makers, and choice opportunities are independent, exogenous streams flowing through a system. Solutions are linked to problems primarily by their simultaneity, relatively few problems are solved, and choices are made for the most part either before any problems are connected to them, or after the problems have abandoned one choice to associate themselves with another" (Olsen, 1991: 92).

Such 'garbage cans' of policy-making do establish path-dependencies, although there is a kind of openness in non-routinized situations which gives room for deviations. It follows from institutional inertia and from the bounded rationality of decision-makers that certain solutions to political problems turn out to be dominant over time in certain countries. In Germany, for instance, social welfare problems tend to be solved by compulsory insurance schemes. In Scandinavia, or the Netherlands, tax-based systems with flat-rate welfare provisions is the selected policy strategy. Only crisis situations, in which complex matchings of actors, problems and solutions occur, give room for new directions in policy-making. Transformations of national policy-styles can, for instance, occur in the wake of mass-unemployment, hyper-inflation, natural or technological disasters or civil unrest. Federalist systems can become centralized or even deferred into authoritarianism during economic depressions as happened in Nazi-Germany. Analyses of political crises show that it proves difficult to regain control of 'social perplexities' by reverting to established rules of policy-making (Czada, 1992b), or, if they do, it leads to diminishing returns in terms of cost-effective decision-making. The discipline of comparative politics, however, lacks systematic studies of institutional break down. The loss of rules, which characterize such situations, extend the strategic options of political actors.

Besides its cognitive-cultural aspects and 'garbage can' characteristics, policies are developed in formal organizations and inter-organizational networks as will be further elaborated in Chapter 7 in this book. Research on corporatist interest-intermediation has shown how organizational structures and interorganizational networks influence the process of governmental decision-making and its policy-outcomes (Lehmbruch/Schmitter, 1982). Lehmbruch (1984) reports on a "neocorporatist logic of exchange" between conflicting but functionally interdependent and institutionally linked interest organizations. This gives way to the idea that the relations between political actors are not solely dominated by zero-sum distributional conflicts. There are also complementary and parallel interests (Scharpf, 1984). Political actors may, in fact, face each other as potential competitors, as exchange-partners, or as associates (Czada 1991: 263). In reality, the recourse to these patterns of behavior is open to strategic choice. On can find them in different mixtures, depending on actors' goals, available resources, changing environments and power-dependencies.

The debate on corporatism shows that the association of convergent or joint interests appears to be much more a theoretical problem than a practical one for explaining relationships of political exchange or competition. Exchanging or competing for political resources like votes, influence, status, power leads to market-like, aggregative processes. In contrast, interest associations supersede the transitory coupling of individual actors. Political authority and an executive body are required in order to maintain and manage an association. Every association of interests requires some kind of governance in order to realize its goals, be it the state or other organizations.

To view politics as an integrative, institutionally shaped process instead of a mere aggregative mechanism has several implications. Institutions have to be seen as autonomous forces. They are public goods, which single actors cannot deliberately create or change for their own convenience. In searching for the rational foundations of political action, one may assume that institutional patterns of interest intermediation offer specific pay-offs for individual and corporate actors that vary from country to country as well as from one sector of policy-making to another. The advantage of viewing systems of interest intermediation as incentive structures (i.e. delineating pay-offs) instead of systemic regulative mechanisms (i.e. adapting to problems) is threefold:

1. The conditions of political stability can be better understood by viewing the motives and choices of specific actors instead of functional adaptive mechanisms. We have seen, for instance, that industrial relations systems do not adapt automatically to specific economic problems, but unions perceive those problems according to the background of their

historical experience and ideological concepts. The choices are influenced by available means and more or less speculative assumptions on the choices of other actors in society and politics. Historically persistent patterns of political choice behavior are due to the rationally motivated resistance of political actors to chance. The rational motive is twofold: change entails uncertainty and high risks with respect to newly emerging social constellations, and it is expensive with respect to moving-costs and the economic as well as the cognitive burdens that are associated with change (Hechter, 1987).

2. Differences between processes of interest intermediation are no longer seen as deviations from a functional ideal-type like the pluralist equilibrium, but are instead viewed as the result of institutional incentives and consequential political action. There are different patterns of interaction like pluralist, corporatist, or sectoralist intermediation with specific rationalities and decision-making-styles. The latter are influenced by cultural orientations.

3. Forecasts and interventions can be made, if one knows how incentive structures and behavioral patterns determine actors' choices, and how these are then translated into public policies by institutional processes of interest intermediation or interest aggregation. This, however, is an ambitious claim. Whereas institutional incentive structures and behavioral patterns of actors can be observed and compared with the aid of conventional techniques of empirical research, it is much more difficult to close the micro-macro link between the choices of actors and public policies resulting from the effects of interaction between those choices. One could, for instance, forecast, that the German unions will discipline the wage-demands of their members in favor of the economic closing-up of the East. It is, however, difficult to say, how important wage-rates are as a determinant for economic growth in the east; and one could only speculate how, for instance, the central bank, will react upon union policies. The bank could ease monetary policy and, thus, support economic growth. It could also take a restrictive course to counter inflationary tendencies originating in global financial markets or international crises, which develop quite independently from German union policies. Thus, one at best can only construct scenarios.

In any case, the prognostic power of an actor's approach appears to be much better than that of pure structuralist or functionalist approaches to politics. The inquiry of the political process should also take into account the cultural and institutional development of the political systems under investigation. Hence, the degree of rationality cannot be detected by a pure, or economic, concept of rational choice, but must instead be analyzed and interpreted on the basis of 'real life' experience. One way to do this, is by developing rational-cum-institutional concepts that can 'travel' cross-nationally. Perhaps this seems a daunting task, but it is one that ought to be undertaken.

6 Restrictions in the Political Control of Science

Dietmar Braun

The political control of economic and social developments has been a major field of interest in comparative public policy research for quite some time. The results which have been presented show that it was not a question of *if* politics did matter but rather *when, how and to what degree*. There are variations in the explanatory power of political variables according to country, policy field and over time, but there seemed little doubt that party control, systems of interest intermediation or types of democratic systems induced concomitant variations in rates of unemployment and inflation or strike behavior (Castles et al., 1987).

From a more general, *systems-theoretical perspective*, however, this overall consensus in comparative public policy has been contested. Disregarding possible variations between countries, the German sociologist *Niklas Luhmann* maintains that there is a growing inability of the political system to control events and developments in subsystems of society. His basic assumption is that society is differentiated into a large number of functional subsystems, each of which develops the tendency to cut itself off from other functional subsystems. The political system is therefore confronted with a complex and multi-faceted environment and loses its traditional position as the center of society. According to systems theory, political control in the sense of determining the 'operational mode' of functional subsystems does not exist. Because this perspective radically revises some of the assumptions concerning political control that comparative public policy has taken for granted, it is worthwhile to assess its basic ideas more thoroughly.

Though I subscribe to the notion of the functional differentiation of society, I reject the strict macro-level explanatory model of systems theory for comparative research. Instead I will present an actor-based model that takes into account the general ideas of Luhmann and his followers. My unit of observation is the actor, which is part of a functional subsystem.

The most prominent example used by German systems theory as a verification of its premises and assumptions is the relationship between politics and science. I will confine my discussion, therefore, to *research policies*. The general question I will take up is: *What are the restrictions that prevent the political system from controlling scientific production?*[1]
After a discussion of the basic ideas of systems theory, the actor-based model of *credibility-cycles* will be introduced. The discussion on research policies is subdivided into two main sections: first, problems of policy-makers to organize policy advise will be analyzed, and second, the transfer of basic research into application is questioned.

My contribution to the general topic of this book is therefore the presentation and discussion of a neglected theoretical approach in comparative public policy, which might render some fruitful insights into options and restrictions of political control as well as may become a heuristic device for hypothesis-building.

6.1 Political Control in the View of the Systems-theory

The core of Luhmann's argument[2] is his *theory of the differentiation of society into a set of subsystems* each based on a specific *meaning*. Such subsystems are manifold in advanced industrialized countries (examples are the scientific system, the legal system, the political system, the economic system, the religious system). In contrast to Parsons, Luhmann does not depart from an analytically defined

---

[1] By the term *control* we mean the link of "decisions on guidelines to the output of actors", which is implementation, and not the setting of "parameters for action (for example by defining standards)" which is policy-formulation and would be denoted by the term "guidance" (Bogason 1991: 194).

[2] It is not possible here to deal with systems theory in a way that would do justice to its complex assumptions and conclusions. In my presentation of Luhmann's theory, I will focus on those elements I find useful from my own point of view.

set of structures or subsystems functional for the stability of society. He considers instead the differentiation of society into subsystems as the evolutionary outcome of a process of *complexity reduction*. In order to cope with the unlimited complexity of the world, social systems are bound to reduce complexity by the selection of information and events. *Meaning* for Luhmann is therefore a kind of selection criterion of social systems. And it is more than that according to Luhmann:

> "Meaning functions as the premise for experience processing in a way that makes possible a choice from among different possible states or contents of consciousness, and in this it does not totally eliminate what has not been chosen, but preserves it in the form of the world and so keeps it accessible....Meaning is not a selective event, but a selective relationship between system and world - although this is still not an adequate characterization. Rather, what is special about the meaningful or meaning-based processing of experience is that it makes possible *both* the reduction and the preservation of complexity" (Luhmann, 1990: 27).

The relationship of functional subsystems of their environment is characterized by *autonomy and integration*. On the one hand all internal processes and activities of a functional subsystem are directed to the specific *point of reference*[3] of a subsystem. This constitutes their autonomy from other subsystems. On the other hand concentration on the production of one function decreases the capability of subsystems to take care of other functions important to their own systemic reproduction.[4] Functional subsystems are dependent on the services of other functional subsystems. This evokes the need for the organization of an exchange of the different services each functional subsystem provides.

---

[3] A point of reference of the scientific subsystem would for example be the scientific development of knowledge (Luhmann, 1977: 20) or in case of the political system the "announcement of collectively binding decisions" or the "authoritative allocation of material and immaterial values" (Luhmann, 1986: 169).

[4] For example, education is a requirement for the ability of the scientific subsystem to recruit human capital, and economic activities are a requirement for all other subsystems to satisfy their financial needs.

Subsystems are therefore characterized by "independence" and "interdependence" (Willke, 1989; see also Morel et al., 1989: 188-189).

What does this mean for political control? According to Luhmann the political system which is embedded into functionally differentiated societies has lost its traditional central position. It can no longer make use of hierarchical procedures to control the delivery of services of other subsystems (Luhmann, 1986: 168-169). The differentiation of society into subsystems, moreover, increasingly deprives the political system of the information necessary to intervene into other subsystems.[5] Subsystems are in many ways *"closed systems"* in the way they process their communication and activities (Luhmann, 1990: 5). Though subsystems do react to one another, this reaction is solely based on their own type of communication and capability of observation. There might be political control if political actors are able to find access to the scientific communication which can initiate a process of change. The dynamic of the ensuing change is, however, determined by the social structures and types of communication inherent to the scientific system. Policy-makers need the aid of functional subsystems in order to achieve political ends.

6.2 An Actor-based Model of Scientific Production

Luhmann deliberately refuses to integrate actors or action into his theory. This assumption has, of course, often been criticized (Scharpf, 1989; Mayntz, 1988; Schimank, 1985). However, one can uphold basic insights of systems theory while simultaneously referring to a more empirically based action theory. A systems theory without actors lacks empirical evidence; an actor perspective without a notion of structured and systemic relationships binding actors (the classical role-concept) is insufficient for understanding the complexity of reality.

The interesting question is to what extent Luhmann's notion of the 'closed quality' of functional subsystems and the subsequent restrictions on

---

[5] Only complete information on the conditions, situations and moves of actors can, as Elinor Ostrom for example has shown for the "common resources problem", lead to successful political control (Ostrom 1990: 8-11). Complete information is, however, never available.

political control can be upheld if we integrate intentions and behaviors of actors into the systemic framework. In what way are functional subsystems able to incorporate their members into a 'self-referential' communication process? What is the 'social glue' of functional subsystems from an actor's perspective?

An elegant answer to these questions could consist of the assumption that all actors in a system identify with the point of reference of the system. Systems would bind their members by powerful normative regulations. Such an assumption would render, of course, a rather simplistic undercomplex view of reality. It would moreover neglect recent theoretical and empirical findings. Individual choices are apparently based on self-interest, rules and regulations, norms and even emotions (Flam, 1989; Elster, 1989b: 61-70; Hohn/Schimank, 1990: 29). How then are individual choices and collective behavior in functional subsystems linked to one another?

The notion of a *credit or credibility cycle*, which has been developed above all by Bruno Latour (1979 with Woolgar; see also Latour 1987) by integrating ideas of Merton (1973: 281-412), Hagstrom (1965) and Bourdieu (1977, 1984), is a useful concept for answering the question raised here.[6]

The basic idea is simple: all actors who try to fulfill a professional role in a functional subsystem are forced to *invest* in their *credibility* in order to "keep producing under the best possible conditions" (Kohler, 1989: 3). Credibility in the scientific subsystem means *reputation* in the scientific community. Such a reputation enables actors "to be trusted with goods or money in expectation of future payment" (Latour/Woolgar, 1979: 194). Just as credibility makes it easier for the businessman to get a loan from his bank, it "concerns scientists' abilities actually to do 'science' when applying for grants and institutional support" (Latour/Woolgar, 1979: 198).

Investments in science resemble investments in economy: they pass through several stages of a transformation process in order to yield returns to the investor. This analogy of social processes in different subsystems caused

---

[6] The idea of a credibility cycle was developed mainly by analyzing the cognitive and social processes in the scientific subsystem. The concept may be a heuristic tool to analyze the relationship of systems and actor behaviour in other functional subsystems of society. It seems possible for example to transplant the ideas of the credibility cycle to the doctor in the health care system or to the politician in the political system.

Bourdieu to compare credibility in the scientific system or in other subsystems with 'social capital' (Bourdieu, 1975: 21).

Kohler summarizes Latour's description of the cyclical investment process as follows:

> "Researchers work to produce results that will be used and thus accredited by other workers; the credibility thus gained in the marketplace is reinvested in getting grants, which buy equipment, laboratories, and co-workers; material resources are reinvested in the production of more results, which get turned into arguments and papers, which earn credibility, which is reinvested in grants, and so on." (Kohler, 1989: 2).

A scientific career "therefore presents itself as a *continuous* process of accumulation ..."(Bourdieu, 1975: 26).

Whatever the personal motivation of the actor may be,[7] once he has decided to participate he is forced to invest in his credibility and through all the transformation stages from investment to return. It is during this transformation process that the point of reference (scientific knowledge) is reproduced. It is therefore not necessary that the individual actor be motivated to contribute to the point of reference of functional subsystem. He may behave like a self-interested and strategic-thinking actor. New knowledge is acquired once he has accepted to invest in his credibility. This argument is summarized in the following figure (see also Latour/Woolgar, 1979: 201):

---

[7] "Scientists are thus free to report interest in solving difficult problems, in getting tenure, in wanting to alleviate the miseries of humanity, in manipulating scientific instruments, or even in the pursuit of true knowledge" (Latour/Woolgar, 1979: 207-08).

Figure 6.1   *The Credibility Cycle of the Scientist*

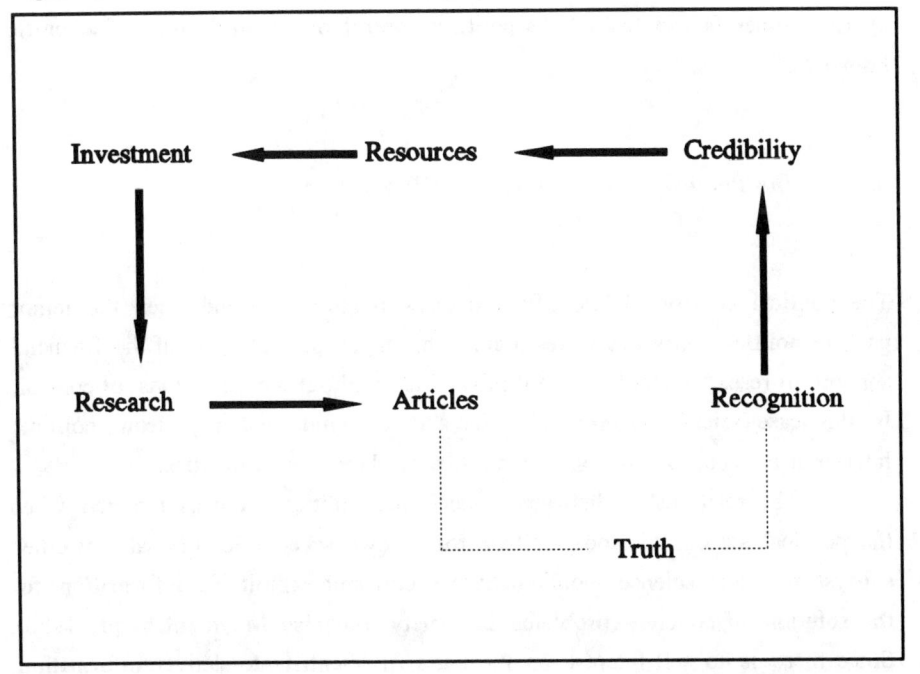

```
Investment  ←——— Resources ←——— Credibility
    │                                  ↑
    ↓                                  │
Research  ———→  Articles         Recognition
                   └·········· Truth ··········┘
```

'Truth' symbolizes the point of reference of the scientific subsystem, the production of scientific knowledge. The figure demonstrates that recognition by the scientific community is a central factor in gaining credibility. It is at the same time an important part of the 'social glue' of the system: the scientist will only be recognized if he has taken into consideration the methodological requirements of the scientific community, anticipated the expectations the scientific community has with regard to the innovativeness of research topics, and so on. The knowledge that the scientist will be evaluated by peers according to the established principles of accumulating scientific knowledge functions as a kind of social control on the behavior of scientists.

    The credibility cycle is thus the social mechanism which links the production of the scientific system to the intrinsic motivations of actors. It has a *conservative influence* on the behavior of actors striving for scientific reputation - and this is the actor-based explanation of the 'closed quality' of societal subsystems - which makes it difficult for policy-makers to change the behavior of scientists according to the external guidelines of politics.

Let us now turn to research policies and see in what way credibility cycles or other factors restrict the political control of the production of scientific knowledge.

6.3 The Political Control of Scientific Production

The political control of scientific processes is only part, and often the minor part, of political activities in research. The major part consists of the financial support of research institutes and universities without any intentions of control. In this case science can organize its activities independently from political interference according to its own rules, procedures and priorities.

The relationship between science and politics becomes strained when the political system demands - either for its own sake or for the sake of other subsystems - that science should deliver useful and exploitable information for the solution of concrete problems in society (see also Mayntz/Scharpf, 1990). Since there is no self-interest on the parts of scientists to deliver information which is scientifically unpromising, it is here political control becomes involved. How to gain the cooperation of scientists in applied research fields contributing to the needs of industry, health care or politics is the major problem for research policy makers.

The political control of scientific knowledge is usually directed either to the organization of scientific information useful for political action (policy advice) or to the organization of a transfer of knowledge from the scientific subsystem to other subsystems. In the first case the political system is a corporate actor with its own interests, in the second case, it is the trustee for other subsystems that put claims on science.

6.3.1 Problems in the Organization of Scientific Policy Advice

The exploitation of scientific information which might improve political action and control is confronted by the different time-horizons of political and scientific activities as well as by the working of the credibility cycle of scientists.

The time-horizon of the scientific subsystem is *long-term*: No one can predict, for example, if and when scientists will find a solution to problems. The success of research in terms of a useful result - not in terms of scientific articles - depends on so many contingent factors that scientists cannot promise to succeed. Luhmann suggests, moreover, that the very logic of the scientific enterprise creates a never-ending spiral of new problems. All answers found in science are regarded as temporary and as the starting point for new questions. In other words, it is not the solution of singular problems science is striving for but the continuous process of problem-solving (Luhmann, 1986: 156; Braun, 1991b: 70).

Other authors stipulate that scientific discoveries follow their own time- and phase-specific course which cannot be influenced from the outside. Only in the last phase of scientific development does political control seem feasible (Böhme/Stehr, 1976; Van den Daele et al., 1979).

The time-horizon of the political system is more limited and often short-term: the political credibility cycle is attached to the time-horizon of parliamentary democracy. It is expected that the politician participates in periodic elections in which the voter assesses policies and political programmes. The political business cycle compels political actors into a rather tight time-straitjacket. Political expectations concerning scientific productions are therefore structured by the time-horizon of the political credibility cycle. The demands for the short-term supply of useful policy advice increase when problems appear on the political agenda which are expected to have clear repercussions on the public credibility of the politician.

Politicians may be compelled to circumvent this time-difference problem by using one of three strategies: hiring, incorporating or instrumentalizing scientists. If political actors try to *hire* a commercial research enterprise they will often find that this may solve the time-difference problem[8] but that the information problem remains. Two factors contribute to this deficit: first, commercial research enterprises often lack the scientific backing and experience needed for carefully tested and scientifically valid information; secondly, for

---

[8] Commercial research enterprises often follow the logic of rentability inherent to the economic system. The short-term time-horizon of investment and return in the economic subsystem is congruent to the time-horizon of the political system.

cognitive and technical reasons, a complex problem is often not solvable within the time-span allowed for by the political system. Politics gets the information 'quick', but it often may be 'dirty'.

Problems arising from the conservative character of credibility cycles are present in the two other strategies used by research policy makers to establish useful information feedback between science and politics. Take for example the political strategy of *incorporating* scientists into research institutes of the political system with the task of answering directly to political demands and information needs. The success of such a strategy is jeopardized for three reasons (Braun/Schimank, 1992):

- The overflow of demands made by politicians and bureaucrats as well as the daily routines of useful information processing absorb most of the time of the incorporated scientists. As their activities are overwhelmingly based on applied research, they may lose the opportunity to make themselves familiar with developments in fundamental and strategic research (Hohn/Schimank, 1990).
- The consumption of time resources by applied research and routineactivities leaves no room to engage in fundamental and strategic research. The services for the political system are, moreover, not recognized by the scientific community as a contribution to the scientific credibility cycle.
  The scientist working at the service of the political system therefore has a position and a guaranteed income but is not able to invest in his or her scientific credibility.
- The longer this situation of estrangement of the scientist from his or her roots continues, the more difficult it gets for him or her to return. Earlier investments in credibility grow pale if they are not permanently reinvested.

The danger of being cut off from their scientific credibility cycle might force scientists to leave the political system as early as possible in order not to lose too much previously accumulated 'social capital' or it might prevent those scientists who are able to climb the ladder of scientific success from entering politically dominated research enterprises at all. In both cases policy-makers will not be able to incorporate 'cream of the crop' scientists. In this way, politics gets information, but it may render it useless for the improvement of political action.

The third strategy consists in financing university researchers (and research groups) for the explicit purpose of establishing a powerful scientific human capital pool within the scientific system which can be exploited if needed (we might call this the 'instrumentalizing strategy'). This, for example, is what the Department of Health and Social Services (DHSS) in the United Kingdom has attempted to do in order to set up health services research, the results of which could be directly applied to the policies of the Ministry (O'Grady 1990; Braun, 1992).

Again, the hybrid position between political imperatives and the scientific credibility cycle did not work out to the advantage of political ends. The research groups had extreme difficulties in receiving recognition from the scientific community as long as they stuck to applied research. If they did not and endeavored to contribute to basic knowledge in their field, which the government expected them to do, they were able to become integrated into the universities but could not be controlled by politics.

In all three strategies, therefore, policy-makers run into profound restrictions, hindering their efforts to successfully build up a direct and exploitable information flow from science to the political system. These restrictions are attributable to the 'operational mode' of science (time-horizon) and the conservative influence of credibility cycles.

6.3.2 *The Organization of the Transfer of Scientific Knowledge to the Health Care Subsystem*

What kind of restrictions exist in the organization of a *transfer of knowledge* from the scientific subsystem to other subsystems? What can policy-makers do to overcome these restrictions?

Since the 1980s governments in many countries have increased the pressure on the scientific subsystem to demonstrate its usefulness and efficiency in terms of cost-benefits. Particular attention was paid to the translation of basic research findings into industrial applications. Another issue involved the knowledge *health research* could deliver with regard to an improvement of the health of the population and of the cost-effectiveness of the health care system. Pushed by the growth of chronic diseases, an awareness of the negative effects of environmental and life-style factors on health, and the apparently uncontainable increase in the costs of the health care system, governments expected quick and applicable solutions and answers from scientists. To give an example I will describe a central area of health research: the transfer of scientific biomedical knowledge into clinical application.

There are two ways to organize the transfer of knowledge from basic research into application in other subsystems:
- By means of the situative differentiation of professional roles
- By means of the establishment of cooperation among actors with different professional roles

It is shown in the following sections that the functional differentiation and conservative influence of credibility cycles restrict the transfer of scientific knowledge into the health care system. Political strategies to overcome these restrictions seem to be confined to the setting of institutional frameworks for action.

6.3.3 Situative Differentiation

An easy solution to the transfer problem in health research would be given if one single actor could combine the knowledge of both the scientist and the physician, and this is indeed expected of the medical professor at a medical school or medical faculty. The transfer then seems to be a mere question of adequate time distribution: for example, the medical scientist does fundamental research in the morning and applies it in the afternoon.

Theories which do not depart from the concept of functional differentiation - for example, the 'structural pose paradigm' (Mandell/Porter, 1991) - and from assessments from politicians, administrators and even the affected actors themselves both easily overestimate the capabilities of actors to adapt to different situative roles and underestimate the centrifugal consequences of role differentiation.

Each functional role demands specific *cognitive abilities* from the actor. These abilities are routinely used in the daily activities. Cognitive psychology for example has found (Evans et al., 1987) that physicians use inductive reasoning and empirical classification for their activities, while scientists make use of deductive and axiomatic reasoning. Different cognitive horizons, it seems, form a major obstacle for actors who seek to combine scientific and practical knowledge in a sequential order.

Another obstacle in this respect is the tendency of functional subsystems to continuously expand their claims on the time and energy of actors. Bourdieu and Latour and Woolgar have demonstrated that scientists are obliged to run through their credibility cycle as quick as possible in order to maximize the profits for their credibility. This acceleration of 'runs' (from investment to return to investment) has - though in combination with other factors - contributed to the increase in specialization of scientific knowledge. The urge to publish at a more rapid pace and the growing need of detailed knowledge for scientific research claims most of the time-resources of actors who want to be successful in the credibility cycle of science.

The health care system puts equivalent claims on its members: the physicians too have experienced a growing specialization in their field, they have to deal with more refined and sophisticated technologies and are often confronted with a growing number of patients. The task of a physician is, moreover, dependent on a profound and thorough knowledge which is gathered through the practice of medicine. This practical knowledge needs to be continuously renewed. The effect is the same as in the case of the scientist: there is no time left for physicians to take into consideration the cognitive developments in other functional subsystems.

The result of this ceaseless devouring appetite of functional subsystems for the performance of its members is - as empirical evidence confirms - a growing inability to find actors who are able to deal successfully with both science and patient-care. Though situation differentiation is in most countries formally upheld in the role of professors, in fact professors are seldom able to fulfill both roles adequately. They are inclined to take on one of the two roles. This stance is supported by negative sanctions of the subsystems: the scientific subsystem does not reward attempts of biomedical scientists to gain a reputation in the development of therapies for patients, neither does the health-care system honor those physicians who start a career as a scientist.

The growing inability to differentiate roles situatively is, finally, nurtured by the *institutional environment* itself in which the actors are working, namely, the universities and medical faculties.

When Abraham Flexner wrote his reports on medical faculties and universities earlier this century (Flexner, 1927; 1930), he was impressed by the "integrative" German university system, where research, teaching and patient-care are integrated into medical faculties. He advised the American universities to copy this system in order to improve research performance.

Organizational co-existence, i.e., the integration of different functional activities under the roof of one organization, appears to be one way to organize the exchange between different subsystems in a coherent and permanent fashion. Though American research universities have indeed demonstrated an astonishing capability to transfer knowledge from biomedical science into clinical application, the European universities, in particular the German and French ones, failed to do so. Why?

Empirical evidence is found that patient-care can systematically dominate the distribution of organizational resources (time, space, money) in its own favor, if it is closely associated to, or even integrated into medical faculties, as for example in France and the FRG.[9]

From a systems-theoretical point of view, an explanation for the tendency of medical faculties to develop 'functional hierarchies' (Braun 1991b) can be found in what Luhmann has labeled the 'priority of urgent activities'. Here again, differences in the time-horizons of functional activities play an important restrictive role in the transfer of scientific knowledge to other subsystems.

Patient-care is able to capture in the prominent place in medical faculties because it does not allow for a delay in treatment. Moreover, there are not any time-limits for patientcare: patients may be admitted at anytime to the hospital, and once they are, they need the immediate help of physicians and constant surveillance during their stay. Urgency and unlimited consumption of time-resources supported by moral imperatives in society justify a constant claim of patient-care on human capital and organizational resources.

Research cannot compete with this claim. Though there are no time-limits to the search for new and more profound knowledge as such, research can

---

[9] There are different models of association between medical faculties or schools and hospitals. The example of the USA and the UK demonstrate that the organizational separation of patient-care from the university *can* make it easier to forego the tendency of patient-care to dominate the other functional activities (Braun, 1990; 1991a).

wait during the night, research projects are designed for several years and there are no 'clients' demanding immediate activities by scientists. Fundamental research needs, as is described above, a long-term horizon.

It is thus understandable that administrators and decision-makers in medical faculties are systematically inclined to support first patientcare and to grant the other functions lesser priority. The consequence of this 'functional hierarchy' is the inability to transfer scientific knowledge into clinical application, since medical professors spend most of their time in patient-care, infrastructural resources at the hospital and the faculty are directed to the aid of diagnosis and treatment of patients, and biomedical scientists are (ab)used for the diagnosis of patients instead of as suppliers of scientific information transformable into clinical knowledge.

Though many American research universities succeeded in overcoming the predominance of patientcare in medical faculties by various institutional facilities (Braun, 1990) the organizational co-existence of functional activities today seems to be an awkward device for the transfer of knowledge into health care. The 'functional hierarchy' does not allow for role integration. Quite the contrary, it enforces role differentiation and thereby fosters the conservative tendencies of credibility cycles.

6.3.4 *Organizing the Cooperation of Actors from Different Subsystems*

If sequential role differentiation fails in establishing the transfer of scientific knowledge, the adequate strategy would be to stimulate the cooperation between biomedical scientists and physicians. There are again, however, restrictions which hamper such cooperation.

In all countries under review, mistrust, and even a contempt, is found between clinical physicians and biomedical scientists. Clinical physicians who dominate the medical faculties in most countries, are not prepared to grant scientists an equal status within the faculty. Scientists are therefore discouraged from entering into medical faculties. They lack infrastructural support and their pay is always inferior to the salaries of physicians. In addition, participating in clinical research is not regarded as a contribution to the scientific credibility cycle. Conversely physicians, have no incentives to participate in a cooperative enterprise with scientists: their status as a physicians is higher than that of scientist, they can earn more by healing patients then by writing articles; and they are primarily bound within the credibility cycle of the health care system and are thus subject to the same conservative effects on their behavior as the scientific credibility cycle has on scientists.

This divide between scientists and clinical physicians is of course not insurmountable. The systemstheoretical tools of observation and the notion of credibility cycles cannot but make comprehensible the dynamics or the *undercurrents* which are at work in the transfer of knowledge from science to other subsystems. They demonstrate the compelling forces of structured interactions on individual choices. This does not mean that it impossible to create *institutional devices* which can induce a deviant behavior. It is here that political control seems to have its task and opportunities.

My empirical studies demonstrate that a quite successful transfer can exist if a number of institutional preconditions are given. In particular, the example of the United States demonstrates that an early integration of scientific research in medical education, a large-scale department system, restrictions on profit-making by treating private patients, monitoring of the research performance of medical professors, a decentralized and competitive scientific system, a 'grants economy' and the supply of sufficient time for research helped to build up the cooperation between scientists and physicians (Braun, 1990). What can we learn from this description with regard to the *political control* of scientific production?

First, attempts of political control to improve the transfer of scientific knowledge into clinical application, which would aim to attract biomedical scientists and physicians systematically into applied clinical research, are confronted with the centrifugal forces of functionally differentiated subsystems. The behavior of actors which fulfill professional roles in functional subsystems are strongly determined by norms, rules and regulations valid within the functional subsystem. It seems difficult for actors fulfilling professional roles to deviate from expectations attached to these roles.

Secondly, though it seems difficult for policy-makers to estrange the scientist from his chosen credibility cycle, there are nevertheless indirect and long-term means that policy-makers can make use of in attempts at political control. As the example of the United States suggests, the transfer of scientific knowledge to other subsystems can be influenced by providing adequate opportunity structures. Role-taking and role-making is embedded into national-specific institutional environments. Institutional reforms are therefore the key to political control to individual and collective behavior (for this argument: Ben-David, 1971).

6.4   *Conclusions*

By referring to concepts from systems theory and the sociology of science it was endeavoured in this article to overcome the structural approach that comparative public policy usually applies to the measurement of political control. Correlations between aggregated variables may point to the significance of political structures or actors, but they do not help in explaining how 'signals' emitted by political actors are received by societal actors and transformed into individual and collective action. In other words, comparative public policy does not account for the so-called 'macro-micro-macro'-link in the explanation of collective action and outcomes (Alexander/Giesen, 1987). Explanations in comparative public policy usually remain confined to the macro-level of collective action.

As the vigorous debates on 'rational choice' and 'new institutionalism' in the political sciences indicate (see: Keman, 1992a; Czada/Windhoff-Héritier 1991; March and Olsen 1989; Alt/Shepsle 1990; Elster 1989a), there is, however, a growing awareness of the need to develop outlines of a political theory of action.

This chapter has followed the questions raised in the ongoing debate. I found it useful, however, to introduce the concepts of functional differentiation and credibility cycles to understand the restrictions policy-makers encounter in their attempts to control collective outcomes. In terms of these concepts, the addressees of political action were conceived as actors bound by professional roles governed by norms, rules and regulations of functional subsystems.

Though March and Olsen (1989) do not consider the concept of functional differentiation, their notion of a 'logic of appropriateness' entails very similar ideas: In order to understand how individual actors behave, it does not suffice to assume a benefit-maximizing actor, rather, we need to take into account the organizational environment and the cultural background actors are bound by, the norms actors adhere to etc. It is therefore the social environment which tells us a lot about actors' choices.

The concepts of functional differentiation and credibility cycles seemed in addition particularly useful for understanding more thoroughly why actors, bound by professional roles (such as those of the scientist, physician or politician), show considerable conservatism in their behavior. Such conservatism can restrict political attempts to achieve desired outcomes in functional subsystems, if it is required that actors accept political ends incompatible with their credibility cycle or if they are supposed to engage in activities not yet recognized as contributing to the actors' credibility.

This point was demonstrated throughout the article by using the political control of science as an example. It was suggested that:

- Political strategies to incorporate or instrumentalize scientists for policy-advise would fail as long as scientists continue to accept the point of reference of the scientific subsystem.
- Sequential role-taking which seemed to be a conducive strategy for organizing the transfer of scientific knowledge into application, comes under increasing strain. It was shown that the internal dynamics of each credibility cycle were extending the demands on time-resources and attention of actors, and thereby forcing them to choose one credibility cycle only.
- The organization of cooperation between scientists and physicians which would be an alternative strategy for the improvement of the transfer of scientific knowledge into application, was similarly subject to centrifugal forces exerted by credibility cycles.

The point stressed here is then that the social processes (norms and expectations) governing the action and behavior of actors in functional subsystems are beyond the intentional control of any single actor. In this sense, credibility cycles can develop a dynamic of their own which leads to the conservative behavior of actors: as long as they choose to fulfill their professional role they submit to 'self-referential processes' at work in functional subsystems.

Policy-makers who attempt to set guidelines incompatible with the norms and expectations of professional roles are therefore - and this is the main message - confronted by tendencies of encapsulation and repulsion. There is no easy and direct way to translate political 'messages' into corresponding behavior of actors in functional subsystems. In order to be 'heard' policy-makers must provide opportunities and incentives which may induce a gradual shift in the 'cognitive maps' of actors and in the norms and expectations guiding their behavior. In other words, the challenge for political control is to build up new institutional frameworks and incentive mechanisms helpful in developing professional roles more conducive to political needs.

The restrictions placed on political control are therefore obvious: policy-makers cannot directly intervene in the social processes regulating the behavior of actors in functional subsystems. Credibility cycles function as a protective shield for actors against the intrusion of external demands. Political action is confined to the shaping of the institutional framework of professional action. Whether addressees actually respond in the way policy-makers want them to is, however, subject to their will as well as well as to the 'social glue' of the functional subsystem.

It will be fruitful to elaborate these ideas. A focus of future research would then be to assess the different credibility cycles governing the behavior of actors in functional subsystems. By comparing different subsystems of political control it may be possible to learn more about the dynamic of political control and its efficiency on different levels of observing units of analysis (i.e. the micro-macro link). We need to understand the manifold 'self-referential' processes in society before we can account for the relationship of political action and collective outcomes in society. It is the transformation process of political attempts of control into individual action and collective outcomes which we need to understand more thoroughly. Only by assessing the transformation process step by step will we be able to really understand what governing power is left to policy-makers in times of a functional differentiation of society.

PART III: *Comparative Political Research*

7 Policy Network Analysis: A Tool for Comparative Political Research

Adrienne Windhoff-Héritier

In recent years policy network analysis has been increasingly used as an analytical approach in political research. This is not just a new fad in political science, but is instead due to the growing insight that public policies emerge from the interaction of public and private actors. Less and less emphasis has been placed on the state as the central actor, state actors dealing with powerful large organizations in all sectors of public policies are instead stressed. What analytical questions are raised by policy network analysis and what advantages does it have to offer? To what extent does policy network analysis lend itself as an analytical instrument to the comparative investigation of politics and policy-making?

The reason why policy network analysis is generally considered to be a promising instrument of political research is twofold. Firstly, it combines explanatory approaches from different theoretical backgrounds and secondly, as previously mentioned, it attempts to explain the emergence of political decisions within the context of interacting public and private actors which are concerned with a specific policy issue. In doing so, it goes beyond the description of formal institutional decision making; it also clearly goes beyond the assumption that one political elite dominates decision processes in all policy fields. These specific virtues of policy network analysis - or so the argument runs - may, within certain limits, also be brought to bear in comparative political research.

What is a policy network? A policy network consists of public and private actors (institutions, organizations, groups, individuals) and their interactions. The members of a network are not only actors holding positions with formal powers of decision, but all 'consequential actors' (Knoke/Laumann,

1978) who direct, coordinate or control material or immaterial resources in a policy field of common concern. The membership and central positions within the network are constantly negotiated and embattled among existing and potential participants. Networks gain stability over a longer period of time if stable expectations concerning calculable exchange relations are developed. The exchange of resources between formal and informal actors within the network is limited and is to a certain extent structured by institutional rules, organizational structures, contracts, informal routines, as well as the governance structure of the network. The latter is defined by political decision and describes the specific policy instruments which are used in the field, such as command-and-control strategies, negotiation mechanisms or market incentives.

In doing so, the governance structure of a network shapes the incentives of the participants and induces the latter to act in a specific way. Moreover, the range and nature of exchange processes, and the limiting and enabling role of institutions are only to be understood within the context of a specific policy field which lays open particular opportunities of action. Furthermore, interaction within the network is influenced by a shared understanding of the adequate mode of problem solving and an adequate style of interaction among actors.

In the first section of following contribution to this volume I shall outline the main theoretical questions linked by policy network analysis. In the second part, I will discuss in which way and to what extent policy network analysis can be used in comparative political research. In a third section, the British and U.S. clean air policy innovations of 1990 will be analyzed to illustrate the network-analytical approach.

7.1 Policy Network Analysis: Linking Different Theoretical Approaches

Four different theoretical backgrounds come to bear in policy network analysis:
a) Rational choice theory in the shape of resource exchange and resource dependence theory, as developed by Aldrich and Pfeffer (1976);
b) the new political institutionalism, as outlined by March and Olsen (1989);

c) symbolic interaction theory, as elaborated by Burns and Flam (1987) for the organizational context;
d) public policy analysis (Windhoff-Héritier, 1987).

The aforementioned four strands of theoretical and conceptual thinking are combined within the framework of policy network analysis in order to explain the development of policies: resource dependence theory assumes that rational actors, each in a position of relative autonomy, interact in a policy field because they depend upon each other to produce a policy (decision) under an overarching collective purpose. Within their own organizations they cannot create all resources and functions required for the policy production, therefore they are required to enter into transactions with other actors in the network. The term of 'generalized political exchange' has been used (Marin, 1990) to give expression to the fact that this exchange may be multilateral and indirect (through circuits of) as well as bilateral and, above all, that it may extend over a variety of resources (Mayntz, 1992: 25).

The actors are engaged in a 'common enterprise' (DiMaggio/Powell, 1983: 149). Membership in the network is, at all times, an object of controversy and bargaining between the dominant actors of the network and those who want to gain influence in the network, or enter the network by offering resources important for the 'problem solution' in the policy field. Each actor, public or private, is interested in maximizing his resources, material or immaterial, in order to influence the outcomes of the policy decision process, to guarantee his survival and to stabilize the relationships with other actors. On the one hand, the resource dependence model portrays the actor-organization as responding to the organizational environment, but, on the other, it also depicts it as an active entity capable of changing the terms of interaction (Aldrich/Pfeffer, 1976: 83).

Since the organizational environment does not impose strict requirements for survival of the organization, there is a range of choices and strategies available (Child, 1972). Therefore, the criteria by which decisions are made within the organization also become problematic. Internal power differences are important and the influence of internal subunits, in interaction with the demands of various external groups in the network, may come to determine the outcome (Aldrich/Pfeffer, 1976: 84). Contingencies in the network environment and ensuing uncertainty are absorbed by forming coalitions with other organizational actors, through merger, the movement of personnel among organizations, ('interpenetration' cf. Laumann/Knoke, 1978), tacit collusion, or legal contracts. Thus, linkages are also structured by organizational interdependencies such as interorganizational bodies or the multi-membership in various organizations of single actors (Laumann/Knoke, 1978: 463). The linkages and contracts serve to minimize transaction costs (Williamson, 1985), i.e. the information costs and costs which may be incurred in exchange relations if the interacting partner proves to be unreliable, or to be 'shirking'. For example: actor A may have invested considerably in the product to be exchanged with actor B, but the latter is opportunistic and fails to pay the agreed price.

The existing linkages between the actors are analytically relevant because they constitute the structure of the network. This structure may be analyzed under aspects of centralization and decentralization, the number of existing sub-networks and their horizontal interdependence. Existing linkages reveal network behavior, the power structure of a network at a given time and the coherence of a network. They are characterized by different degrees of intensity, frequency, formalization and standardization of interaction (Laumann et al., 1978: 465). What is 'transported' in these linkages are material and immaterial resources such as financial means, information etc. (Tichy/Fombrun 1979:927). The exchange of resources is to an important degree influenced by the dominating governance structure, that is, the dominant mode of guidance and control are defined by the policy instrument used. The latter may have the nature of incentives, negotiation patterns or command-and-control strategies. A governance structure offers reference points to the individual actor which allow the decision maker to weigh up of costs and benefits of particular courses of action (Döhler, 1989: 350).

The existence of governance structures and formal interorganizational linkages indicates that within the network resources are not freely exchanged, rather than revealing that their exchange is restricted by institutional rules. That is where the new political institutionalism comes in. This approach emphasizes that not only rules and traditions, but also routinization and 'sunk costs' of customary exchange relations set limits to the rational resource exchange decisions of the network actors. So do, of course, existing formal institutions, such as given interorganizational contracts defined by the constitution, by law or administrative ruling. It was above all the new statists (Evans et al., 1985;

Krasner 1988) and some organization theorists (March/Olsen, 1989) who emphasized the importance of state structures, institutions and rules in the shaping of policy decisions by trying to stem the tide of exclusively economic explanations of policy decisions. They underline the importance of the 'rule of appropriateness', according to which decisions in unstructured situations are fitted to existing rules, traditions etc., as opposed to the rule of 'consequentiality', where decisions strictly follow cost and benefit calculations (Olsen, 1991).

In the institutionalist view, political and policy decisions must be in part derived from political institutions as 'irretrievable sources' of political action, institutions being defined as interconnected rules and routines which define the adequate action as a relationship between a role and a situation (March/Olsen 1989). From this point of view, politics is only in part to be understood as a rational and consequence-oriented process, and is also to be seen as process oriented in itself: decision processes are just as much concerned with the attribution of status as with the definition of truth and virtue, and the maintenance of loyalty and legitimacy (March/Olsen, 1975: 12). Rules, such as standard operating procedures,

> "...affectthe substantive outcomes of choices by regulating the access of participants, problems, and solutions to choices, and by affecting the participants' allocation of attention, their standard of evaluation, priorities, perceptions, identities, and resources." (Olsen 1991:93)

It would be a mistake, however, to consider the resource exchange approach and the institutional approach as mutually exclusive. Rather more, they are closely linked, simultaneously enabling and limiting each other, for choosing among different courses of action according to one's preference is only possible if there are a limited number of options. This limitation is given through the institutional context restricting the range of choice of possible alternatives of action by setting rules, creating organizational hierarchies etc. Vice versa, institutions may be understood as developing from individual choice decisions: bi-lateral or tri-lateral contracts may be drawn up, or hierarchical organizations are established in order to save transaction costs (Williamson, 1985). However, once institutions are in place, they tend to develop a certain inertia, an interest in themselves, and unfold their own dynamics; they go beyond the scope of individual economic decisions.

> "...Institutions have such wide span in time and space that they evade the control of individual decisions" (Giddens, 1988: 78; see also: Windhoff-Héritier, 1991)

Interactions amongst network actors are not only guided by the actors' rational interests augmenting their resources through exchanges with other actors, as well as by the limits set to these exchanges by organizational and legal rules, but also by, if you will, softer rules. A common understanding about the appropriate approach of problem solving is circumscribed as 'the operating ideology' (Sharpe, 1990), or as a 'belief systems' defined as a "configuration of ideals and attitudes in which elements are bound together by some form of constraint of functional interdependence" (Converse, quoted in: Czada, 1991). Burn and Flam (1987), finally, see it as the appropriate way of dealing with each other, as the 'social rule system'.

These collective belief systems are, of course, closely linked to existing institutions, for institutions are created as a result of interests, dominant ideas and the perpetration of the value systems linked to them (Czada, 1991). The "social rule systems", if they are backed "...to a greater or lesser extent by social sanctions and networks of power and control, ...are referred to as rule regimes" (Burns/Flam 1987: 13). Since social rule systems are collectively shared, they permit supra-actor descriptions and analyses of the patterning of social transactions and social structure in the sphere to which they apply. Thus, for example, prevention has become the dominant idea and value system in fighting juvenile crime while punishment has increasingly been questioned as an appropriate problem approach. Or, to give another example, 'compliance by consensus' has for a long time been regarded as the appropriate way of inspectors' dealing with industry in British environmental policy.

Finally, policy network analysis uses the concepts and classifying patterns of public policy analysis. Policy analysis conceives of political and policy decision making as a dynamic process which follows specific stages of the policy cycle, although not necessarily in an orderly manner. Thus, the phases of problem definition, agenda setting, policy formulation, policy implementation and policy feedback are distinguished in order to explain the emergence and transformation of policies and the underlying political processes. Although all actors who are engaged in the policy field at one or another of those stages 'belong' to the network, their relative importance and influence may vary depending on the phase of the policy cycle; so do the dominant coalitions and cleavage structures, that is, the 'policy arena', which is structured by the expected costs and benefits of a specific policy (Windhoff-Héritier, 1987). Accordingly, the transformation of the policy network in each phase needs to be investigated.

Moreover, policy analysis assumes that the nature of the policy at hand, the specific features of the problem to be solved, is systematically related to features of the policy network. Thus, it is expected that redistributive policies tend to produce polarized cleavage structures in the policy arena of the network; they pit those who benefit from a policy against those who have to bear its costs and therefore give rise to a polarized network structure, with this being so it is assumed that redistributive policies only have a chance to be implemented, if they are based on 'command-and-control', i.e.: precise regulation followed by sanctions in case of non-compliance. Hence policy strategies and the specific opportunities of action open to the network actors can only be understood in the context of a particular policy and the specific policy instruments used.

Policy networks often emerge during historical 'watershed situations' (Skowronek, 1982). When under 'external shocks' such as wars or economic crisis, specific patterns of interaction between the state and society arise. In these situations, the state often plays an active role in creating specific network structures, or structures of interest intermediation (Lehmbruch, 1991). Under state leadership policy networks are created in new fields of activity such as nuclear power policy (Czada, 1991), although the state need not necessarily play a dominant role in the field, once the new developments have taken off. New networks gain stability because the actors involved with each other are regularly interacting over a longer period of time and are evolving calculable exchange relations (Döhler, 1989) which are based on past experience. Subsequent policy changes tend to develop within the structures of the existing network ('path-dependency') which reveal a considerable resistance towards new innovations.

To briefly summarize, policy network analysis explains the development of public policies in terms of complex exchange and transaction processes between network actors within given institutional restrictions. The structure and dynamics of these interactions vary in the different phases of the policy cycle. Networks as analytical tools are conceived for specific policy areas[1]. The policies under discussion and the policy instruments used offer specific incentives to the concerned actors who, simultaneously, in their interaction with other network actors are guided by a specific problem solving ideology and 'social rule system'.

7.2   Policy Network Analysis in Comparative Research

How can the instruments of policy network analysis be used in comparative political research? What are its advantages and its limits? Comparative politics faces a general dilemma: it perpetually has to navigate between Scylla and Charybdis. On the one hand, it must avoid the trap of ending up with idiosyncratic, highly detailed 'thick descriptions' of single cases; yet, on the other, it should not limit itself to collecting highly aggregated cross-national data such as the number of unemployed, or the resources spent for welfare purposes and so forth. In the first instance, much insight and information is gained about the political decision processes and policy features of a specific country, yet one becomes hopelessly entangled in infinitesimal details and all attempts of comparison between countries have to be abandoned. In the second case, comparable macro-data is at hand. However, we know very little about the processes that lie behind this data; it remains, beyond the scope of analysis, 'a black box'. Clearly, policy network analysis is prone to make the first mistake. How can this error be avoided, or how can the danger of ending up with idiosyncratic case studies at least be managed?

If two or more countries are compared, one can proceed in two phases. Following "the most similar systems approach" (Teune/Przeworski 1970), the units which are compared are characterized by a large number of similar independent variables, such as the level of economic and technological development and the basic political institutions and so forth; the compared units are different by only a smaller number of variables which - it is assumed -

---

[1]   Policy area and issue area overlap only to a certain extent, since issues are more limited than policies; in other words, a policy area comprises a variety of issues.

explain part of the cross-national differences in network processes and their policy outcomes. The independent variables may be of either short-term or long-term nature. Departing from the "most similar systems approach", the first phase 'takes stock' of central common and distinct features of the compared networks (standard comparative independent variables).

The policy networks of the research units may also be compared with regard to their outputs-outcomes-impacts, which are treated as dependent variables. The question is: how do differences in the structure and the operation of policy networks explain different policy results? The latter may differ on the level of policy outputs, that is political decisions, (e.g. on the allocation of resources), on the level of policy outcomes (first tangible implementation activities), or the level of long-term policy impacts (i.e. is changes in the state of the environment, human behavior or human health). Naturally, the first and the second are much easier to measure and to relate back to the explanatory variables.

The following comparative independent variables are commonly used to describe important features of the analyzed units or nation-states (Feick/Jann, 1988).

Long-term features of political, economic and socio-cultural development:
- the level of economic and technological development
- the basic features of political institutions
- long-term values
- the central features of the policy problem at hand (such as the high technical complexity of the problem to be solved, the redistributive character of policy etc.)

Short-term features of political, economic and socio-cultural developments:
- changes in the world-economy: recession or boom
- external shocks such as
- international political crisis
- crisis in the natural environment
- technological innovation.

The above common long-term and short-term factors, typical for all units under investigation, facilitate the comparability of countries (or sub-national units).

By contrast, distinctive long- and short-term features, such as the following, may explain differences in policy outcomes.

Long-term country-specific political, economic, socio-cultural variables are:
- specific aspects of the political institutions (presidential versus parliamentarian democracy; bi-chamber system or one-chamber system; unitary or federalist system, electoral system etc.)
- the role of the courts in the political process
- the party system (e.g. polarized or not, multi-party etc.)
- the associative structure (the number and structure, e.g. centralized or decentralized, of organized interests, such as manufacturers' and employers' associations, trade unions, workers' organizations, environmental organizations etc.)
- the patterns of public-private cooperation in the implementation of policies
- the policy instruments used in the policy field of research

Short-term country-specific variables are:
- electoral outcomes
- changes of parties in government
- crisis of the national economy; structural crisis in the national economy
- national crisis in the natural environment
- national cultural 'shocks'

Long-term versus short-term variables are used in order to distinguish the possible effects of short-term independent variables in a longitudinal analysis of policy networks. This first stage, describing structural differences and similarities of the units under comparison (standard variables of cross-national comparison), provides an impression of structural aspects and typical patterns of the policy network. The standard variables can be matched to the routine checklist of questions used for the description of networks:

a) The standard comparative variable, 'formal political and administrative institutions', corresponds with the description of the formal structure of the network. It describes the particular formal powers which actors in specific positions have specifies the nature of their formal relationships. It also describes the degree of centralization or decentralization of the formal institutional structures within the network.

b) The description of all 'consequential actors' within the network includes the formal positions described under a), goes beyond this by including all actors disposing of resources relevant for the policy problem, even though they may have no formal powers. It is in part covered by the standard variable describing public-private patterns of cooperation in policy formulation and implementation.

c) The network feature analyzing coalition structures of the network by which actors try to influence the outcome of policy events by pooling their resources has no corresponding standard comparative variable. Neither does the description of the centrality of actors which is not exclusively based on formal powers, but other material and immaterial resources.

d) The network feature 'governance structure' corresponds to policy instruments used in the policy field under investigation.

e) The dominating 'operating ideology' guiding the problem solving approach in the field is, to some extent reflected in the analysis of the dominating social and cultural values in this specific field of public intervention.

A comparison of the network-analysis checklist questions with the standard comparative variables shows that the latter partially cover the first. Only partially, because one important aspect of network analysis focussing on the dynamics of interaction between formal and informal actors, their exchange processes, their coalition building, their conflicts and the ensuing cleavage structures cannot be grasped by the standard variables. This is the aspect of the networks that one author had in mind when he said: "Network analysis is like trying to take a picture of the Mississippi River". Yet, the use of a grid of 'objective' network aspects (or: standard variables) may serve as a starting point for the analysis of the particularities of policy network dynamics. Often enough, the distinctive structural network aspects may be the very reasons why the dynamics of the network processes develop in a specific way and, in consequence, produce specific policy outcomes.

7.3   *Policy Innovations In Clean Air Policy Networks:*
      Comparing British and American Clean Air Policy

How can comparative policy network analysis explain why and how an important environmental policy innovation came about in both Britain and the United States, independently? In 1990, the British Parliament passed the Environmental

Protection Act; also in 1990, the United States Congress enacted the new Clean Air Act. Both laws, the dependent variable to be explained in terms of policy outputs and outcomes, are comprehensive and ambitious in scope and objectives. It is not so much the details of the laws which are of interest here, as incisive as they may be to both countries, but the very fact that an innovative departure in policy making occurred in both countries.

In the policy case to be discussed, the comparative analysis - on the basis of the most similar systems approach - shows that the network processes that unfolded in the two countries and brought about the innovation may be partially traced back to distinctive network structures. With respect to basic long-term system variables, the United States and Great Britain fit within the context of the "most similar systems approach" i.e., both countries have a similar level of economic and technological development and they both have democratic political institutions and similar socio-cultural value systems. However, there are significant differences in the finer structure of their political institutions as well as their problem solving approach in environmental policy.

In the British system, which on account of its unitarian political and administrative structure may qualify as a centralized network, new initiatives in environmental policy making flow, as a rule, from the executive, or administrative, leadership of the central government. Initiatives also may be developed at the local level, but since the central governments legal and financial grip on local authorities tightened during the 1980s, there has been less room for action by local governments. If central government is unwilling to respond to local initiatives, it can repress the latter more easily than before, and a policy stalemate may ensue. This was the case during the 1980s under the Thatcher government.

By contrast, the U.S. federalist and decentralized policy network offers a multiplicity of political arenas. The single states can use their far-reaching powers of decision making to develop new policy initiatives, even if the Federal government has decided to take no action in a specific policy field. This was the case under the Reagan administration in the 1980s. Access to the court system always offers the possibility of changing the political arena.

In the British case, the question therefore arises, where did the innovation emerge from? In retrospect, it may be demonstrated that the absence of subnational, powerful political actors in Great Britain, was however compensated by its embeddedness in the supranational decision structure of the European Community. It was mainly the European Community which brought pressure on the British government to change its environmental policy in many significant respects. As one official said: "The influence of the European Community on British environmental policy can hardly be overestimated in the past years" (Interview, London December 1991, Her Majesty's Inspectorate of Pollution). Policy objectives and policy instruments, as applied in some of the other member states such as Germany, functioned as a model in shaping the Community and in turn Great Britain's policy.

This pressure 'from above' was complemented by growing political mobilization and activities deployed at the grassroots level by environmental organizations. Interestingly, these political actors increasingly use the supranational institutions, such as the Community's Court and the Commission, as leverage points in order to push for innovations in environmental policy. Thus, local groups and environmental associations, such as 'Friends of the Earth', have been directly addressing the Commission to secure the implementation of the Community Directives by local authorities. Both factors, the Community legislation and the environmental movement contributed to the modernization of British environmental policy as it was enacted in the new Environmental Protection Act.

In the United States the pressure from grassroots movements has also been a political factor in the policy network for quite some time. However, it gained additional weight during the 1980s in view of the stagnation of environmental policy during the Reagan administration. Local actors developed their initiatives in conjunction with single states. Support was sought from the Courts which were addressed by members of environmental groups. Within a few years the activities unfolded by single states, California foremost among them, served as examples which were followed by other states. They developed such a political momentum that the Federal government found itself under pressure to engage in new environmental activities. As a result, the new administration under President Bush decided to push for a significant amendment of the old Clean Air Act.

In both countries the policy innovation was, to some extent, favored by a change in the occupation of governmental key positions. In the U.S. the advent of a new Republican administration brought about a change in central positions of the Environmental Protection Agency, the chief bureaucratic actor in the network, which facilitated policy innovations. What we can see, is that - due to the distinctive institutional network structures - the pressure from below (and from above in the case of Britain) is translated differently into formal political power in the two countries. In the case of the U.S., initiatives of grassroots movements, local environmental organizations, which were supported by the courts, are channelled and shaped by single states. Subsequently, the cumulative impact of the pace-setter functions of several states brought pressure to bear on federal policies.

The events in California serve to illustrate how a modification of the governance structure changed the coalition structure and exchange processes in a subnetwork. The relative inactivity of the Reagan administration set in motion a conflict between California and the Federal government, in the course of which environmentalists from California literally forced E.P.A. to implement the Clean Air Act more strictly. A key role was played by the courts, a very important latent actor in the policy network because citizens can turn to the courts to sue the agency for inaction (Bryner, 1984: 318). In California, in 1984 a member of an environmentalist group sued E.P.A. for failing to implement the Clean Air Act in Greater Los Angeles. After three years, the court decided in favor of the litigant. This judgment sparked off a change in the regional policy network and initiated developments which had repercussions in other states, encouraging them to also undertake policy initiatives, by-passing the Federal government, and thus also changing the clean air policy in the national network.

In Great Britain, by contrast, initiatives from below used the European Community as a vehicle in order to influence national policy. Quite independently, however, the pressure from above, from the supranational level, has to be considered as a factor of influence in its own right. A closer look into the policy-network in Britain also reveals how - with the new institutional structures - the stakes in the decision process in clean air policy have changed. The establishing of 'public access' in administrative procedures opens new possibilities of access to the network and new possibilities for environmental associations to bring their resources to bear in the network exchange processes.

'Public access' means that for the first time the new Environmental Protection Act opens the administrative decision process to the public which is offered extensive information about the applications of process operators and subsequent bureaucratic authorizations. 'Public access' means, for instance, that the application for operation is listed in a 'public register' and responses to the application can be made within twenty-eight days. Additionally, the applicant must advertize the application in the local newspaper and again the public can comment upon the application during the twenty-eight days following publication.

With 'public access', a kind of leverage is offered to environmental organizations so that they may critically scrutinize the administrative authorization procedures and play a critical role of surveillance in clean air administration. Even more so, since all industrial plants also have to publish their emission monitoring data in the 'public register'. However, after a year and a half of practical experience with the new act, public interest in using these opportunities are not yet very pronounced. Rather more the new possibilities have been taken advantage of by industrial competitors of the applicants which try to gain information about product components and the quantities produced by their market competitors. Yet, the Department of the Environment, by means of a very active information policy, attempts to increase public interest in clean air policy by daily advertizing air quality measurements in the news, by offering telephone advice for pollution problems and distributing abundant information material. Even if it will take some time for a more active participation of environmental organizations and citizen groups to materialize, the institutional possibilities of public information offered by the Environmental Protection Act is - by comparison with other countries - far-reaching indeed.

The network dynamics producing the new legislation also brought about changes in the traditional governance structures in the two countries. In the United States, where command-and-control strategies have been the central strategy since the 1970s, even stricter elements of hierarchical guidance and control were established; however, extensive market incentives were also introduced in some fields. In Britain, with its tradition of 'consensus by compliance', we find slightly more 'command-and-control' and precise standard setting, more accountability of inspectors' activities and less negotiating between inspectors and firms and, as described, the opening up of the system for 'public access'. Linked to the change in governance structure, we therefore find a partial change of the 'social rule' system in Britain. The style of interaction between the actors and the problem-solving approach have both been redefined. In the

United States this change has been more moderate. The basic problem approach remains the same, but was however enlarged by the completely contrasting governance type of market strategies.

If we relate the analysis of the two case studies back to the above set of independent variables, it becomes clear that long and short-term distinctive features of the two policy-networks go some way in explaining why innovations were brought about in the clean air policy of both the United States and Britain. In summary, the following long-term distinctive institutional features seem the most important: the federalist structure in the United States and in the British case the embeddedness into the supranational network of European environmental policy which set into motion the dynamics of innovation. In the United Kingdom, the European Court also plays an important role since national and subnational actors gained new avenues of influence by having access to it. In the United States, the courts also had an important impact in speeding up the decision-process in California, which, in turn, triggered off innovations in other sub-networks and, finally, in the entire national network.

As to the short-term variables, the electoral outcomes in the United States, although not involving a change in the governing party, offered the possibility of choosing new leading personnel with new policy ideas (head of the E.P.A.). In the case of Britain, the relatively high percentage of votes obtained by the Green Party in the European election put Margaret Thatcher's government under considerable pressure to take some action in environmental policy.

Not surprisingly, the state of the national economy had, and has an important impact on network innovations in environmental policy. The new Clean Air Act, in its most ambitious version was shaped before the on-set of the recession in the United States in 1989/90, subsequently was diminished in its requirements during the economic down-turn. The British Environmental Protection Act was passed before the recession hit Britain.

'External shocks' clearly played a role in the United States spurring legislative action, e.g. the Prince William Sound accident with the oil spilling of the Exxon Valdez which sharpened public attention for environmental issues in general. Also, the rapidly deteriorating air quality in California, especially in the Los Angeles Basin ("Los Angeles is fighting for breath"), gave rise to alarmed policy reactions in the state.

Thus, going through the standard comparative variables of the two air policy fields in the United Stated and Britain, important similarities and differences in the network structure become apparent which - to a large extent - explain policy innovation.

7.4 Conclusions

In summarizing we may say that a systematic comparison of policy network processes can be implemented, to the extent that common and distinctive long- and short-term features in formal network structures are controlled. Beyond this framework of comparable and distinctive, mostly structural, network aspects, specific dynamic processes unfold which are less accessible to a comparative analysis. Yet, aspects of the basic network structure to a considerable extent explain the specific nature of the network processes, the resulting policy developments and their results.

A longitudinal cross-national comparison of policy networks is especially insightful because it permits the identification of country-specific divergences and convergences of policy patterns and the effects of short-term independent variables or events. It reveals cross-national diffusion processes in the application of social rules and technologies in problem solving over the course of time, as well as their impact on the underlying political patterns. Also, supranational institutional influences may be identified, such as the impact of EC directives on national policy patterns of the member states, as well as the impact of economic changes in the world economy. 'External shocks' may entail innovative phases or 'watershed phases' in policy making which in turn initiate a restructuring of the network.

Despite the aforementioned limits to comparison, policy network analysis offers considerable advantages: It systematically links all 'consequential actors' in a policy network, be they public or private, and - in the case of public actors - on all political and administrative levels. By including private actors, this approach draws attention to non-state organizations employing problem solving strategies which present competing strategies to those of the state. To mention a case in point, the mass media with their activities may also play an important role in clean air policy and significantly enhance the effectiveness of state measures; so may also whole-sale trade in the field of waste-disposal policy.

Furthermore, by comparing different networks under the question *how are similar policy problems solved in different countries or subnational units*, policy network analysis draws attention to equivalent functions. In the field of clean air policy, for instance, SO^2 (sulphur dioxide) standards, as they are released into atmosphere by coal-fired power plants, are set by administrative decision in Germany. However in Great Britain, they were for a long time decided by the Chief Inspector who set them individually for each plant under his jurisdiction. Therefore, the British Chief Inspector was the functional equivalent of the SO^2 standards in other countries[2].

At the end of the day, we may conclude that whomsoever expects stringent causal evidence, rendering possible precise 'technological' policy recommendations, from comparative policy network analysis will be disappointed. But whoever, more modestly, makes an attempt to answer the question: which policy features and actor patterns, which contextual variables do countries have in common, that, with reasonable success, solve specific policy problems may consider policy network analysis as a useful analytical tool of comparative politics.

---

[2] Contribution of Weidner to a discussion at a workshop on environmental policy organized by "Fachtagung Umweltpolitik", 16/17.9.1991 at the Wissenschaftszentrum Berlin.

8 The Politics of Managing the Mixed Economy

Hans Keman

One of the core domains within the relation between politics and society concerns economic development. In particular in the wake of the first and second oil-shock (1973 and 1979), that hit the advanced industrialized democracies, the politics of economic management received prime attention from economists and political scientists (Paloheimo, 1987; Keman/Lehner, 1984). However, other reasons can be mentioned for the increase of analyses of economic policy formation and economic performance:

- The growing economic interdependence as indicated by the rising proportion of imports and exports in the national product has been a strong motive on examining the relationship between domestic politics and dependance on the world market (e.g.: Cameron, 1978; 1984; Keman et al., 1987).
- The growth and spread of the social welfare state became more and more dependent on the growth of the economy, as well as it simultaneously incurred a strong increase in the size of the public economy. Given the economic recession that has occurred since the early 1970s this has affected the fiscal policy performance of most OECD-countries. Reason enough for economists and political scientists to delve into the question whether or not fiscal policies were (still) manageable (e.g: Tarschys, 1983; Cowart, 1978; Dunleavy, 1991).
- A manifest characteristic of the economic development since the early 1970s has been the new phenomenon of 'stagflation' crisis (i.e. the simultaneous occurrence of growing rates of inflation and unemployment, resulting in a stagnating economic growth). This has generated a debate on the causes and conditions of economic growth (e.g.: Boltho et al., 1982; Olson, 1982) on the one hand, and on the question which policy strategy would produce economic

recovery and eventually a more manageable national economy, on the other (Castles et al., 1987; Keman, 1988).

The debate on managing the 'mixed economy' centers around two questions: firstly, 'do political institutions matter' regarding a country's economic performance (Shonfield, 1982; Lindberg/Mayer, 1985); secondly, which institutional arrangements can account for the strong variation in unemployment and inflation throughout the western world (Schmidt, 1983; Scharpf, 1984; Cameron, 1985). This debate has led to a theoretical reappraisal of the linkage between the 'political' and economic development in advanced capitalist democracies. In addition, it became equally clear that empirical research into this relationship should be cross-national in order to discover the patterns of variation of the relation between politics and the 'economy' and to validate potential explanations of this variation. Hence it may be expected, as Strümpel and Scholz claim, that:

> "the promise of internationally comparative economic research as a field rests not only on the need of policy-makers to raise their sights above and beyond national frontiers, but also on its theoretical potential (...) and (...) reflect the need for comparison and generalization inherent in the scientific method."
> (Strümpel/Scholz, 1987: 264-265)

In this chapter the relationship between the political process and related economic policy formation will be discussed and investigated in an attempt to account for the variation in economic performance of eighteen advanced capitalist democracies between 1965-1988. The focus will be at a 'political' explanation of the politics of economic policy-making in a mixed economy. In addition this exercise will demonstrate how helpful the comparative approach as a 'scientific' tool for analyzing public policy formation and performance can be.

8.1 Explaining Variations in Economic Development

Academic interest only slowly shifted towards the political process of decision-making in relation to policy outputs. The emergence of economic stagnation in the advanced industrial world and its detrimental consequences for upholding the social welfare system was a cause of this shift. Also the rapid increase in unemployment and inflation led to an increasing interest for the shaping of economic policy in the western world and the outcomes of this process (Keman et al., 1987; Castles et al., 1987; Goldthorpe, 1984). A closer inspection of the cross-national variation in policy outputs and policy outcomes revealed that the evolving pattern could not satisfactorily be explained by economic factors alone, nor was the relationship between policy outcomes and output consistent. Strümpel and Scholz (1987) and Schmidt (1987) have indicated that the remaining variation could very well be a result of the impact of political factors. Broadly three groups of potential political explanation can be identified:

1. Political behavior of actors holding conflicting views on the economic management of capitalism (Schmidt, 1982a; Cowart, 1978; Scharpf, 1987);

2. Political-institutional arrangements influencing the options for developing an 'appropriate' economic policy formation (Schmidt, 1987; Keman, 1984; Katzenstein, 1985; Scharpf, 1984; Olson, 1982);

3. Policy formation viewed as a necessary, but intermediary link between politics and economic development (Lindberg, 1985; Andersson, 1987).

In addition to these three groups of political factors explaining the variation in economic performance, some authors have pointed to non-political factors affecting the relationship between politics and economic behavior: on the one hand, this concerns the growing international interdependence, exemplified by foreign trade (Cameron, 1978) and the relative weight of a nation in international economic relations (Keohane, 1984; Strange, 1988); on the other hand, the impact of technological and industrial development is mentioned as well as psychological and cultural factors that may contribute to the cross-national differences in economic performance (Maddison, 1982; Boltho, 1982).

Overlooking this array of possible explanations of economic development in advanced industrial societies it is not surprising that many conclusions have been drawn, but only few appear conclusive. Yet, some explanatory trajectories seem more promising than others: firstly, research designs that focus on the interrelationship between political behavior and the working of institutions have been quite successful in explaining the process of policy formation, but are only weakly related to the corresponding variation in economic performance. Hence, what can account for the choice of an economic policy in a country does not necessarily lead to a recovery from its economic 'misery'[1].

Fritz Scharpf (1987) has pointed at this weakness in much of the existing research. Instead of assuming a straightforward relation between policy formation and subsequent performance, he puts forward that, on the one hand, institutions are variables containing the options open to political actors to choose the 'best' or 'optimal' policy (Scharpf, 1984; 1987; 1992); on the other hand, he suggests that 'best' or 'optimal' policy strategies are dependent on political compromise and societal co-operation. Without these, even the 'best' policy is not feasible (Scharpf, 1991). This is an important argument, because it shows that those economic policies, however well-founded in economic theory, are often inappropriate in reality due to *non*-economic factors (see also: Whiteley, 1987; Lehner, 1987; Lindberg/Mayer, 1985). Hence, the first alternative explanatory route to follow is to analyze the *institutionalized* behavior of political and societal actors in relation to economic policy formation.

The second trajectory that may be promising to account for the cross-national and inter-temporal variation in economic development is to pay more attention to the underlying dimensions of political behavior which are manifested in ideological and issue-related differences between political and societal actors. Manfred Schmidt (1982b; 1983) has been among the first to elaborate this aspect on the basis of comparative public policy analysis (but see also: Castles et al., 1987; 1989; Cameron, 1984; 1985; Esping-Andersen, 1987; Therborn, 1986). In his model Schmidt brings together the way socio-economic conflicts are articulated on the level of politics (respectively in parliament and government) and the way these conflicts can be managed by means of institutional arrangements (see also: Czada, 1987; Keman, 1988; Braun, 1989). His research demonstrates that this combination is quite powerful in accounting for the shaping of economic policy as well why it leads to a more or less successful economic *performance*. It will be obvious that this approach is one that aims at a *political explanation* of the possibility of managing a mixed economy.

---

[1] This expression is adopted from the 'misery-index' developed by OECD; i.e. the sum of the rates of unemployment and inflation in a country, divided by 2; see: Keman/Van Dijk, 1987, for an elaborated version.

Basically I agree with the 'models' of Scharpf and Schmidt. The first emphasizing the institutional behavior of actors involved in the policy-making process (which view is by and large comparable with the network approach of Windhoff-Héritier; see chapter 7 of this book), the other stressing the impact of societal conflicts on both the policy formation and related economic performance. Both models are, however, not yet completely satisfactory. What is lacking is a specification of the extent to which institutions *indeed* facilitate coalescent and cooperative behavior of policy-actors and in what way issue-related ideological controversies *actually* influence political decisions. Therefore, whilst adopting the basic tenets of the models of Scharpf and Schmidt I propose to give more room to the underlying dimensions that conduct political and societal actors in shaping economic policy that is capable of producing a favorable economic performance. These amendments will hopefully not only make the models more comprehensive, but also make it possible to attain a more satisfying explanation. To this end it is necessary to discuss the research design that will be employed to analyze the significance of these models as explanations of the 'politics of economic management'.

8.2 Analyzing Cross-national Variation in Economic Policy and Performance

In this chapter our main concern will be to what extent and in what way the 'political' (process) *influences* the cross-national variation in economic policy-making, and to what extent this *accounts* for the economic performance. The leading research question is therefore: 'do politics and institutions matter' regarding the management of the 'mixed economy' and the related economic performance in capitalist democracies, in particular in periods of crisis?

In contrast to many studies, in which the dependent variable concerns often either a policy indicator or a performance related indicator, both elements will be analyzed here simultaneously. Conversely, Scharpf focusses on variations in unemployment and inflation only, whereas Schmidt uses primarily policy output indicators. However, in both cases this still leaves the question unanswered whether or not policy-making is indeed related to economic performance.

Secondly, in many studies the various possible indicators of economic policy-making are utilized separately. That is to say, the impact of the political process is analyzed for each indicator (e.g.: size and growth of public spending, level and growth of government employment, increases in public debt service, control of money supply and interest rates etc.; e.g. Cowart, 1978; Andrain, 1980). However, it is essential to view the policy instruments as a segment of a encompassing policy strategy.

Thirdly, often the time dimension is not considered as a variable or is operationalized for one specific period (covering the time span before and after a crisis, e.g. before and after the 'oil-shock'). In other studies researchers try to cope with this problem by means of a time series analysis (Whiteley, 1987). However, this often confines the comparison to one or two countries and will not reveal the patterned diversity of the link between politics and the economy within the universe of discourse (see also: Castles, 1987).

In the fourth place there is the problem of both refinement of analyzing the political process as variable that is also influenced by country-specific features. In other words, the problem of Scylla and Charybdis: performing a broad cross-national investigation as well as taking into account the specific features of a country concurrently, which may account for the actual working of a system that is seemingly similar to others (i.e. Galton's Problem: Przeworski, 1987; see: Chapter 2 of this book).

Point of departure is that the answer to the research question is to model the political process of policy formation by focussing on the relevant political and societal actors within the context of the political institutions in which they (must) operate. In addition, it is important to take into account the (underlying) conflicting motives of the relevant actors with respect to the 'problem' at hand, which has apparently to be solved by actions of the state (Skocpol, 1985; Therborn, 1986; Schmidt, 1987; Scharpf, 1987). Hence, the basic model of investigation, relating theory to empirical analysis, will be:

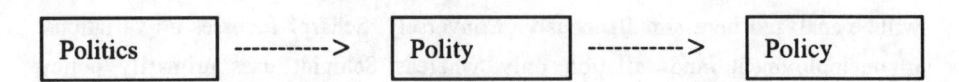

| Politics | ----------> | Polity | ----------> | Policy |

This triad, which was at the core of Chapter 2 in this book, will direct the choice of variables and the modelling of the relationships representing the politics of economic management in advanced capitalistic democracies.

The latter specification immediately defines the unit of analysis as well as the choice of the cases involved: by capitalist democracies we mean those countries that are characterized by a parliamentary mode of decision-making within the limits of democratic-liberal "Rule of Law" and a socio-economic system of production and consumption that is by and large operating via market procedures, but is also more or less controlled and influenced by public means of intervention (Lane, 1985; Keman, 1988). In short, only countries with a 'mixed economy' and where the use of 'public power' is democratically exercised (cf. Shonfield, 1982) make up the 'universe of discourse'[2].

The period of investigation is 1965-1988. Partly this choice is dictated by the availability of reliable data. Yet, this period suits the aim of our research, namely examining the relevant changes in economic developments. In order to cope for the variation in time, this period is divided into three: 1965-1972, 1973-1979 and 1980-1988. The obvious reason for this is mentioned in the introduction to this chapter: all capitalist democracies (among others) were affected by the respective 'oil-shocks' of 1973 and 1979. A second reason for this periodization is the fact that it is often put forward that after 1980 in many countries the political debate changed with respect to the 'nature' of the crisis: from a cyclical view regarding economic recovery to a more structural interpretation of the economic development in capitalist democracies (Lindberg/Scharpf/Engelhardt, 1987; Keman et al., 1987; Castles et al., 1987).

Next, let us consider the variables that will be employed to analyze empirically the research question. The political process of decision-making is captured by the following categories:

1. *Politics*: political actors in terms of motivated behavior.
2. *Polity*: Structuration and working of Parliamentary Democracies.

Actors are all those organized collectivities that aim at representation and at influencing decision-making. It concerns political parties, socio-economic interest groups and governments. Their motives are operationalized in two ways: one, by means of assuming that the left versus right-dimension is a valid indicator of political behavior with respect to economic management and

---

[2] The term 'universe of discourse' signifies an artificially, closed group of cases and not a 'sample'. Hence, statistical tests of significance have little meaning in terms confirming hypotheses.

performance. Secondly, that the intensity of this conflict is revealed by examining the 'salient issues' that prevail in a political system (Budge/Farlie, 1983). In other words, we expect that 'salient issues' are the 'revealed preferences' of the actors involved and indicate their choice of policy. The leading hypothesis is then that ideological differences do matter according to their being a salient issue. Parties are therefore represented in terms of electoral strength of the ideological party-blocs in parliament, and the same holds for the participation in government of the left, right and center blocs. Socio-economic interests are measured by the size of trade unions (Armingeon, 1992).

The occurrence of issues related to the socio-economic situation are taken from Lane/Ersson (1991) and Budge (1991). There are three types of issues:
1. concerning state-intervention (conservatism);
2. the importance of socio-economic problems (economy);
3. the effects of economic policy (redistribution).

The extent to which actors are driven by these motives will influence the decision-making process and with it the choice of the policy strategy of managing the mixed economy. The way and the extent actors are successful in their policy pursuit is supposed to be dependent on the structure and working of the existing democratic institutions. These institutions, by and large, indicate the room for manoeuver of the actors involved. Three types of institutional arrangements will figure in this analysis:
1. The *cleavage* structure of party systems;
2. The working of party systems in terms of *consociationalism*;
3. The existence and degree of *corporatist* modes of conflict-resolution.

The *cleavage* structure of a society (Lipset/Rokkan, 1967) directs the division of a party system on the basis of social-cultural features of a society (e.g. ethnicity, language, religion etc.; see: Lipset/Rokkan, 1967; Von Beyme, 1985). *Consociational* politics is the result of multi-dimensional, issue-related differences in multi-party systems. Essentially it follows the logic of coalescent behavior on the basis of sharing the spoils in the allocation of policy outputs (Lijphart, 1977). *Corporatism* is seen as a more or less informal negotiation system, which binds socio-economic actors to the political system (Schmidt, 1982b; Katzenstein, 1985). The basic assumption is that the 'public welfare' is better served by cooperative behavior and can be achieved by means of policy agreements between the policy actors (i.e. trade unions, employer organizations and government).

The first indicator is considered to influence the degree of adversarial behavior as a consequence of the relative strength and number of parties in parliament. The second is more specific in terms of the effects of the working of a party system in reaching compromises and the development of cooperation between parties. The third variable is a disputed one with respect to its occurrence and impact (Therborn, 1987; Czada, 1987). Nevertheless, it is hardly questioned that this phenomenon exists and may have an impact on policy performance of advanced capitalist democracies (Lehner, 1987). Bot the features of party systems and corporatism represent here the 'polity' and will be scrutinized in relation to both economic policy formation and economic performance.

An optimal operationalization of the final part of the 'triad' of the political process, policy strategy and related performance is therefore vital. Instead of relying on separate indicators of policy action (i.e. outputs) and or economic performance (i.e. outcomes) we have chosen to construct composite indexes of policy strategy and economic performance.

Economic policy is generally indicated by means of fiscal and monetary instruments (Andrain, 1980; Hibbs, 1985). In theory these instruments are seen as different, whilst in practice they operate in 'concert' and are not decided upon in isolation. That is to say, it may be expected that the politics of economic management is shaped more or less as a 'package deal' and its effect on the economy is of a compound nature. Factor analysis of the main economic policy instruments in the countries under review showed that two *strategies* can be discerned: a 'monetary restrictive' (MRS) one, and a 'tax & saving' (TSS) one[3]. The difference between the two is that the first strategy aims at avoiding deficit-spending by government as well as keeping official interest rates under control

---

[3] Based on Principal Component Analysis with a varimax solution (i.e. orthogonal rotation); communality (h^2) is respectively 41.7% and 34.7% for the two factors found; factor loadings are:

Policy Instruments:	TSS	MRS
Government Spendings	0.87	-0.23
Level of Taxation	0.90	0.22
Discount Rate	0.12	0.77
Deficit Spending	-0.37	0.82

simultaneously, whereas the second strategy attempts to control the public economy by keeping the government outlays and revenues in balance (the so-called 'extraction-distribution cycle'; cf. Goldscheid/Schumpeter, 1976). The result of the factor-analysis shows that in most countries an economic policy has been developed in which a combination of 'monetarist' and 'Keynesian' policy instruments are used simultaneously. In addition it appears that over time and across countries there is a strong variation in the combined use of these instruments.

Finally, the economic performance of OECD-countries is measured according to the indicators commonly used; they are: economic growth, rates of inflation and unemployment. Following Schmidt (1987) we add to this list labor market performance (i.e.: growth of employment controlled for demographic development) and world market (inter)dependence (Cameron, 1978). As is the case with policy instruments, we cannot and should not expect that these indicators emerge and develop separately. Therefore we constructed an index of economic performance by means of factor-analysis for each period under investigation and used the factor-scores (i.e. the estimate for each case) in the ensuing empirical analysis.

To sum up: the research design is developed in close relation with the theory guided research question in order to explain the cross-national and intertemporal variation of the politics of economic management in advanced capitalist democracies. To that end we have operationalized the political process by distinguishing actors, institutions and policy formation and performance in three periods: 1965-1972, 1973-1979 and 1980-1988. In the following sections we shall analyze the research question by examining the variation within politics, polity and policy in relation to economic policy formation and economic performance. In this way we will demonstrate the advantages of comparative research in political science as well as enhancing our knowledge of the relationship under review here.

8.3 Economic Development and Economic Management

Between 1965 and today there have been three turning points in the economic development of the advanced industrial societies:
1. A situation of 'stagnation', that followed the strong growth of most national economies since the late fifties.
2. After 1973 this stagnation turned into a 'stagflation' which was by and large due to the quadrupling of energy prices and the development and spread of laborsaving' techniques.
3. With the second 'oil-shock' of 1979/1980, accompanied by the emergence of the NIC's (newly industrializing countries) economic recovery slowed down and the economic situation was now labelled as a 'recession' (Maddison, 1991; Schmidt, 1987; OECD, 1990).

This general description seems to fit the economic data available:

Table 8.1: Economic Development in 18 OECD-Countries

	Levels			Change		
	65-73	73-79	80-88	65-72	73-79	80-88
EG	4.67%	2.97%	2.27%	-0.28%	-2.23	1.32%
SD	1.42	1.02	0.8	2.02	2.17	2.31
IN	5.30%	10.43%	11.29%	4.70%	-1.71%	-6.52%
SD	0.94	3.70	2.7	2.18	5.11	3.62
UN	2.51%	4.02%	6.92%	0.92%	1.62%	1.78%
SD	1.81	2.37	3.79	0.89	2.74	2.15

Source: OECD: Economic Outlook; Historical Abstracts (various issues); based on own computations of yearly figures; EG = Economic Growth; IN = Inflation; UN = Unemployment; Level = cross-national average of all years; Change = first difference; SD = Standard Deviation from the Mean.

The table shows that indeed the first 'oil-shock' has been a kind of a watershed in the western world and that, contrary to economic belief in the Phillips-curve, unemployment and inflation seem to go hand in hand since then. Although economic growth appears to pick up, the rate of inflation has on average doubled, and unemployment even tripled between 1965 and 1988. However, the Standard Deviations are even more interesting. They demonstrate the cross-national spread of the economic indicators. There is a considerable variation in the economic development of the different countries ranging from a growth rate of 2% (Switzerland) to 6% on average between 1965 and 1988 (Japan). The same observation holds for the rates of inflation (Range = 7%) and unemployment. In this case the average level of unemployment in Switzerland is 0.3%, whereas this is 9.8% in Ireland.

These differences and the countries mentioned defy conventional macroeconomic wisdom. For example, Switzerland and Ireland are seen as opposites in terms of economic performance, and one would expect Switzerland to do well in all respects. However, its growth rate is low and yet its rate of unemployment is the lowest within the world of OECD (see on this: Schmidt, 1985). Ireland is often depicted as a 'third world' country, which is on most accounts an exaggeration, and yet is able to survive economically. In a number of respects its economic performance is indeed not top-ranking from a comparative perspective, but other countries are in the same league also (e.g. Italy, the United Kingdom and New Zealand). Table 8.1 allows for the conclusion that there is ample cross-national and intertemporal variation in economic performance to account for, and we expect that the 'politics of economic management' might well have to do with this. In addition, the differences between these performance indicators over time and within countries demonstrate that economic explanations are insufficient to account for this development (Mayer/Lindberg, 1985; Castles et al., 1987).

The first matter to investigate is, naturally, the relation between the politics and policies of economic management that have been employed and the variation in economic performance.

Table 8.2: *Relationship between Economic Policy and Economic Performance* (N = 18)

Policy Strategy	Economic Performance		
	1965-72	1973-79	1980-88
MRS	0.61	-0.68	0.80
TSS	-0.14	0.46	-0.18

MRS = Monetary Restrictive Strategy; TSS = Tax and Saving' Strategy
It concerns Pearson Product Moment Correlations; A result of ≥ .40 as is considered to be 'significant' (see note 3).

Obviously 'policies do matter' with regard to economic performance. What is interesting is that apparently the period between 1973 and 1979 is quite different from the other two: 'monetary restrictivism' is paying off before 1973 and after 1979. Between 1973 and 1979, it seems, the pay-offs had to be attributed to the degree of Keynesian management of the economy. As we already stated, in reality both strategies co-exist in each country and in different degrees in each period. Hence, the above correlations only demonstrate the extent to which each strategy performs in general. Let us therefore examine in what way and in which period the various countries made us of a combination of both strategies.

Figure 8.1: *Strategies of Economic Management between 1965 and 1988*

	Low TSS	High TSS
Strict MRS	Australia (65-72; 80-88) Canada (73-79) Finland (80-88) France (73-79) Germany (80-88) Ireland (73-79) Italy(73-79);Japan (80-88) New Zealand (80-88) Switzerland (65-72;80-88) UK (73-79)	Austria (65-72;80-88) Belgium (73-79;80-88) Denmark(65-72;73-79;80-88) Finland (65-72) France (65-72;80-88) Netherlands (73-79) Norway (65-72;80-88) Sweden (65-72;73-79;80-88) UK (80-88)
Moderate MRS	Canada (80-88) Germany (65-72;73-79) Italy (65-72;80-88) Japan (65-72;73-79) New Zealand (65-72) US (65-72;73-79;80-88)	Australia (73-79) Austria (73-79) Belgium (65-72;80-88) Canada (65-72) Finland (73-79) Ireland (65-72;80-88) Netherlands (65-72;80-88) Norway (73-79) UK (65-72)

MRS = Monetary Restrictive Strategy; TSS = Tax & Saving' Strategy. Based on the results of the factor analysis concerning economic policy dimensions.

The countries in the left-upper cell represent those with predominantly a monetarist restrictive course; those in the right-lower cell are the cases that represent a Keynesian tendency of economic management, whereas the countries in the left-lower cell can be considered as rather inactive in economic policy-making; finally, the countries mentioned in the right-upper cell are using an unusual combination of strict monetarism and Keynesian instruments simultaneously. All types of economic policy have been used in each period. Only in three countries, Denmark, Sweden and the U.S., had the same type of policy throughout the whole period. Many countries, however, have changed their compounded use of policy instruments exactly during this period. Few countries were prone to 'monetary restrictivism' before 1973 (N = 2), whereas the 'Keynesian' option was hardly chosen after 1980. Conversely, the more mixed strategies were utilized all the time and became widespread after 1973 (N = 17). The information presented Figure 8.1 also gives us a clue as to why the period between 1973 and 1979 has been different from the other two in terms of the reversed correlation between type of economic policy and economic performance (see Table 8.2 again). Comparing the policy choice for each period by country it appears that some countries opted for a return to their original strategy (i.e. Australia, Austria, Ireland, Italy, Norway, France, the Netherlands and Switzerland), or they choose yet another option after 1979 (Canada, Germany, Japan and the United Kingdom). Hence, most countries attempted to cope with the crisis by choosing another policy strategy between 1973 and 1979.

A further question with respect to the relation between policy formation and economic performance is, of course, to what extent each combination of economic policy-instruments has contributed to the economic performance of a country and what weight each of them yielded in the process.

Table 8.3: *The combined impact of Monetary Restrictive and Tax & Saving Strategies on Economic Performance*

Period	R^2	Beta:MRS	Beta:TSS	DW	p
1965-72	39.4%	0.61 (3.04)	-0.14 (-0.70)	1.89	0.02
1973-79	62.7%	-0.68 (-4.60)	0.46 (3.07)	1.96	0.00
1980-88	66.7%	0.80 (5.34)	-0.18 (-1.22)	2.16	0.00

Based on the following equation: Y (= performance) = a + b(MRS) + B(TSS)
R^2 = Adjusted Squared Multiple r; DW = Durbin-Watson Statistical Test; p = 2-tailed significance test; T-values are between brackets.

The degree of 'explained variance' (R^2) demonstrates that the both policy strategies do have a bearing on economic performance. The monetarist type is seemingly more effective, except for the period between 1973 and 1979. These results sustain the observation that the years between 1973 and 1979 apparently were a period of transition, during which policies were transformed or renewed. This view is supported by looking at the signs and the beta-weights in the equation. Only between 1973 and 1979 the 'tax & saving' strategy seemed to add to the result. This part of the analysis supports the view that policies do matter with reard to economic performance.

The significance of this finding is that, sooner or later, most countries attempt to cope with the economic circumstances by choosing a policy strategy that fits their situation best. The conclusion can be therefore that the relation between policy formation economic performance is quite straightforward in general, but at the same time is probably taking shape in a rather variable manner in the various OECD-countries. It may well be that political and institutional factors account for this patterned variation. In the next sections this will be investigated in more detail.

8.4   *Parties and Governments and Economic Policy Formation*

In this section we shall examine the role and impact of the different ideological party-blocs (i.e. left, right and center). Hence, we shall investigate the extent to which the left versus right controversy is indeed an underlying dimension that directs the actions of these actors in relation to economic policy formation. In addition another factor that figures pre-eminently in the research of economic policy are, of course, trade unions (Hibbs, 1977; Korpi, 1983; Cameron, 1984; 1985. They are considered as an important feature of the organized class conflict, influencing the efficacy of a policy strategy (Katzenstein, 1985; Scharpf, 1987; Czada, 1987; Keman, 1990). Without the cooperation of trade unions and without a certain degree of coalescence with non-left parties it seems difficult to develop a policy strategy regarding economic management that is politically feasible and can be carried out effectively (Armingeon, 1987; Braun, 1989; Pennings, 1991). It is thus important to know to what extent these policy actors are motivated by conflicting views on the economic situation and in what degree there is room for cooperation and compromise.

Below in Table 8.4 the relation between policy actors (i.e. parties, trade unions and parties in government) and 'salient' issues is reported. Salient issues represent those societal conflicts that are considered to be politically relevant in differing degrees for political actors (Budge/Farlie, 1983). The more salient an issue, it can be expected, the stronger it will direct the behavior of a policy actor in terms of cooperative or adversarial actions.

Table 8.4: Relations between Policy Actors and Conflict Dimensions

	Issues		
Actors	Conservatism	Redistribution	Economy
1. Parties			
- Left	0.08	0.22	0.59
- Center	0.22	0.06	-0.01
- Right	-0.26	-0.18	-0.43
2. Trade Unions	-0.15	0.41	0.18
3. Government			
- Left PC	-0.38	0.31	0.25
- Center PC	0.40	-0.16	-0.18
- Right PC	-0.05	-0.18	-0.43

Issue-variables are based on Budge (1989), Division of Parties and Party Control (PC) of Government, on Keman (1988). All correlations are Pearson Product Moment Correlations.

These three issues, Conservatism, Redistribution and Economy, appear to be relevant to most of the policy actors involved. So, it may be expected that these policy actors consider them as a course for political action. The correlations reported in this table confirm the generally held view that parties of the left and right do indeed differ on the running of the economy, but contrary to such general views, much less so regarding the issue of the redistribution of economic growth. It is in this domain that the presence and strength of trade unions appears to be relevant with respect to the process of policy formation. Conservatism, indicating a preference for a moderate degree of state intervention, is not a dominant feature of party competition. It is, however, a relevant factor on the level of government. In particular parties of the center are sensitive in this respect and it may therefore influence their behavior in government, especially in terms of choosing a specific type of economic policy formation whilst in coalition government (Budge/Keman, 1990). Finally, on the level of parties in government, it is obvious that there is a difference between the left and other parties with respect to managing the economy and the related effects in terms of redistribution. Given these results, it seems plausible to expect that ideologically different parties will have a different impact on economic policy formation according to their issue-related views. The extent to which this can be observed will be shown by relating the different party-blocs to the different economic policy strategies in each period.

Table 8.5.a.: The Impact of Parties in Parliament & Government

Parties in Parliament (legislative strength)					
Policy Strategy	beta Left	beta Center	beta Right	R^2	p
MRS 65-72	2.94	2.76	3.31	26.8%	0.06
MRS 73-79	0.24	0.34	0.26	0.0%	0.96
MRS 80-88	2.73	2.54	3.42	12.9%	0.12
TSS 65-72	1.42	1.52	1.62	0.0%	0.64
TSS 73-79	3.94	3.98	4.69	42.7%	0.01
TSS 80-88	2.33	2.17	2.46	21.8%	0.10

Table 8.5.b Party Control Government	Left PC		Center PC		Right PC	
	b	R^2	b	R^2	b	R^2
MRS 65-72	0.72	52.4%	(-0.29)	8.5%	(0.34)	11.7%
MRS 73-79	(0.16)	2.5%	(0.10)	0.9%	(-0.22)	4.9%
MRS 80-88	0.46	20.8%	-0.55	30.1%	(0.12)	1.4%
TSS 65-72	0.46	20.7%	(0.04)	0.1%	-0.41	17.1%
TSS 73-79	0.81	65.2%	(-0.25)	6.0%	-0.45	20.6%
TSS 80-88	0.77	59.4%	(-0.13)	1.6%	-0.53	28.2%

Explanation: basic equation: Policy = a + b(party 1) + b(party 2) + b(party 3); results in brackets are not significant *Beta*-weight (standardized coefficients); R^2 = adjusted multiple squared r; p = 2-tailed significance test; results between brackets are not significant at a level of ≤ 0.10.
MRS = Monetary Restrictive Strategy; TSS = Tax & Saving Strategy.

Table 8.5.a reports the extent to which the legislative strength of parties are related to the type of policy strategy that is prevalent in a country. In terms of explained variance (R^2) the relation is not strong. In fact, the impact of parties is only notable before 1973 regarding 'monetary restrictivism'. It could be suggested that all parties were more or less conservative in fiscal matters, avoiding deficit spending and inflation-pushing policies. Of course, during this period this could be accomplished more easily than later on. For in most countries economic growth and employment were at a sound level. In other words, prudent economic management was sufficient to combine the development of the public sector and the market sector without having negative effects on the performance of either sector (Lane, 1985). Furthermore, policy aims in other domains of the state (e.g. social welfare) could be realized without creating counter-productive effects on economic developments.

After 1972, however, this situation changed dramatically. There appears to have been a tendency to opt for a 'Keynesian' course of action, which - judging the Beta-weights - was supported by all parties, particularly in the period 1973-1979. This outcome is by and large according to the afore-described developments in policy formation and economic performance (see Figure 8.2 and Tables 8.2 and 8.4), namely, that after the second oil-shock a reorientation took place and new combinations of policy strategiescame to the surface.

This development can be traced by looking how parties in government have influenced the choice of policy strategy. Table 8.5.b is quite informative in this respect. First of all, it can be noted that party control is a better predictor of the direction of policy-making. This need not to surprise us, as this is what parties are supposed to do, when in government. What is surprising, to some extent, is the fact that the tendency towards 'monetary restrictivism' is apparently not a contested option among parties in government. It seems then that this strategy of economic management is less disputed in reality than is often assumed in the literature (e.g. Gould et al., 1981; Whiteley, 1987). This is not the case, however, with respect to the 'tax & saving' option. Here the parties in government are divided about utilizing it. Table 8.5.b demonstrates that leftwing parties consistently promote this strategy, whereas the rightwing parties oppose it. It is telling to see, in addition, that the center parties do not take a clear position in this respect. In short, the left vs. right distinction matters with respect to economic policy formation and the way parties influence this process is predominantly manifested in their behavior whilst in government.

Another feature of parties in government in many countries, under review here, is that they have to participate in coalitions and thus collaboration by compromise is the name of the game (Laver/Schofield, 1990; Strom, 1990). Table 8.5.c shows in what way and how successful parties have thrown in their weight with respect to the choice of economic policy.

Table 8.5.c   Party Behavior in Coalitions

Policy	Left PC + Center PC	Center PC + Right PC		R^2	p
MRS 65-72	0.71	-0.04 -0.82	-0.85	46.3% 46.3%	0.00 0.00
MRS 73-79	(0.22)	(0.18) (-0.07)	(-0.26)	0.0% 0.0%	0.67 0.67
MRS 80-88	(0.30)	-0.44 -0.77	(-0.36)	29.7% 29.7%	0.00 0.00
TSS 65-72	0.53	(0.22) (-0.36)	-0.64	15.0% 15.0%	0.12 0.12
TSS 73-79	0.82	(0.05) -0.85	-0.98	60.8% 60.8%	0.00 0.00
TSS 80-88	0.83	(0.17) -0.74	-0.99	56.7% 56.7%	0.00 0.00

Explanation: see Table 8.5.a & b

The emerging picture is quite clear and conforms nicely with the widely held view that the left-right distinction in capitalist democracies is relevant and important for understanding the policy-making process. During the whole period, but in particular after 1972, parties of the left promote an active policy stance in a more 'Keynesian'-guided direction. Conversely, parties of the right behave in an opposite direction. They seem to be inhibited with respect to state intervention and are strongly opposed to the 'tax & saving' strategy. However, the most interesting finding is the way parties of the center behave in a coalition: when in government with the left, they apparently go along with their ideas; when in government with the right the opposite situation occurs. Again, this result fits with generally held views on the role and position of center parties (Wilensky, 1981; Van Kersbergen, 1991; Budge/Keman, 1990). In addition, this outcome is supported by the relationship between salient economic issues discussed earlier (see Table 8.4). Center parties are simply less prolific on these matters. This shows how important it is not to analyze parties in static terms of established party families only, but also to examine the different underlying motives of parties with respect to a policy domain, here that of economic management.

Just as this aspect is important for the understanding of party differences and its impact on party behavior in government, it is considered to be of great weight regarding the role of trade unions and the feasibility of economic management. Recall that the issue of redistribution is important to trade unions and to a lesser degree to leftwing parties. The following table shows the extent of the combined impact of leftwing party control and the weight of trade unions:

Table 8.5.d: Left Wing Party Control, Trade Unionism and Economic Policy

Policy strategy	Left in Government	Trade Unions	R^2	p
MRS 65-72	0.94	-0.35	53.7%	0.00
MRS 73-99	(-0.11)	(0.43)	1.1%	0.36
MRS 80-88	0.88	-0.66	41.9%	0.01
TSS 65-72	0.33	0.19	11.0%	0.17
TSS 73-79	0.87	(-0.08)	62.8%	0.00
TSS 80-88	0.61	(0.23)	54.4%	0.69

Explanation: see Table 8.5.a & b; Left in Government & Trade Unions: Beta's

Trade unions have indeed an impact on policy formation. However, the influence is more limited than is often taken for granted (e.g. Korpi, 1983). With respect to the monetary restrictive strategy it seems plausible to suggest that trade unions are constraining leftwing parties in government. The latter, often in a coalition, tend to serve the general interest or may have agreed on a compromise of which the 'monetary restrictivism' is part and parcel (see Table 8.5.c). The trade unions appear to function as a countervailing power, in particular after 1979. This can be understood within the context of the salient issues that direct the behavior of policy actors, whereas leftwing parties favor economic policy, the trade unions are more interested in economic redistribution. It makes sense therefore, that these actors will promote a 'tax & saving' strategy rather than a monetary restrictive one. This view is supported by the results of Table 8.5.b & c where leftwing party control is a positive influence on this type of economic management. All in all, however, the relative weight of trade unions may be important, but its influence seems to be of an indirect, constraining nature.

To conclude: parties in parliament and government do matter with regard to economic policy-making. In particular the strength of both the left- and rightwing parties is notable. The center bloc apparently performs an intermediary role, whereas trade unions play a constraining role in the policy-making process. The impact of the policy actors involved can *inter alia* be understood on the basis of their ideological differences, which are enhanced by the extent to which socio-economic issues are relevant within a political system. The degree and way the various policy actors have a bearing on the policy-making process is more often than not interdependent and sometimes indirect. It may very well be that the cross-national differences in the organization of the 'polity' (i.e. political institutions) account for the variation in the behavior of policy actors.

8.5   Political Institutions and Policy-making

Among others, both Schmidt and Scharpf have emphasized the *intermediary* function of political institutions with regard to the relation between politics and policy (also: Braun/Keman, 1986; Czada/Windhoff-Héritier, 1991). Institutions are defined as those formal and informal 'rules of the game' that direct the behavior of the policy actors involved (March/Olsen, 1989; Keman, 1992a). The 'rules of the game' are to some extent similar in most liberal democracies, but differ in their details and their actual working. Hence, similar institutions may well produce dissimilar processes of policy formation, and may even affect the performance of countries differently (Olson, 1982; Schmidt, 1985; Czada, 1987; Keman, 1988; Braun, 1989; Castles, 1989). If institutions do matter, they may help to explain the puzzling observation that countries with an identical pattern of issues, party differences, government composition and relative strength of political actors do differ in their choice of policy strategy and/or the related performance.

With respect to the domain of economic management the following institutional arrangements will be examined: corporatist arrangements, consociational politics and the cleavage structure of the party system (see Section 8.2 for an elaboration). Institutions mold the behavior of policy actors, because they are existing independently from actors in the political system and constrain the strategic behavior of those actors. For example 'exiting' from corporatist decision-making can very well turn an actor into a 'loser'. Not complying with consociational practice will often be punished by the other players. Not taking into account a cleavage-related interest may lead to veto-situations in the process of policy formation. Hence they limit the options for choice, but at the same time these institutions can help to avoid stalemates and zero-sum solutions in the process of policy formations.

All three institutional arrangements are cross-national variables and indicate the room for manoeuver of all actors involved. By definition they cannot be considered as explanatory (or: causal) factors. They are intermediating variables influencing the behavior of actors with respect to policy formation. As these variables are interrelated and since we wish to avoid 'overdetermination', we shall inspect the impact of each institutional arrangement separately in relation to the relevant policy actors (i.e. party control of government) with respect to policy formation indexes (MRS and TSS).

Table 8.6: Party Control of Government, Institutional Arrangements and Choice of Economic Policy

Policy	Actors	Institutions	R^2
MRS 65-72	Center PC	Cleavages	18.2%
	Center PC	Consociationalism	26.9%
	Left + Center PC	Cleavages	49.2%
MRS 73-79	Left PC	Corporatism	30.3%
	Right PC	Corporatism	21.4%
	Left + Center PC	Corporatism	38.8%
	Center + Right PC	Corporatism	38.8%
MRS 80-88	Center PC	Consociationalism	34.5%
	Center PC	Corporatism	46.9%
	Right PC	Corporatism	40.9%
	Left + Center PC	Corporatism	44.2%
TSS 65-72	None	None	
TSS 73-79	Left PC	Consociationalism	69.4%
	Center PC	Consociationalism	52.6%
	Center + Right PC	Consociationalism	67.9%
	Left + Center PC	Corporatism	58.0%
TSS 80-88	Left PC	Corporatism	60.9%
	Left + Center PC	Corporatism	64.4%
	Center + Right PC	Corporatism	64.4%

The regression equation is: Policy Strategy = $\alpha + \beta 1(\text{actor}) + \beta 2(\text{institution})$; it is computed for each period. The N of equations = 90, exploring all combinations of Table 8.5.b & c. Only the significant results ($p \leq 0.10$) are reported.

The main conclusion is that, although institutions do matter, they do not matter all the time and not always in the same way and degree. In addition, it is obvious from this regression analysis that the 'cleavage structure' of society has little impact on the politics of economic management. Apparently is the extent to which these conflict-dimensions are relevant already intermediated by means of political parties themselves. Moreover, although an indirect effect was supposed, it seems that these socio-cultural features do not affect economic affairs. This only signifies the importance of the left-right distinction with respect to the politics of economic management.

This conclusion partly explains the minor role and influence that parties of the center have in government regarding economic policy-making (or wish to have?). Both the left and rightwing parties in government are more influential. However, it appears that their room to manoeuver is modified when and where consociational and corporatist arrangements exist. Corporatism is an important factor after 1972, in particular regarding the role of the left in government, but also in relation to coalitions with center parties (see also: Keman, 1988; Budge/Keman, 1990; Van Kersbergen, 1991). The statistical results show that corporatist arrangements play a *modifying* role in choosing a policy strategy. Both strategies: the restrictive (i.e. 'monetarism') and the expansionary (i.e. 'Keynsianism') one, are influenced by the corporatist 'rules of the game'. On the one hand, it appears to constrain the leftwing and make these parties accept monetary restrictive policies. On the other, the same process appears to take place with respect to parties of the right concerning the 'tax & saving' option as part and parcel of economic management. Hence, both consociational and corporatist practices affect, particularly after the first oil-shock, the formation of economic policies in advanced capitalist democracies.

Both modes of conflict-resolution add significantly to our understanding why certain strategies are chosen, and make it understandable why in situations of economic stagnation and under conditions of *non*-left party control expansionary policy strategies are an option for choice. This observation also helps to understand as to why leftwing party control of government often induces a more restrictive and monetarist policy strategy. In the latter situation, the corporatist mode of conflict-resolution appears to play an important part. The overall conclusion may be therefore, that the politics of economic policy formation is indeed strongly influenced by parties of the left and right. However this influence is by and large modified by their room for manoeuver within government, particularly in coalitions, and depends additionally on existing pattern of institutional arrangements. This conclusion holds in particular for the development after 1972.

8.6 The Politics of Economic Management in Capitalist Democracies

This chapter has served a dual purpose. On the one hand, the extent to which features of the political process in parliamentary democracies can account for the cross-national and intertemporal variation in economic policy-making and how this is related to the economic performance of the various 'mixed economies', was the research question under examination. On the other hand, the research design developed here was meant to demonstrate the possibilities of a comparative research in order to develop an empirical model of 'politics & policies' in democratic 'polity'.

The final task of this chapter is therefore to tie together the several findings and to attempt to 'model' these in terms of the 'triad', which have directed our line of reasoning with respect to the explanation of 'politics of economic management'(see: Figure 8.1). A fruitful point of departure may be to continue where Scharpf (1987) and Schmidt (1987) have left off. Recall that both authors used models of economic policy-making in which actors and institutions play an important role with regard to the policy-making process.

Scharpf emphasizes the room for manoeuver of policy actors in terms of rational action and institutional constraints in relation to political choice. Schmidt focusses on the institutional features without explicitly using rational action as an explanatory force. He rather stresses the complex interdependence of political actors, institutions and, what he calls, "structural obstacles" to an effective policy performance (Schmidt, 1987: 14-17). Apart from flaws in their research design I challenged the comprehensiveness of their models.

Fritz Scharpf concludes that only certain policy strategies are effective, namely those that promote a consensus among the policy actors and will lead to concerted policy-action. In other words: those policy strategies that are *politically* not feasible (however proper they may be in terms of macro-economic theory) will be counter-productive in terms of performance. In his view 'Keynesian' policy strategies (here typified as: TSS) will do the 'trick', if, and only if, there is a political consensus and cooperation form the policy actors involved. As will become clear in this section, this assertion is not a completely tenable view in the light of the analysis carried out here.

Manfred Schmidt argues differently. he observes that both 'labor-dominated' governments and 'conservative-reformists' can produce a satisfactory performance. The feasibility and efficacy of economic management depends, for example, on the availability of social welfare programs in order to gain cooperation from the trade unions. Or a political compromise can be reached by means of subsidizing certain economic sectors. To paraphrase Schmidt: there is a 'progressive' and a 'conservative' approach to economic recovery, and an 'expansionary' (Keynesian) and a 'restrictive' (monetarist) road to economic recovery. Again, although Schmidt's argument is convincing, our analysis shows that this not necessarily leads a neat, cross-national division of economic policy-making within the OECD-countries that warrants such a conclusion.

Partly this has to do with the research-design employed by both authors. By employing a premeditated, i.e. historically founded, periodization of the period under review (1965-1988), and by developing policy profiles that are sensitive to national developments, it has been demonstrated that the cross-national pattern of the 'politics of economic management' and the related policy performance is quite diversified and variable across and within those countries. Hence, we need a more dynamic interpretation of *what* has happened in order to clarify *why* it happened.

The main findings of this chapter will be presented in three models that fit best the relations between politics, the polity and policy with respect to economic performance.[4] The basic format of each model is similar for each period, incorporating the various actors and institutions that were relevant to both the policy strategies that have figured throughout this chapter. In addition the direct impact of these actors and institutions has been related to economic performance for each period:

[4] In the remainder I shall specify the 'models' by means of stepwise regression analysis. It should be reminded that the causal implications should not be overestimated. The aim is to develop a parsimonious model summarizing our findings.

Table 8.7   Politics and Policies of Economic Management (1965-1972)

Politics	Policy		Economic Performance
	MRS	TSS	
Left PC	.98	.24	.65
Consociationalism	-	.51	.18
Trade unions	-.38	-	-.62

Explained Variance of the equations used: Politics -> Policy (MRS): 55.1 %; Politics -> Policy (TSS): 21.8 %; Politics + Policy -> Economic Performance: 39.4%; *Note*: Based on Tables 8.2 and 8.6; all coefficients are Beta-weights; variance is Adjusted Multiple Squared r; (-) = variable not in equation.

Apparently leftwing politics and the organizational strength of trade unions were dominant during this period and got their way to a large degree. Recall, however, that the rightwing exerted influence on policy-making as well (see Table 8.5.a & b), but their impact is apparently either constrained by the force of the trade union movement or has been modified by coalescent leadership behavior. To some extent this can be understood as a result of the fact, although economic stagnation was observed, that it was considered to be a problem that could be easily resolved by means of Keynesian demand-management; a strategy strongly advocated by labor and other leftwing parties, and one that made other parties unpopular, if they resisted it. Hence, 'leftwing' politics were considered to be both economically and politically feasible during this period. It made the 'left' a dominant policy actor.

Table 8.8   Politics and Policies of Economic Management (1973-1979)

Politics	Policy		Economic Performance
	MRS	TSS	
Left PC	.75	.61	.30
Consociationalism	-	.34	.05
Corporatism	-.84	-	.99

Explained Variance of the equations used: Politics -> Policy(MRS): 30.3%; Politics -> Policy(TSS): 69.4%; Politics + Policy -> Economic Performance: 62.7%; *Note*: see Table 8.7 for explanation.

The emerging model is quite similar to that of the previous period in terms of the actors and institutions involved: the leftwing parties appear still to dominate the politics of policy formation. What is interesting during these years is, that apparently the institutional arrangement of a country made a difference: 'consociationalism' contributed to the choice of a Keynesian type of policy, whereas 'corporatism apparently made the 'monetarist' option not only feasible, but also - judging its relationship with performance - an effective one. It may be concluded therefore that the leftwing parties in government appeared to be able to redirect their priorities best, if corporatist or consociational institutions were available and through which compromise with and cooperation from other actors could be gained. Notwithstanding political controversy and strongly differing opinions on which policy strategy to employ during these years, the political process appeared capable to cope with it.

Table 8.9   Politics and Policies of Economic Management (1980-1988)

Politics	Policy		Economic Performance
	MRS	TSS	
Left PC	-.55	-1.02	-.05
Right PC	-	-1.39	-.41
Trade unions	-.52	-	.06
Consociationalism	-.45	-	.01
Corporatism	-.44	.43	.93

Explained Variance of the equations used: Politics -> Policy (MRS): 62.0 %; Politics -> Policy (TSS): 64.4 %; Politics + Policy -> Economic Performance: 66.7 %; *Note*: see Table 8.7 for explanation.

The last decade has been one of genuine change. The era of the leftwing dominance in government and with it its predominance in directing economic policy formation is apparently over. Given this development, some authors (e.g. Merkel, 1991; Padgett/Paterson, 1991) have already proclaimed the downfall of Democratic Socialism today. It is too early to warrant such conclusions, but it is obvious that the other political actors have gained weight in the policy process and that the choice of strategy is now clearly in favor of monetary restrictivism. This can be observed in the grown impact of the center and the right, relative to the left and the trade unions, with regard to policy making. In addition, the negative signs indicate their attitude toward the 'tax & saving' strategy. Finally, the results of this model show that both the political *and* the socio-economic institutions remain important in relation to the behavior of parties regarding the choice of a policy strategy. Without taking these modes of conflict-resolution into account, it is difficult to understand the process of political change in relation to policy formation and the related economic performance after 1980.

In general, it can be concluded that 'politics does matter', but the way it does, in particular in times of crisis, can only properly be understood, if the institutionalized modes of behavior of political actors are taken into account. In particular corporatism and consociationalism are important factors that shape the process of decision-making and influence the room for manoeuver the actors involved. The very changes that were taking place in the different periods under review have demonstrated this. The analysis carried out in this chapter helps, therefore, to understand more fully how politics plays its role in a capitalist democracy and furthermore how it directs important choices in policy formation; choices that affect the economic welfare in capitalist democracies.

9 The Political Trinity: Liberty, Equality and Fraternity

Jan-Erik Lane and Svante Ersson

States are human made social organizations that constrain individual activity in a way that may lead to a reified concept of the state, to the fallacy of misplaced concreteness, or to treating the state as if it were an entity exterior to the persons who belong to the state. Basically, there is a clear principal-agent problem in the state organization as the rulers may deviate from publicly stated goals or begin to pursue ends that are to their own interests, but are also hardly in the public's interest. The public contract needs to be clarified in democratic elections and monitored against the dangers of moral hazard and adverse selection, i.e. political opportunism (Lane/Nyen, 1992).

The famous slogan from the French revolution: Liberté, égalité and fraternité, may be interpreted as an attempt to define the principal-agent problem in politics. Any government should pursue exactly these three principles in order to be legitimate to the population. Evaluating state activities in this area is a method for monitoring the activities of the elite as the agent and hold it accountable to the population as the principal. What, more precisely, could count as state performance with regard to the principles of liberty, equality and brotherhood of man? In this chapter we will discuss the principles of the French revolution in relation to present day data about the countries of the world, evaluating state performance and probing their interrelationships.

Fundamentally there is no limit to the various outputs of a state (i.e polities that are being recognized as sovereign organizations by the international community) or outcomes to be included in a state evaluation inquiry (Lane, 1992). What matters is system importance or relevance, i.e. evaluation criteria that may be justified from some normative point of view concerning what constitutes a good or a bad polity in terms of a principal-agent framework. The crucial question is, thus, whether the normative criteria selected are generally considered the legitimate ones to employ, for example by the inhabitants themselves, their elites or the international community.

Starting from the political trinity, in particular liberty and equality we focus here upon the occurrence of civil and political rights on the one hand and welfare state expenditures as well as income distribution on the other hand. What is the cross-national variation in these aspects of 'liberté' and 'égalité' among a set of 130 states in the world, i.e. countries with a population larger than 1 million in 1990?

Liberty and equality are highly desirable human ends according to main stream ethical theory, but how about brotherhood? Not only human brotherhood matters, as in international endeavors to end war as a mechanism of conflict resolution between states. The concept of fraternity also implies that states should be characterized by concord between its major groups. Referring not the least to the French revolution, Tocqueville argued that equality is a major determinant in social life (Tocqueville, 1969: 9), in particular with regard to liberty. Looking at the relevance of the Tocqueville model, we wish to add fraternity to the basic equation of liberty and equality.

Firstly, we present an overview of the occurrence of the political trinity values in the world. Secondly, we discuss their interrelationships to search for how internally compatible the political trinity values are. Is equality a condition for liberty, as the Tocqueville model implies (Pope, 1986)? What are the implications of fraternity for liberty and equality? Knowing how important the general level of affluence is for state properties (Lane/Ersson, 1990), we add data on GDP per capita to the evaluation analysis.

9.1 Liberty

Liberty is related to democracy as a means as well as an end, involving government of the people, for the people and by the people as Abraham Lincoln stated in 1863. In order to qualify as government of the people and by the people a specific set of institutions has to be introduced and maintained in a country. Democratic institutions would be of two types. First, there are the participation rules that lay down the presuppositions for the principal-agent interaction between the electorate and the voters. Second, there are the power rules that specify the procedures for how the political elites may compete for and exercise power.

Essentially, this would involve human rights of various kinds. There is a connection between the first and second types of institutions pointing towards the relevance for democracy not only of basic liberties but also of the rules for competition. What matters more than constitutional rules such as voting techniques is the real position of the opposition and the actual probability that the power position of the ruling elite may be contested (Dahl, 1971).

That liberty as a human right is a crucial element in a democratic regime is taken for granted among several scholars analyzing democracy. However, when indices are constructed in order to measure the occurrence of democracy, then the central place of human rights becomes evident. In particular some human rights are sine qua non for any democracy: freedom of thought, speech, association and the freedom of the press. Other human rights such like habeas corpus are perhaps not directly relevant for democracy, but certainly are in an indirect way. Table 9.1 presents two indices on liberty covering the post Second World War period. Civil or political liberty may be handled as a quantitative variable, allowing us to rank states of the world according to how democratic they tend to be.

Table 9.1   Liberty around the World 1973-1978 (Averages)

Area:	Gastil's civil liberties index	Gastil's political rights index
Africa (N=42)	5.5	5.8
America (N=24)	3.5	3.6
Asia (N=35)	5.0	4.9
Oceania (N=3)	1.4	1.4
Europe (N=24)	3.2	3.3
Esq	.32	.29

Note: The scale orders countries in relation to the degree of human rights such that a higher score indicates less of liberty among other things. N=number of cases; Esq = the eta-squared statistic. *Source*: Gastil, 1987; 1990.

In contrast to Oceania the two continents where liberty is not very obvious are Africa and Asia. Listing the few countries there that have or have had some kind of liberal regime though not fully institutionalized during the post-War period, we could point out the following: India, Sri Lanka, Japan, Malaysia and Singapore. There is no freedom in Africa, not even Liberia scores high on any of the indices despite their historical legacy. Yet, tiny Mauritius and Botswana constitute interesting positive exceptions.

The situation is quite different on the American continent. Here, we have not only the US and Canada with their long democratic experience, but also a number of countries that have institutionalized liberty for specific periods of time.

The concept of Latin-Americanization is resorted to in order to pin down a swing back and forth between liberty and coercion, i.e. in most cases military rule, which is characteristic of several countries in Central and Latin America. It implies not only that liberty has been fragile in countries like Argentina, Brazil, Chile and Peru, but also that civil coercion is not easily maintained for longer periods of time in these countries. Military regimes are fundamentally instable because their claim to legitimacy is difficult to uphold over time since they involve the suppression of liberty (Blondel, 1990).

In Europe the divide between civil and political liberty on the one hand and coercion on the other has been a different one in the sense that it was remarkably stable up until 1989. The iron curtain separated the democracies in Western Europe from the so-called people's democracies in Eastern Europe. One could find traces of some type of Latin American pattern in Southern Europe. In Greece, liberty was fragile up until the introduction of the new regime in 1974 following the collapse of the military regime installed in 1967. Portugal (1926-1974) and Spain (1939-1975) have had long experiences of authoritarian rule, but the risk for Latin-Americanization could now exist mainly in the new democracies in Eastern Europe.

In both Portugal and Spain civil and political coercion proved to be strong and long-lived. The Franco regime installed after the civil war between 1936-39 and the Salazar regime formed in 1932 did not fall prey to the vacillation typical of many military regimes in Latin America. On the contrary, the Franco regime remained intact up until the very death of the Caudillo, when typically the successor problem proved impossible to solve. The Portuguese dictatorship foundered on the independence wars in the Portuguese colonies in Africa.

It may be predicted that liberty will grow substantially during the 1990s. Not only have the former East European countries and the many new states in the former giant Soviet Empire attempted to establish stable democratic rule, but there is also in Latin America, as well as in Asia, a general trend towards democracy. Constitutional rule may increase also in Africa, e.g. in South Africa. There is now a new wave of democratization spreading liberty all over the world. Huntington identifies the following waves: (1) 1828 - 1926; (2) 1943 - 1962; (3) 1974 - 1990 (Huntington, 1991: 16). If the hopes for a strong movement towards liberty come true, then almost 50 per cent of the countries of the world would institutionalize civil and political liberty. Yet, there is cause for a warning of a possible occurrence of a third reverse wave, as the events in Peru in the spring of 1992 testify.

However, even if the prospects look bright now for liberty as well as the increasing dissemination of political rights across the world, things may change rapidly, as it is far from evident that each and every attempt to introduce new democracies will be successful. Not simply installing a democratic regime, but maintaining it in the face of economic hardship, social problems and cultural diversity requires not only political skill, but also a favorable economic and social environment. Is economic equality, or a deep-seated sense of brotherhood, a necessary condition for liberty in a state?

9.2   Égalité

When democracy is looked upon as a means to promote government for the people, then there is the hope that government will be for the common good of the people in a general sense. Thus, besides civil war the worst that could happen is that a state becomes a warrior or a police state, either conducting war with its neighbors or engaging in genocide. Positively, a democracy would attempt to increase the general level of affluence in the country either by supporting a welfare state or promoting a welfare society, especially enhancing equality between its citizens. Equality could be a measuring rod of the extent to which states have accomplished major socially legitimate targets.

Equality may be enhanced by government activity as reflected in the size of the public sector as well as in the composition of the public sector. States vary in the size of their public sectors as well as in the orientation of these in terms of policy outputs targeted towards equality such as health and education expenditures as well as transfer payments. Table 9.2 presents an overview of government size.

Table 9.2   The Size of the Public Sector (in % of GDP)

	General Government Final Consumption					Military Expenditure		Health and Education	
Year	'55	'60	'65	'70	'81	'60	'86	'60	'86
Africa	8.9	12.1	13.5	14.5	17.2	1.1	3.7	3.3	5.6
America	9.6	9.9	10.5	11.7	14.4	2.4	3.0	4.0	6.6
Asia	11.0	11.4	12.3	14.1	14.6	5.0	9.5	3.7	6.2
Oceania	10.4	10.2	19.4	18.6	20.3	1.9	2.1	5.1	9.8
Europe	12.8	12.2	13.4	14.2	18.3	4.0	3.5	5.8	9.7
Esq	.19	.06	.14	.08	.09	.26	.23	.26	.23

Note: The number of cases varies at the separate times of measurement: Africa from 17 in 1955 to 41 in 1986; America from 19 in 1955 to 24 in 1986; Asia from 12 in 1955 to 27 in 1986; Oceania from 2 in 1955 to 3 in 1986; Europe from 16 in 1955 to 23 in 1986. *Source*: World Bank, 1983 (first 5 columns); United Nations Development Programme, 1990 (last 4 columns).

Public sector growth is a universal phenomenon. The expansion of government during the post-War period is to be found in countries on all the continents. Generally speaking, it is a matter of a strong upward trend in the relative size of government on each continent.

The public sector consists of the activities of governments on various levels and with various functions. One the one hand, there are the classical functions of the state: internal and external order. On the other, there is the set of welfare state functions. In Table 9.2, the share of military expenditures would belong to the guardian state concept whereas the share of educational and health expenditures would constitute part of the welfare state, which is intended to promote equality by providing access for most of the population to these services. Both type of state expenditures have risen sharply since the 1960s. Among the countries in Asia the increase in military spending is very pronounced, which to some extent is also true of African states. In Europe the main trend is the relative expansion of the welfare state and the relative decline in the military budgets.

Some states allocate a considerable part of the resources of the country to military efforts. In the 1986 data the really big spenders on military items include: Iraq (32%), Iran (20%), Israel (19%), Oman (28%), Saudi Arabia (23%), Yemen (22%), Syria (15%), USSR (12%), Liberia (12%), Mongolia (11%), North Korea (10%), United Arab Emirates (9%) and United States (7%). As a matter of act, the concentration on military spending in the countries situated in the Middle East is enormous, as a matter of fact.

On the other hand, some states focus heavily on equality enhancing welfare state expenditures, on programmes such like health and education. Such countries are the following according to the 1986 data: Austria (11%), Belgium (11%), Canada (14%), Denmark (13%), Finland (12%), France (12.5%), Germany or FRG (11%), Ireland (15%), the Netherlands (14%), New Zealand (11%), Norway (12%), Saudi Arabia (14.5%), Sweden (15.5%), Switzerland (12%). A welfare *state* is not synonymous with a welfare *society*. Welfare societies or countries with a high standard of living may be market orientated, trusting voluntary exchange mechanisms more than budget allocation in the provision of welfare services to its population.

A welfare state not only provides a number of services virtually without cost to its citizens. The allocation of education of various kinds includes obligatory primary education and a variety of opportunities with regard to secondary and higher education. Health care comprises both open and closed somatic care involving a large number of medical specialties. The allocation of social services consists of both old age care and services to a variety of clientele. In addition, a welfare state operates transfer payment programmes, the size of which is indicated in Table 9.3.

Table 9.3   The Redistributive State

Social Security Benefits expenditure in % of GDP in 1980	
Africa (N=11)	0.6
America (N=19)	3.1
Asia (N=19)	3.1
Oceania (N=2)	10.4
Europe (N=20)	15.4
Esq	.76

Source: United Nations Development Programme, 1991; note that the N of Cases is lower as a result of lack of data.

A large scale welfare state can only be found in Europe and in Oceania. Economic poverty is a definitive barrier to cash payments as the low score for Africa indicates. But there exist patterns of public resource allocation in Third World countries that are welfare state orientated (MacPherson/Midgley, 1987). One cannot bypass the existing financial constraints in any state, particularly not in an analysis of countries in the Third World (Jackman, 1975). However these states do have a few social policies dating back to colonial times, although in the developing countries they tend to be directed towards urban elites.

Economic affluence is a necessary but not sufficient condition for extensive transfer payments. In very rich Japan cash payments amount to 6 per cent of GDP and in rich Singapore they only make up about 3 per cent of GDP, whereas in the Netherlands with 22 per cent, Denmark with 19 per cent and Italy with 13 per cent transfer payments loom large. Although the number of countries covered in Table 9.3 is not as large as could be hoped for, it is true that countries differ considerably in their effort to run welfare programmes enhancing equality across society.

Equality refers not only to policy outputs but it also involves policy outcomes. The measurement of equality as outcomes presents a number of problems that are not easily resolved. The set of relevant outcomes with regard to the evaluation of equality is large, meaning that it is necessary to concentrate on a few outcome criteria that are as broad as possible. The level of affluence as well as economic growth would be of interest. However, direct measures on social equality would include indicators on the distribution of incomes, measuring the extent of equality in a more straightforward manner.

Table 9.4 shows that inequalities of income are larger in poor countries than in rich ones, whatever measure of income differentials one may employ - a controversial issue in itself. Actually, income equality was larger in the West European welfare states than in the former communist states. Generally speaking, the higher the scores the more unequal is the distribution of income.

Table 9.4   Income Inequality

Area:	HDR10 1990(N)	HDR20 1990(N)	OEB 1990(N)	OWH 1983(N)	MUS20 1979(N)	INDEX 1988(N)
Africa	32 (9)	52 (15)	41 (19)	58 (16)	59 (17)	55 (29)
America	34 (10)	54 (16)	38 (18)	55 (16)	57 (19)	21 (21)
Asia	31 (14)	46 (15)	35 (18)	50 (14)	49 (16)	28 (26)
Oceania	28 (2)	44 (2)	29 (2)	40 (2)	40 (2)	-87 (2)
Europe	24 (13)	41 (14)	24 (20)	40 (16)	45 (14)	-83 (22)
Esq	.37	.32	.49	.48	.34	.61

Note: The inequality indices measure the income share of the top 10 per cent or top 20 per cent of the population.
Source: HDR = Human Development Report, 1990; EB = Encyclopedia Britannica, 1990; WH = World Handbook, 1983; Musgrave, 1979; INDEX = Dye and Zeigler, 1988.

It must be underlined that income distribution data is beset by problems of reliability as well as validity when employed across such a large set of countries. Yet, it clearly stands out that countries with an advanced economy tend to have more of income equality than poor countries. The implication would then be that income inequalities could be accepted much more easily in rapidly growing economies than in stagnating ones, because over time economic prosperity would increase income equality. In any case, the finding is that one of the major human values of the French revolution - égalité - has its best chances in states with an advanced economy, meaning so-called capitalist institutions (Williamson, 1986).

The amount of equality in the distribution of income is related to the level of economic affluence by means of the so-called Kuznets' curve. It predicts that income inequality will rise in a process of rapid economic development only to decline as a higher level of economic affluence has been reached. Are there significant traces of the operation of the Kuznets' mechanism among states in the late 1980s after a long-term process of economic growth in most countries, as well as in the world economy at large since the end of World War Two? Figure 9.1 presents the plotted relationship between income inequality (HDR20) and the level of affluence (GDP per capita 1987) in the 1980s:

Figure 9.1   *The Kuznets' Curve: income distribution and level of economic affluence*

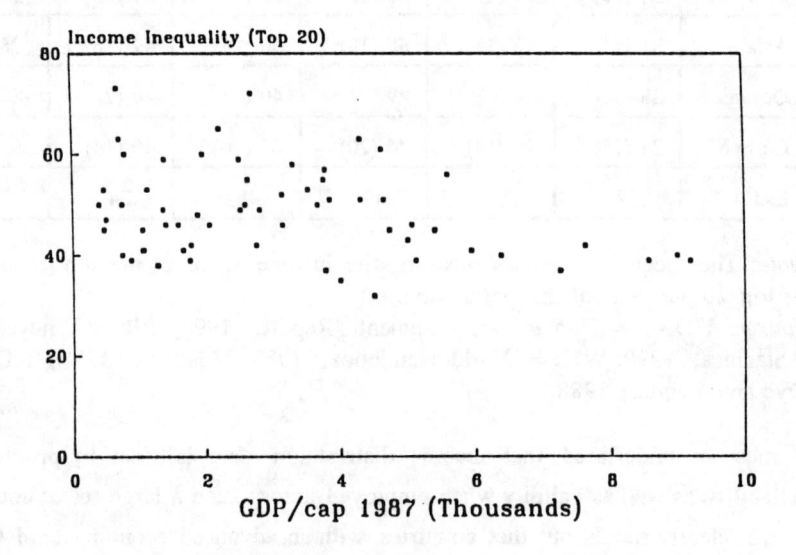

It is thus impossible not to bring up affluence when discussing equality. There are two contrary hypotheses, one stating that income differentials would matter less, if the level of affluence is generally high. The other hypothesis claims that poverty would be more acceptable to the population, if it is shared among all. Let us look at the variation in human predicament among polities.

9.3 Affluence

The level of economic affluence may be measured in various ways. Table 9.5 presents both Gross Domestic Product and Gross National Product on a per capita basis from 1950 to 1989.

Table 9.5　　Level of Affluence (US dollars per capita)

Gross Domestic Product				Gross National Product		
	1950	1960	1970	1980	1985	1989
Africa	684	589	734	850	866	784 (N=39)
America	1949	2295	3046	3607	3410	3099 (N=23)
Asia	816	1290	2127	3578	3847	4874 (N=24)
Oceania	4431	3920	5201	5747	6075	9043 (N=3)
Europe	2577	3753	5503	7302	7823	13832 (N=19)
Esq	.38	.51	.51	.45	.48	.43

Note: The number of cases for GDP varies: Africa from 9 in 1950 to 41 in 1985; America from 18 to 23; Asia from 12 to 27; Oceania from 2 to 3. *Source*: GDP per capita 1950-1985: Summers/Heston, 1988; GNP per capita 1989: World Bank, 1991.

Using data from 1987 (Human development report, 1990), there certainly are poor countries and rich countries as well as a number of countries in between (all figures represent US$). In Europe the rich states are all situated in Western Europe, in particular in the North, except to super affluent Switzerland (15 403) and well-off Austria (12. 386). The economic well-being of the East European countries is very difficult to tap in a more precise way. Most probably the GDP has been overestimated for a long period of time. The large differences between Norway (15.940), Sweden (13.780), Denmark (15.119), FRG (14.730), the Netherlands (12.661) on the one hand, and former GDR (8.000), Poland (4.000), Czechoslovakia (7.750), Hungary (4.500) in the 1987 data are certainly not overestimated (United Nations Development Programme, 1990). In the data for the early 1990s they will have grown even larger, as the system change away from a command economy has proved to be a difficult process to administer, resulting in considerable losses in output.

Similarly, the economic separation between Southern West-Europe and Southern East-Europe is a sharp one and the distance will grow even wider. Former Yugoslavia (5.000), Romania (3.000), Bulgaria (4.307) cannot expect to catch up with Portugal (5.597), Spain (8.989), Italy (10.682) and Greece (5.500). Counting the former USSR (6.000) as part of Europe, the same observation applies to it. The question here is how much of the real affluence level that will be reduced in the process of economic system transformation.

On the American continent there is the clear-cut economic north-south divide. The United States (17.615) and Canada (16.375) have a standard of living which is several times as high as that in the Latin American countries: Uruguay (5.069), Brazil (4.307), Argentina (4.647), Venezuela (4.306) and Chile (4.862) among the better off countries and Peru (3.129), Colombia (3.524), Paraguay (2.603) and Bolivia (1.380) among the less well off. In Central America there are both states doing fairly well such as Mexico (4.624), Costa Rica (3.760) but also states that are not doing so well like Honduras (1.119), Cuba (2.500) and Haiti (775).

Characteristic for the states on the African continent is extreme poverty. Actually, only a few countries in the North have moved out of the poor predicament of African countries where Gabon (2.068) and South Africa (4.981) are also the exceptions. Thus, Egypt (1.357), Algeria (2.633), Morocco (1.761) and Tunisia (2.741) differ from Nigeria (452), Kenya (794), Tanzania (405), Malawi (476), Zambia (717) and Zaire (220). In several states economic conditions must be characterized as extremely harsh, in particular in countries that have experienced long civil wars.

The variation in affluence on the gigantic Asian continent differs from that of the African continent as there are besides the poor states of the Third World, also some very rich countries. On the one hand the oil exporting countries are affluent, some of them more than the others. Saudi Arabia (8.320), Oman (7.750) and United Arab Emirates (12.191) have standards of living comparable to the OECD countries whereas Iran (3.300) and Iraq (2.400) are closer to the conditions in several Third World countries, in particular the latter after the economically devastating Gulf war.

In Southeast Asia, besides Japan, the so-called Baby Tigers have shown that the gap between rich and poor countries may be closed in a relatively short time period (Balassa, 1991). The level of affluence in Japan (13.135) as well as in the newly industrializing countries - Singapore (12.970), Taiwan (3.500), South Korea (4.832) and Hong Kong (6.272) - may be compared with several West European countries. The contrast to the predicament of the huge Asian states: China (2.124), India (1.053), Pakistan (1.585), Bangladesh (883), Thailand (2.576), Indonesia (1.660) and Burma (450) is stark, but Asian poverty is not quite as bad as African poverty.

In Oceania Australia (11.782) and New Zealand (10.541) belong to the rich set of OECD countries whereas Papua New Guinea (1.843) belongs to the Third World. Typical of Australia and New Zealand is not that they belong to the so-called rich world, but that their level of affluence has grown at such a slow rate. Table 9.6 contains the growth rate data.

Table 9.6   Economic Growth: average yearly rates

Area:	1950-60 (N)	1970-81 (N)	1965-89 (N)
Africa	1.51 (29)	.58 (42)	.86 (37)
America	2.04 (18)	1.98 (23)	1.17 (22)
Asia	2.77 (17)	3.00 (29)	2.81 (20)
Oceania	.85 (2)	.60 (3)	.90 (3)
Europe	3.77 (15)	2.75 (17)	2.71 (15)
Esq	.14	.13	.16

Source: World Bank, 1983: annual growth in GDP/cap 1950-1960, 1970-1981; World Bank, 1991: annual growth in GNP/cap 1965-1989.

Rapid economic change on a long-run basis has occurred in Asia and Europe. It is true that yearly growth rates in national economies fluctuate considerably as a response to short-run conditions, but economic growth rate measures averaged out for a number of years are telling indicators on sustainable dynamic economic processes in a country. The substantial long-term growth rates for the two continents of Europe and Asia are all the more impressive as they cover an immense country variation between truly dynamic economies and countries where the economy displays long-run sluggish growth.

The dismal development on the African continent is apparent in the data. Not much better is the data for Oceania, whereas the American data hides both strong economic expansion as well as economic retardation. Let us list the countries that stand for high average rates of economic growth between 1965 and 1989 and contrast it with a list of the countries whose economies have changed slowly, if not negatively, during the same time period of roughly 25 years:

Table 9.7 *Average Growth Rates 1965-1989 (per cent)*

Rapidly growing countries		Slowly growing countries	
1. Botswana	8.5	1. Kuwait	-4.0
2. South Korea	7.0	2. Libya	-3.0
3. Singapore	7.0	3. Uganda	-2.8
4. China	5.7	4. Niger	-2.4
5. Lesotho	5.0	5. Zaire	-2.0
6. Switzerland	4.6	6. Zambia	-2.0
7. Indonesia	4.4	7. Madagascar	-1.9
8. Japan	4.3	8. Ghana	-1.5
9. Thailand	4.2	9. Jamaica	-1.3
10. Egypt	4.2	10. Chad	-1.2
11. Malaysia	4.0	11. Venezuela	-1.0
12. Canada	4.0	12. Senegal	-0.7
13. Burundi	3.6	13. Mauritania	-0.5
14. Tunisia	3.3	14. Peru	-0.2
15. Finland	3.2	15. Tanzania	-0.1
16. Yugoslavia	3.2	16. Argentina	-0.1

17. Italy	3.0
18. Mauritius	3.0
19. Mexico	3.0
20. Sri Lanka	3.0

Source: World Bank, 1991.

It is difficult to narrow down the exact meaning of a long-run economic growth process, but it sets a tone for the conduct of life within a state that affects all spheres of life. The level of affluence may be more important than the rate of change in the economy, but a sustainable growth rate at about 3-5% per year means a lot for the standard of living within a decade. Just as countries with a strong economic growth can climb up from the set of poor states towards the rich countries, so can rich countries tumble downwards. The developments in South East Asia and their counter-examples in Latin America testify to the fuzzy borderline between rich and poor countries.

Although the GDP and GNP indicators tap much about country conditions they do need to be complemented by a set of social indicators that describe more about quality of life and human development as well as about the distribution of welfare in a society. What matters is how economic affluence translates into general conditions of living among the population. The economic capacity of a state may be employed for various purposes, only one of which could be the reduction of mass poverty. A description by means of the GDP and GNP measures is most adequately combined with some measure such as the human development index or an income distribution index. We start with the first indicator.

Quality of life is the most crucial aspect of the human condition. It denotes a variety things such as health and sanitary conditions, communications, education, birth rates and life expectation. One indicator on quality of life is the human development index, which focuses on people's deprivation in life expectancy, literacy and income for a decent standard of living (Human Development Programme, 1990: 13). The index allows us to portray an alternative picture of the sharp differences in the human predicament on earth.

The human predicament in Africa and Asia is on the whole worse than in America, Oceania and Europe. Conditions are not rosy, particularly not in Africa. At the same time there are exceptions which must be noted. In Africa the distance between unhappy circumstances and more happy ones is tremendous and at the same time as the average values for the African continent is far below that of Oceania and Europe. Angola, Benin, Bhutan, Ethiopia, Guinea, Liberia, Niger, Sierra Leone, Somalia, Zaire are the unfortunate cases whereas prospects are brighter in Algeria and Tunisia in the North, Gabon in Central Africa and South Africa in the South. In Asia there is immense mass poverty but it tends to be not as bad as in Africa, with the exception of Bangladesh and Burma. Thus, India, Pakistan and Indonesia score low on the indicators, but not as low as the unfortunate countries in Africa or Bangladesh and Burma.

The distance between a miserable and a well-to-do situation on the American continent is quite substantial, but yet not as huge as that between the poor countries in Asia on the one hand and Japan, Singapore, South Korea and Hong Kong on the other. What matters are life opportunities, and they tend to be low in countries such as Bolivia, Peru, Ecuador, Haiti and Honduras, but not in terms of African standards. The United States and Canada outdistance the other states by far, but in terms of general conditions of life Argentina, Brazil and Uruguay are more close to the fortunate American states than to the destitute ones.

To be more specific, the major finding comparing economic indicators with general social ones is that in Europe the vast differences in economic affluence between the West and the East do not translate into sharply separated life conditions. There is an interesting curvilinearity in the connection between economic affluence and general quality of life. Very low levels of affluence result in truly miserable social conditions, but as the GDP indicator scores ascend towards higher levels, the quality of life indicator measures at first rise proportionately but then the curve evens out. Figure 9.2 displays the asymptotic nature of the relationship between levels of affluence (GDP per capita 1987) and the human condition (Human Development Index).

Figure 9.2   *Human Development Index and Level of Economic Affluence in the 1980s*

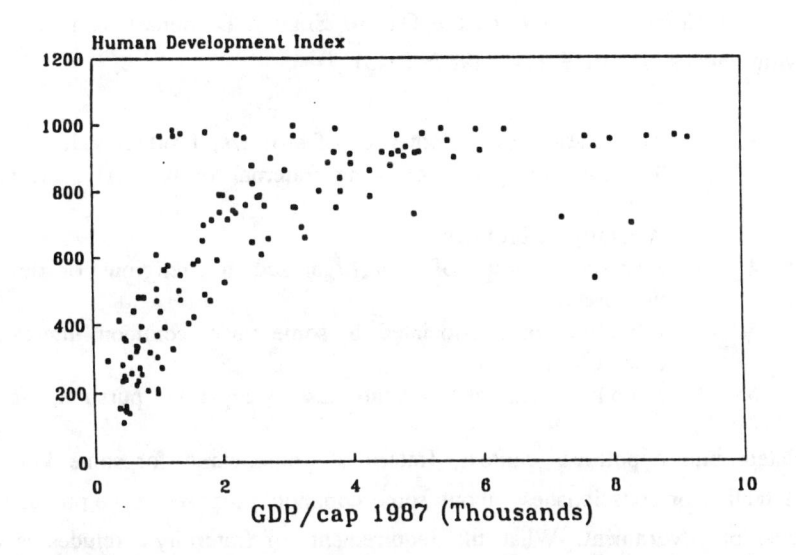

The distribution of income is an important aspect when analyzing the human predicament, at least so the political trinity model claims. The use of income distribution scores is a caveat against any simple conclusion that increases in total economic output must result in more affluence for the entire population. At the same time one must be aware that rapid processes of economic growth most likely are beneficial for broad masses in the population, even if the income distribution is skewed to the advantage of the rich. The finding is that affluence in general matters more than simply equality in income distribution, because it improves the general human predicament and also reduces income inequality.

9.4 Fraternity

To the French revolutionaries a desirable state was not only a republic where liberty and equality ruled. They also required fraternity. The emphasis on fraternity has not stood up as well as the requirements for liberty and equality in the history of normative political principles. As a matter of fact, we may ask somewhat astonishingly whether there really is a core political principle behind the argument for brotherhood. Before we try to map the occurrence of fraternity in the world, we must briefly pin down its double meaning in political discourse.

The Compact Edition of the Oxford English Dictionary contains the following entries on 'fraternity' (1987: 1043):

1. The relation of a brother or of brothers; brotherhood.
2. The state or quality of being fraternal or brotherly; brotherhood.
3. A family of brothers.
4. A body or order of men organized for religious or devout purposes.
5. A body of men associated by some tie or common interest; a company or guild.
6. A body of men of the same class, occupation, pursuits, etc.

Translated into a political context, fraternity would stand for some kind of shared feeling or consciousness about some common purposes to be pursued at the level of government. What the requirement of fraternity excludes is the political body where citizens are either indifferent towards each other, political apathy or alienation as expressions of such a predicament, or alternatively, where citizens are in severe conflict with each other about the ends and means of the political community, as e.g. in civil war.

Fraternity as a political ideal would amount to something like brotherhood in a republic. The Oxford English Dictionary mentions as one of the key meanings of 'brotherhood':

"Fellowship; community of feeling uniting man and man; also concretely those united in such fellowship" (1987: 284)

Yet, what unites man may be entirely different sorts of things. Amongst other things solidarity based on a shared identity could also very well enhance this type of behavior. On the one hand there is the notion of universal fellowship and on the other hand there is national fellowship or simply nationalism. A political community may be focussed on what unites its members such as national identity making them different from other men. Or a political community may be orientated towards universal principles that could unite all men, as e.g. human rights and international cooperation being widely conceived.

These two interpretations of brotherhood may run into a violent clash with each other. National identity could become the basis for large scale state atrocities towards internal so-called enemies or groups with a different ethnic identity. And it may trigger imperialist wars aiming at the dominination of one fraternity by another. However, nationalist theory has also harbored a soft thesis claiming that national identification is a source of popular sovereignty that could very well foster respect and cooperation between nation states - as stated already in Meinecke's *Weltburgertum und Nationalstaat* (1907).

National fellowship is often considered to be a vital part of a compound republic. A nation-state is not simply an administrative entity but involves a community of equals acting in liberty towards fellow goals. What is the use of equality if the society is torn apart by conflict between different fellowships? How can liberty last when communities and factions take steps to crush each other? Fraternity may be regarded as value addition or value condition: it could add an independent value to liberty and equality, or it could be looked upon as a means to, or a condition for a stable regime based upon liberty and equality.

A happy state could not possibly be one where there was strong dissent among major social groups about the direction of the political community. In addition, such collective disagreement could topple both liberty and equality within a political body. At the same time strong national consensus could be harmful as it may cause nationalist attitudes and aggressive behavior. To some, fraternity denotes a universal brotherhood independent of state boundaries, whereas to others it stands for national unity. The developments of the French revolution indicate this ambiguity in the concept, for the process of "Napoleonization" implied that the idea of brotherhood could serve as the basis for the building of a French empire, offsetting the emergence of other national fraternities:

> "it is indeed true that modern nationalism is a product of the
> French revolution and as a concept was born out of the failure
> of the revolution's universalism." (Szporluk, 1988: 81)

Fraternity may be measured in two different ways, either directly or indirectly. Firstly, attitudes toward groups and the nation may be surveyed. Secondly, one could look at the amount of fragmentation in the social structure, measuring the probability that two randomly selected individuals belong to the same ethnic or religious group as well as to a social class. Table 9.8 presents rough estimation data for a number of countries using the second kind of indicator on the occurrence of fraternity in a state.

The ethnicity fractionalization index - ELF - is a composite of two such indices, one for the 1960s and the other for the 1970s. One may assume that the fractionalization scores would hardly have changed rapidly over the last decades, if not increased. The ethnic fragmentation index is scaled the other way around with regard to the ethnic domination index, which measures just how large the share of the population is that belongs to the dominating language group.

Table 9.8   Ethnic and Religious Homogeneity versus Heterogeneity

	1. (N)	2. (N)	3. (N)	4. (N)	5. (N)
Africa	.61 (42)	51 (41)	51 (43)	51 (42)	.48 (43)
America	.37 (24)	86 (24)	66 (24)	71 (24)	.22 (24)
Asia	.40 (29)	77 (34)	74 (36)	75 (35)	.16 (36)
Oceania	.33 (3)	84 (3)	83 (3)	90 (3)	.49 (3)
Europe	.24 (24)	84 (24)	83 (24)	84 (24)	.33 (24)
Esq	.25	.32	.25	.26	.32

Source & Explanation: 1 = ELF: ethno-linguistic fractionalization, Taylor/Hudson, 1972, Barrett, 1982; 2 = DOM1: size of dominating ethno-linguistic group, Rustow, 1967; 3 = DOM2: Barrett, 1982; 4 = DOM3: Vanhanen, 1990; 5 = R1: religious fractionalization, Barrett, 1982.

Among the various social cleavages - ethnicity, religion and class - especially ethnic but also religious fragmentation may break the brotherhood of a country into severe dissent. In particular this may be the case if both socio-cultural dimensions occur within a country. On average, ethnic fragmentation tends to be high in Africa, somewhat lower in America and Asia whereas it is generally low in Europe and in Oceania. The religious fragmentation is calculated on the basis of the relative population size of protestants, roman catholics, moslems and other religions. High religious fragmentation scores are to be found mainly in Africa, but also in Europe and Oceania.

Since the intra-group differences are larger than the inter-group differences it is worthwhile to identify countries that score very high on these two fractionalization indices, which means that their fraternity may face severe difficulties (Tables 9.9 and 9.10):

Table 9.9   Ethnic Fragmentation

Belgium	.55	Bolivia	.70
Benin	.75	Ghana	.72
Cambodia	.82	Burkina Faso	.72
Cote D'Ivoir	.87	Canada	.79
Gabon	.76	Central Afr Rep	.74
India	.90	Chad	.80
Indonesia	.77	Colombia	.67
Iran	.78	Congo	.69
Kenya	.89	Ecuador	.60
Liberia	.86	Ethiopia	.70
Nigeria	.88	Guinea	.70
Philippines	.79	Kuwait	.73
Senegal	.77	Laos	.61
Sierra Leone	.78	Malawi	.64
Namibia	.78	Malaysia	.71
Uganda	.93	Mali	.82
Togo	.72	Mexico	.60
(F)Yugoslavia	.78	Mozambique	.74
Zambia	.79	Nepal	.69
Angola	.80	Pakistan	.63
Afghanistan	.63	Peru	.63
Bhutan	.61	Sudan	.72
Guatemala	.58	Niger	.74
Senegal	.77	SouthAfrica	.68
Tanzania	.95	USSR	.68

Note: Only those countries are reported that have an Ethnic Fragmentation Index of > .055.

A few countries score very high on the ethnic - fragmentation index - Uganda, Tanzania, India, Kenya, Nigeria - meaning that the brotherhood would come under severe strain. The same applies to religious fragmentation in countries like Togo, Malawi, Kenya, Ethiopia and Tanzania (Table 9.10).

Table 9.10   Religious Fragmentation

Iraq	.45	Liberia	.64
Angola	.49	Madagascar	.64
Australia	.57	Malawi	.73
Benin	.52	Malaysia	.55
Botswana	.54	Mauritius	.62
Bulgaria	.52	Mozambique	.62
Burkina Faso	.59	Pap New Guinnea	.51
Cameroon	.73	Rwanda	.64
Canada	.57	Sierra Leone	.57
Cen Afr Rep	.63	South Africa	.48
Chad	.70	Tanzania	.73
Cote D'Ivoir	.67	Togo	.64
Cuba	.50	Trinidad	.70
Ethiopia	.61	Uganda	.66
GDR	.53	USSR	.59
FRG	.56	U.S.	.55
Hungary	.54	Uruguay	.49
Indonesia	.59		
Kenya	.69		
Lebanon	.51		
Lesotho	.61		

Note: Only those countries have been reported that a Religious Fragmentation Index of > .45. Source: Taylor and Hudson, 1972; Barrett, 1982.

Some very large countries have had to accommodate ethnic or religious fragmentation: Indonesia, the former USSR, South Africa and Malaysia. The fact that most of these countries have had large difficulties in maintaining some sort of state shows that fraternity may be very difficult to arrive at in countries with extensive and intensive ethnic or religious fragmentation. Often there is both ethnic and religious fragmentation in a country, as the two indices tend to co-vary to some extent ($r = .41$).

9.5 Internal Consistency of the Trinity Model

Evidently, the identification of liberty, equality and brotherhood as the basic political values was based on vague notions about the possibility to achieve these values. Are there tensions in the political trinity? To some political liberties are a condition for a developmental process towards more of equality. To others a certain level of equality guarantees the introduction of democracy and its liberties must be procured for all citizens. Finally, is brotherhood a condition for both political liberty and economic equality? It may be argued that a lack of fraternity may hamper the evolution of democratic institutions and reinforce inequalities.

We shall now look at the interaction between our indicators on liberty, equality and fraternity. Table 9.11 records both equality as a set of outcomes but also on equality as an ambition. A large public sector contains several redistributive programs which enhance equality. However, it is probably true that equality of results depends more upon general economic factors such as the level of affluence, which are also included in the table. Whereas human rights may be established by fiat and equality promoted by the public sector, fraternity is a different kind of social entity. Although it may certainly be fostered by various activities, it has a strong ground in the social structure and its cleavages. Here, we tap fraternity by focussing on ethnic fragmentation which appears to be one of the most divisive type of cleavages.

Table 9.11   Consistency of Trinity Values: correlation between indicators

	(1)	(2)	(3)	(4)	(5)	(6)	(7)	(8)
Political rights (1) (Tab 1)	1.00							
Income ineq. (2) (Tab 4)	.19 (62)	1.00						
Fraternity (3) (Tab 8)	.27 (121)	.38 (61)	1.00					
GGFC81 (4) (Tab 2)	-.14 (91)	-.09 (55)	-.17 (89)	1.00				
HED86 (5) (Tab 2)	-.50 (118)	-.35 (62)	-.40 (113)	.50 (90)	1.00			
SOCB80 (6) (Tab 3)	-.37 (63)	-.59 (41)	-.46 (63)	.32 (53)	.66 (62)	1.00		
GDPC85 (7) (Tab 5)	-.56 (117	-.46 (61)	-.38 (112)	.17 (89)	.64 (114)	.76 (61)	1.00	
EG6589 (8) (Tab 6)	-.29 (97)	-.01 (56)	-.30 (96)	-.07 (83)	.21 (97)	.23 (52)	.24 (95)	1.00

Note: On the indicators see Tables 9.1-8. The liberty indicator is scaled from high to low while the other indicators are scaled from low to high. Fraternity is measured by means of the ethnic fractionalization index, as the religious fragmentation index matters little for the above variables.

The overall finding is that the French revolutionaries were right: liberté, égalité and fraternité are possible to accomplish, but it will not come about without effort. Empirically, the various aspects of the political trinity are related to each other as the indicators on liberty, equality and fraternity tend to go together. At the same time the correlations are not that pronounced which means that the three entities in the trinity reinforce each other, but there certainly is a meaningful pattern of interaction. We may draw two strong conclusions about feasibility, i.e. the policy possibilities of implementing a regime of liberty, equality and fraternity.

Firstly, we should underline the absence of sufficient conditions. The main negative finding is that liberty, equality and fraternity do not automatically reinforce each other. The degree to which freedom and political rights have been institutionalized is only related to the extent of income equality in a weak manner (r=.19). The same is true of the relationship between liberty and fraternity (r=.27), as well as of equality and fraternity (r=.38). Yet, the direction of the connections are in accordance with the trinity model, meaning that these three entities tend to support each other.

Secondly, one positive finding is that there is a necessary condition between liberty and equality. Thus, it is not likely that states which do not respect the principles of liberty will score high on equality, but at the same time the reverse does not hold. States with a high degree of equality tend to be liberal states, but states that score high on freedom need not be states that promote income equality by means of either policy outputs or real policy outcomes. Fraternity is not a necessary condition for either liberty or equality.

Thirdly, another positive finding is the existence of a necessary condition between fraternity on the one hand and liberty or equality on the other. Countries that score very high on ethnic fragmentation are with few exceptions authoritarian states with unequal societies. However, low scores on ethnic fragmentation do not automatically translate into liberty and equality, because other, mainly economic, factors matter.

Fourthly, the impact of economic affluence is considerable with regard to all of the trinity values. We find that there are correlations between affluence and political rights ($r = -.56$), with equality ($r = -.46$) and fraternity ($r = -.38$) with the correct sign. One may dispute the existence of a causal connection, but it remains true that democracy, income equality and fraternity tends to be higher in affluent rich societies. Most important is also that policies aiming at enhancing equality tend to be stronger in countries with a high level of affluence.

In terms of desirability liberty, equality and fraternity may appear appealing. However, in terms of public policy-making in both the short and long term policy measures that promote one of the trinity entities will not markedly spill over into increasing scores on the other trinity entities. But, and this is the crux of the matter, desirable policies targeted to enhance the trinity values - égalité, liberté and fraternité - will not prove self-defeating, because there is no internal incompatibility in the political trinity model.

Summarizing our argument: the three basic political ideals from the French revolution could constitute the starting point for systematic state performance evaluation. Here, we have a few great puzzles for comparative inquiry: why are some states fortunate in scoring high on all three dimensions? We have seen that the currently existing states of the world differ tremendously in the extent to which they have successfully institutionalized liberty, égalité and fraternity. There is a small set of better-off countries which manifests this political trinity. At the same time some states also score low on all three, characterized by dictatorship, poverty and discord in civil society. There exists a mechanism that to some extent interrelates the three dimensions, counteracting any tendency towards goal conflicts or incompatibility between these macro political values. Thus, liberty is a necessary condition for equality and fraternity constitutes likewise a necessary condition for liberty and equality.

Bibliography

Abrams, P. (1982)
Historical Sociology, Ithaca (NY), Cornell UP.
Almond, G.A. (1956)
Comparative Political Systems, in: *Journal of Politics*, 18: 391-409
Almond, G.A. (1968)
Comparative Politics, in: *International Encyclopedia of the Social Sciences*, New York, MacMillan, Vol. 13: 331-336.
Almond, G.A. (1983)
Pluralism, Corporatism and Professional Memory, in: Almond ed., *A Discipline Divided, Schools and Sects in Political Science*, Beverly Hills, Sage: 173-188.
Almond, G.A./Coleman, J.S. eds. (1960)
The Politics of the Developing Areas, Princeton, Princeton UP.
Almond, G.A./Verba, S (1963)
The Civic Culture: Political Attitudes and Democracy in Five Nations. Princeton: Princeton UP.
Almond, G.A./Powell, G.B. (1966)
Comparative Politics, A Developmental Approach, Boston, Little & Brown.
Alt, J./Chrystal, K. (1983)
Political Economics, Berkeley/London, The University of California Press.
Alt, J./Shepsle, K. eds. (1990)
Perspectives on Positive Political Economy, Cambridge, Cambridge UP.
Althusser, L. (1983)
Schets van het begrip historiese tijd, in: *Te Elfder Ure*, 31: 341-380.
Andersson, J.O. (1987)
The Economic Policy Strategies of the Nordic Countries, in: Keman et al. eds..
Andersen, B.R. (1988)
Rationalität und Irrationalität des nordischen Wolfahrtsstaates, in: Graubard ed., *Die Leidenschaft für Gleichheit und Gerechtigkeit*, Baden, Nomos: 11-42.
Andrain, C.F. (1980)
Politics and Economic Policy in Western Democracies, North Scituate, North Duxbury Press.
Apter, D.E., (1965)
The Politics of Modernization, Chicago, Chicago University
Apter, D.E./Andrain, C.F. eds. (1972)
Contemporary Analytical Theory, Englewood Cliffs, Prentice Hall.
Arrow, R.J. (1951)
Social Choice and Individual Values, New York, Wiley.
Axelrod, R. ed. (1976)
Structure of Decision, The Cognitive Maps of Political Elites, Princeton, Princeton UP.
Axelrod, R. (1984)
The Evolution of Cooperation, New York, Basic Books.
Balassa, B. (1991)
Economic Policies in the Pacific Area Developing Countries, London, Macmillan.

Baldwin, P. (1990)
The Politics of Social Solidarity, Class Bases of the European Welfare State 1875-1975, Cambridge, Cambridge UP.
Barnes, S.H./Kaase, M., eds. (1979)
Political Action: Mass Participation in Five Western Democracies, London, Sage.
Barrett, D.B. ed. (1982)
World Christian Encyclopedia, A Comparative Study of Churches and Religions in the Modern World AD 1900-2000, Nairobi, Oxford UP.
Barrington Moore Jr., (1966)
Social Origins of Dictatorship and Democracy, Harmondsworth, Penguin Books.
Barry, B. (1975)
Sociologists, Economists and Democracy, London, Collier-Macmillan.
Bartolini, S./Mair, P. (1990)
Identity, Competition, and Electoral Availability, The stabilisation of European electorates 1885-1985, Cambridge, Cambridge UP.
Bartolini, S. (1991)
On Time and Comparative Research, Maunuscript, University of Trieste.
Beck, P.A. (1986)
Choice, Context and Consequence: Beaten and Unbeaten Paths Toward a Science of Electoral Behavior, in: Weisberg, H.F. ed., *Political Science*: The Science of Politics, New York, Agathon Press: 241-283.
Beer, S./Ulam, A. eds. (1958)
Patterns of Government: The Major Political Systems of Europe, New York, Random House.
Ben-David, J. (1971)
The Scientist's Role in Society, A Comparative Study, New Jersey, Prentice-Hall.
Berger, S. ed. (1981)
Organizing Interests in Western Europe, Pluralism, Corporatism and the Transformation of Politics, Cambridge, Cambridge UP.
Berg-Schlosser, D./Müller-Rommel, F. eds. (1987)
Vergleichende Politikwissenschaft, Opladen, Leske/Budrich.
Bertrand, A.F.M. (1981)
Politieke democratie en welzijn, Alphen a/d Rijn, Samsom.
Binder, L. et al. (1971)
Crises and Sequences in Political Development, Princeton, Princeton UP.
Black, C.E. (1968)
The Dynamics of of Modernization: A Study in Comparative History, New York, Harper & Row.
Blondel, J. (1969)
Introduction to Comparative Government, London, Weidenfeld and Nicholson.
Blondel, J. (1981)
The Discipline of Politics, London, Butterworths.
Blondel, J. (1990)
Comparative government, Hemel Hempstead, Philip Allen.

Bogason, P. (1991)
Control For Whom? Recent Advances in Research on Governmental Guidance and Control, in: *European Journal of Political Research*, 20: 189-208.
Bogdanor, V. ed. (1983)
Coalition Government in Western Europe, London, Heinemann.
Bogdanor, V./Butler, D. eds. (1983)
Democracy and Elections, Electoral Systems and Their Consequences, Cambridge, Cambridge UP.
Böhme, G./Stehr, N. eds. (1976)
The knowledge society, Dordrecht, Kluwer.
Bolaffi, A. (1989)
Souveränitätszerfall oder Pluralismus? - Italienische Fragen an die Weimarer Verfassungsdebatte, in: Luthardt/Söllner eds., *Verfassungsstaat, Souveränität, Pluralismus*, Opladen, Westdeutscher Verlag.
Boltho, A. ed. (1982)
The European Economy, Growth & Crisis, Oxford, Oxford UP.
Bourdieu, P. (1975)
The Specificity of the Scientific Field and the Social Conditions of the Progress of Reason, in: *Social Science Information*, 14/6: 19-47.
Bourdieu, P.(1984)
Homo Academicus, Paris, Les editions de Minuit.
Braun, D. (1989)
Grenzen politischer Regulierung, Der Weg in die Massenarbeitslosigkeit, Wiesbaden, DUV.
Braun, D. (1990)
Health Research and Health Funding in the United States, A Model of Its Kind?, Köln, Max-Planck-Institut für Gesellschaftsforschung.
Braun, D. (1991a)
Die Einflußmöglichkeiten der Forschungsförderung auf Strukturprobleme der Gesundheitsforschung in der Bundesrepublik, Schriftenreihe zum Programm der Bundesregierung Forschung und Entwicklung im Dienste der Gesundheit, Band 15, Bremerhaven, Wirtschaftsverlag NW.
Braun, D. (1991b)
Health Research and Health Funding in France, Köln, Max-Planck-Institut für Gesellschaftsforschung.
Braun, D. (1992)
Probleme und Perspektiven der Gesundheitsforschung in den USA, Frankreich und England, Schriftenreihe zum Programm der Bundesregierung Forschung und Entwicklung im Dienste der Gesundheit, Bremerhaven, Wirtschaftsverlag NW.
Braun, D./Keman, H. (1986)
Politikstrategien und Konfliktregulierung in den Niederlanden, in: *Politische Vierteljahresschrift*, 27/1: 78-99.

Braun, D./Schimank, U. (1992)
Organisatorische Koexistenzen des Forschungssystems mit anderen gesellschaftlichen Teilsystemen, Die prekäre Autonomie wissenschaftlicher Forschung, Köln, Max-Planck-Institut für Gesellschaftsforschung.

Browne, E. C./Dreijmanis, J. eds. (1982)
Government Coalitions in Western Democracies, New York, Longmans.

Bryce, L. (1929)
Modern Democracies, (2 volumes), London, MacMillan.

Budge, I. (1989)
Issues, Dimensions and Change in Postwar Democracies, Paper presented at the University of Rochester.

Budge, I./Farlie, D.J. (1977)
Voting and Party Competition in Ten Democracies, London/New York, Wiley.

Budge, I./Farlie, D.J. (1983)
Explaining and Predicting Elections, Issue effects and party strategies in 23 Democracies, London, Allen and Unwin.

Budge, I./Robertson D./Hearl, D.J. eds. (1987)
Ideology, Strategy and Party Change, Election Programmes in 19 Democracies, Cambridge, Cambridge UP.

Budge, I./Laver M.J. (1986)
Office-Seeking and Policy Pursuit in Coalition Theory, in: *Legislative Studies Quarterly*, 11: 485-506.

Budge, I./Laver M.J. (1992)
Party Policy and Government Programmes, Basingstoke, Macmillan.

Budge, I./Keman, H. (1990)
Parties and Democracy, Coalition Formation and Government Functioning in twenty States, Oxford, Oxford UP.

Burin, F.S./Shell K.L. eds. (1969)
Politics, Law and Social Change: Selected Essays of Otto Kirchheimer, New York, Columbia UP.

Butler, D./Penniman, H.R./Ranney, A. eds. (1981)
Democracy at the Polls. A Comparative Study of Competitive National Elections, Washington DC, American Enterprise Institute

Cameron, D.R. (1978)
The Expansion of the Public Economy, in: *American Political Science Review*, 72: 1243-1261.

Cameron, D.R. (1984)
Social Democracy, Corporatism, and Labor Quiescence in Advanced Capitalist Societies, in: Goldthorpe ed., 143-178.

Cameron, D.R. (1985)
Does Government Cause Inflation? Taxes, Spending and Deficits, in: Lindberg/Maier eds.: 224-279.

Castles, F.G. ed. (1982)
The Impact of Parties, Politics and Policies in Democratic Capitalist States, London/Beverly Hills, Sage.
Castles, F.G. (1986)
Social Expenditure and the Political Right: a methodological note, in: *European Journal of Political Research*, 14/5-6: 669-676.
Castles, F.G. (1987)
Comparative Public Policy Analysis: Problems, Progress and Prospects, in: Castles et al. eds.: 197-224.
Castles, F.G. ed. (1989)
The Comparative History of Public Policy, Oxford, Polity Press.
Castles, F.G. (1991)
Democratic Politics, War and Catch Up: Olson's Thesis, in: *Journal of Theoretical Politics*, 3: 5-25.
Castles, F.G./Lehner F./Schmidt, M.G. eds. (1987)
Managing Mixed Economies, Berlin/New York, Walter de Gruyter.
Cohen, M./March, J/Olsen, J. (1972)
A Garbage Can Model of Organizational Choice, in: *Administrative Science Quarterly*, 17:1-25.
Coleman, J.S. ed. (1965)
Education and Political Development, Princeton, Princeton UP.
Coleman, J.S. (1990)
Foundations of Social Theory, Cambridge (Mass)/London, Belknap Press of Harvard UP.
Connolly, W.E. (1983)
The Terms of Political Discourse, Oxford, Martin Robertson.
Converse, P.E. (1975)
Public Opinion and Voting Behavior, in: Greenstein,F.I./Polsby, N.W. eds., *Handbook of Political Science*, vol. 4: Nongovernmental Politics, Reading (Mass), Addison-Wesley: 75-169
Cowart, A.T. (1978)
The Economic Policies of European Governments (part I: Monetary Policy; part II: Fiscal Policy), in: *British Journal of Political Science*, 8: 285-311 & 425-439.
Crewe, I./Denver, D. eds. (1985)
Electoral Change in Western Democracies, London/Sidney, Croom Helm.
Crouch, C. ed. (1979)
State and Economy in contemporary Capitalism, London, Croom Helm.
Crouch, C. (1979)
The State, Capital and Liberal Democracy, in: Crouch ed.: 13-54.
Czada, R. (1987)
The impact of Interest Politics on flexible Adjustment Policies, in: Keman et al. eds.: 20-53.

Czada, R. (1991)
Ökonomisches Kalkül und strategisches Handeln im Staat, Institutionelle Differenzierung, Autonomisierung und Leistungssteigerung als handlungstheoretische Probleme, Manuskript, Universität Konstanz.

Czada, R. (1992a)
Administrative Interessenvermittlung am Beispiel der kerntechnischen Sicherheitsregulierung in den Vereinigten Staaten und der Bundesrepublik Deutschland, Habilitation thesis, Konstanz, Faculty of Administrative Sciences.

Czada, R. (1992b)
Muddling through a nuclear-political emergency: multilevel cris management in West Germany after radioactive fallout from Chernobyl, in: *Industrial Crisis Quarterly*, 5: 294 - 322.

Czada, R./Lehmbruch, G. (1990)
Parteienwettbewerb, Sozialstaatspostulat und gesellschaftlicher Wertewandel, in: Bermbach/Blanke/Böhret eds., *Spaltung der Gesellschaft und die Zukunft des Sozialstaates*, Opladen, Leske & Budrich: 55 - 84.

Czada, R./Windhoff-Héritier, A. eds. (1991)
Political Choice, Institutions, Rules and the Limits of Rationality, Frankfurt am Mainz/Boulder (Col), Campus/Westview.

Daalder, H. (1966)
The Netherlands: Opposition in a Segmented Society, in: Dahl ed.: 188-236.

Daalder, H. (1979)
Stein Rokkan 1921-1979: A Memoir, in: *European Journal of Political Research*, 7: 337-355.

Daalder, H. (1974)
The Consociational Democracy Theme, in: *World Politics*, 26: 604-621.

Daalder, H./Mair, P. eds. (1983)
Western European Party Systems, Continuity and Change, London etc., Sage.

Daalder, H. (1983)
The Comparative Study of European Parties and Party Systems: An Overview, in: Daalder/Mair eds.: 1-28.

Daalder, H. (1987)
Countries in Comparative European Politics, in: *European Journal of Political Research*, 15: 3-21.

Daalder, H./Irwin, G. eds. (1989)
Politics in the Netherlands: How much Change?, London, Frank Cass.

Dahl, R.A. (1971)
Polyarchy, Participation and Opposition, New Haven/London, Yale UP.

Dalton, R.J./Flanagan, S.C./Beck, P.A. eds. (1984)
Electoral Change in Advanced Industrial Democracies, Princeton (NJ), Princeton UP

Dean, J.W. (1984)
Interest Groups and Political X-inefficiency, in: *European Journal of Political Research*, 12/2: 191-212.

Diamond, L./Linz, J.J./Lipset, S.M. eds. (1988)
Democracy in Developing Countries, Boulder, Westview Press, 4 vols.
Dierkes, M./Weiler, H./Antal, A.B. eds. (1987)
Comparative Policy Research, Learning from Experience, Aldershot, Gower.
Doel, J. van den/Velthoven B. van (1989)
Demokratie en Welvaartstheorie, Alphen a/d Rijn, Samson.
Dogan, M. ed. (1988)
Comparing Pluralist Democracies, Strains on Legitimacy, Boulder (Col), Westview Press.
Dogan, M./Pelassy, D. (1990)
How to compare nations, Strategies in Comparative Politics, Chatham (NJ), Chatham House.
Douglas, M. (1986)
How Institutions Think, Syracuse, Syracuse University Press.
Downs, A. (1957)
An Economic Theory of Democracy, New York, Harper.
Dunleavy, P. (1991)
Democracy, Bureaucracy & Public Choice, Economic Explanations in Political Science, New York/London, Harvester/Wheatsheaf.
Duverger, M. (1951)
Les Partis Politiques, Paris, Armand Colin.
Duverger, M. (1954)
Political Parties: Their Organization and Activity in the Modern State, London, Methuen.
Dye, T.R./Zeigler, H. (1988)
Socialism and Equality in Cross-national Perspective, *Political Science and Politics*, 21, 45-56.
Easton, D. (1965)
A Systems Analysis of Political Life, New York, Wiley
Eckstein, H./Apter, D.E. eds. (1963)
Comparative Politics: A Reader, Glencoe, Free Press.
Eckstein, H. (1966)
Division and Cohesion in Democracy: A Study of Norway, Princeton, Princeton UP.
Eijk, C. van der (1992)
Verkiezingen, politieke communicatie en democratie, in: Eijk, C. van der/Geest, I. van/Kramer, P./Tiddens, L. eds., *Verkiezingen zonder mandaat*, 's Gravenhage, SDU: 12-18
Eijk, C. van der/Niemøller (1984)
Het potentiële electoraat van de nederlandse politieke partijen, in: *Beleid en Maatschappij*, Vol. 11: 192-204
Eijk, C. van der/Niemøller, K. (1985)
The Netherlands, in: Crewe, I./Denver, D. eds.: 342-371

Eijk, C. van der/Oppenhuis, E. (1991)
European Parties' Performance in Electoral Competition, in: *European Journal of Political Research*, Vol. 19, no.1: 55-80
Eijk, C. van der/Schmitt, H. (1991)
The Role of the Eurobarometer in the Study of European Elections and the Development of Comparative Electoral Research, in: Reif, K./Inglehart, R. eds., *Eurobarometer. The Dynamics of European Public Opinion*, London, Macmillan: 257-274
Eijk, C. van der/Franklin, M.N. (1993)
The European Electorate on the Eve of Unification, Ann Arbor, University of Michigan Press (forthcoming)
Eijk, C. van der/Franklin, M.N./Mackie, T./Valen, H. (1992)
Cleavages, Conflict Resolution and Democracy, in: Franklin, M.N./Mackie, T./Valen, H. eds.: 406-431
Eisenstadt, S.N. ed. (1971)
Political Sociology: A Reader, New York, Basic Books.
Eisenstadt, S.N. (1973)
Tradition, Change and Modernity, New York, Wiley.
Elster, J. (1979)
Ulysses and the Sirens, Studies in Rationality and Irrationality, Cambridge, Cambridge UP.
Elster, J. (1985)
An Introduction to Karl Marx, Cambridge, Cambridge UP.
Elster, J. (1989)
Nuts and bolts for the Social Sciences, Cambridge, Cambridge UP.
Encyclopedia Britannica (1990)
Britannica World Data, Chicago, Encyclopedia Britannica.
Esping-Anderson, G. (1985)
Politics against Markets, The Social Democratic Road to Power, Princeton/New Jersey, Princeton UP.
Esping-Anderson, G. (1987)
Institutional Accommodation to Full Employment: a comparison of policy-regimes, in: Keman et al. eds.: 83-110
Esping-Andersen, G. (1990)
The Three Worlds of Welfare Capitalism, Cambridge, Polity.
Evans, P./Rueschemeyer, D./Skocpol, T. eds. (1985)
Bringing the State Back In, Cambridge, Cambridge UP.
Evans, D.A./Patel, V.L. eds. (1989)
Cognitive Science in Medicine, Biomedical Modeling. Cambridge (Mass), MIT.
Ewing, K. (1987)
The Funding of Political Parties in Britain, Cambridge, Cambridge UP
Farago, P. (1987)
Verbände als Träger öffentlicher Politik, Aufbau und Bedeutung privater Regierungen in der Schweiz, Gruesch, Ruegger.

Finer, H. (1949)
Theory and Practice of Modern Government (revised edition), New York, Holt.
Finer, H. (1932)
The Theory and Practice of Modern Government, London, Methuen, 2 vols.
Finer, S.E. (1970)
Comparative Government, Harmondsworth, Penguin.
Flam, H. (1989)
Emotional Man, A Third Perspective on Collective and Corporate Action, Köln, MPIfG Discussion Paper: 89/7.
Flexner, A. (1927)
Die Ausbildung des Mediziners, Eine vergleichende Untersuchung, Berlin.
Flexner, A. (1930)
Universities, New York, Oxford UP.
Flora, P. (1974)
Modernisierungsforschung, Zur empirischen Analyse der gesellschaftlichen Entwicklung, Opladen, Westdeutscher Verlag.
Flora, P. (1975)
Indikatoren der Modernisierung: Ein Historisches Datenhandbuch, Opladen, Westdeutscher Verlag.
Flora, P. (1983)
State, Economy, and Society in Western Europe 1815 - 1975. Vol. I, The Growth of Mass Democracies and Welfare States, Frankfurt/London/Chicago, Campus/Macmillan/St. James
Flora, P. ed. (1986)
Growth to Limits, The Western European Welfare States Since World War II (Volumes 1 & 2), Berlin/New York, Walter de Gruyter.
Flora, P./Heidenheimer, A.J. eds.. (1981)
The Development of Welfare States in Europe and America, New Brunswick/London, Transaction Books.
Franklin, M. (1985)
The Decline of Class Voting in Britain: Changes in the Basis of Electoral Choice, Oxford, Oxford UP
Franklin, M.E./Th. Mackie/H. Valen et al. (1992)
Electoral Responses to Evolving Social and Attitudinal Structures in Western Countries, Cambrdige, Cambridge UP.
Frey, B. (1983)
Democratic Economic Policy, A Theoretical Introduction, Oxford, Basil Blackwell.
Friedrich, C.J./Brzezinski, Z.R. (1956)
Totalitarian Dictatorship and Autocracy, Cambridge Mass, Harvard UP.
Friedrich, C.J. ed. (1954)
Totalitarianism, Cambridge (Mass), Harvard UP.

Friedrich, C.J. (1941)
Constitutional Government and Democracy: Theory and Practice of Modern Government, Boston, Little Brown.
Friedrich, C.J. (1937)
Constitutional Government and Democracy: Theory and Practice in Europe and America, New York, Harper.
Fusilier, R. (1960)
Les Monarchies Parlementaires. Étude sur les Systèmes de Gouvernement: Suède, Norvège, Danemark, Belgique, Pays-Bas, Luxembourg, Paris, Editions Ouvrieres.
Gallagher, M./Laver, M./Mair, P. (1992)
Representative Government in Western Europe, New York, McGraw Hill.
Gastil, R.D. (1987)
Freedom in the World, Political Rights and Civil Liberties 1986-1987, New York, Greenwood Press.
Gastil, R.D. (1990)
The Comparative Survey of Freedom: Experiences and Suggestions, in: *Studies in Comparative International Development*, 25, 25-50.
Goldscheid, R./Schumpeter, J. (1976)
Die Finananzkrise des Steuerstaats, Beiträge zur Politischen Ökonomie der Staatsfinanzen, Franfurt aM, Suhrkamp.
Goldthorpe, J. ed. (1984)
Order and Conflict in Contemporary Capitalism, Oxford, Clarendon Press.
Goldthorpe, J.H. (1984)
The End of Convergence: Corporatist and Dualist Tendencies in Modern Western Societies, in: Goldthorpe ed.: 315-343.
Goodwin, R.E. (1976)
The Politics of Rational Man, New York, John Wiley.
Gould, G./Mills, J./Stewart, S. (1981)
Monetarism and Prosperity?, London/Basingstoke, MacMillan.
Grafstein, R. (1991)
Rational Choice, Theory and Institutions, in: Renwick Monroe ed.: 259-278.
Granberg, D./Holemberg, S. (1988)
The Political System Matters. Social Psychology and Voting Behavior in Sweden and the United States, Cambridge, Cambridge UP
Grew, R. ed. (1978)
Crisis and Political Development in Europe and the United States, Princeton, Princeton UP.
Hagstrom, W.O. (1965)
The Scientific Community, London/Amsterdam, Feffer & Simons Inc.
Hechter, M. (1987)
Principles of Group Solidarity, Berkeley, University of California Press.
Heckscher, G. (1957)
The Study of Comparative Government and Politics, London, Allen & Unwin.

Hermens, F.A. (1941)
Democracy or Anarchy? A Study of Proportional Representation, South Bend, Ill., University of Notre Dame Press.
Hening, S. ed. (1979)
Political Parties in European Community, London, George Allen & Unwin.
Hibbs, D.A. (1977)
Political Parties and Macro-Economic Policy, in: *American Political Science Review*, 71: 1476-1487.
Hibbs, D.A. (1985)
Inflation, Political Support, and Macroeconomic Policy, in: Lindberg/Maier eds.: 175-194.
Hirschman, A.O. (1970)
Exit, Voice and Loyalty, Responses to Decline in Firms, Organizations and States, Cambridge (Mass)/London, Harvard UP.
Hirschman, A.O. (1977)
The Passions and the Interests, Political Arguments for Capitalism Before its Triumph, Princeton, Princeton UP.
Hobbes, T. (1951)
Leviathan, Oxford, Blackwell.
Hoetjes, B.J.S. (1990)
Vergelijkende Politicologie, in: van Schendelen ed., *Kernthema's van de politicologie*, Amsterdam, Boom: 257-279.
Hofstede, G. (1980)
Motivation, Leadership and Organization: Do American Theories Apply Abroad?, in: *Organizational Dynamics*, summer 1980: 42 - 63.
Hofstede, G. (1984)
Culture's Consequences, International Differences in Work Related Values, Beverly Hills, Sage.
Hohn, H-W./Schimank, U. (1990)
Konflikte und Gleichgewichte im Forschungssystem, Akteurkonstellationen und Entwicklungspfade in der staatlich finanzierten außeruniversitären Forschung, Frankfurt/New York, Campus.
Holt, R.T./Turner, J.E. eds. (1970)
The Methodology of Comparative Research, New York, The Free Press.
Huntington, S.P. (1968)
Political Order in Changing Societies, New Haven, Yale UP.
Huntington, S.P. (1991)
The Third Wave, Democratization in the Late Twentieth Century, Norman, University of Oklahoma Press.
Huyse, L. (1970)
Passiviteit, Pacificatie en Verzuiling in de Belgische Politiek: Een Sociologische Studie, Antwerpen, Standaard, 1970.

Inglehart, R. (1977)
The Silent Revolution: Changing Values and Political Styles among Western Publics, Princeton, Princeton UP.
Inglehart, R. (1990)
Culture Shift in Advanced Industrial Society, Princeton, Princeton UP.
Irvine, J./Martin B.R./Isard, P. (1990)
Investing in the Future, An International Comparison of Government Funding of Academic and Related Research, Brookfield (Vermont), Edward Elgar.
Jackman, R.W. (1975)
Politics and Social Equality, A Comparative Analysis, New York, John Wiley
Kalleberg, A.L. (1966)
The Logic of Comparison: A Methodological Note on the Comparative Study of Political Systems, in: *World Politics*, 19: 69-82.
Kaltefleiter, W. (1970)
Die Funktionen des Staatsoberhauptes in der Parlamentarischen Demokratie, Cologne, Westdeutscher Verlag.
Katz, R.S./Mair, P. eds. (1992)
Party Organizations in Western Democracies, London, Sage.
Katzenstein, P. (1985)
Small States in World Markets, Industrial Policy in Europe, Ithaca/London, Cornell UP.
Kelley, S./Mirer, T (1974)
The Simple Act of Voting, in: *American Political Science Review*, 68: 572-91.
Kelman, S. (1981)
Regulation America, Regulating Sweden, A Comparative Study of Occupational safety and Health Policy, Cambridge (Mass), MIT Press.
Keman, H. (1984)
Politics, Politics and Consequences: A Cross-National Analysis of Public Policy formation in Advanced Capitalist Democracies (1967-1981), in: *European Journal of Political Research*, 12/2: 147-170.
Keman, H. (1988)
The Development toward Surplus Welfare, Social Democratic Politics and Policies in Advanced Capitalist Democracies (1965-1984), Amsterdam, CT-press.
Keman, H. (1990)
Social Democracy and Welfare Statism, in: *The Netherlands Journal of Social Sciences*, 26/1: 17-34.
Keman, H. (1992a)
Over Politicologie,maatschappelijke conflicten en politieke consensus als paradox, Amsterdam, VU-Uitgeverij.
Keman, H. (1992b)
Theoretical Approaches to Social Democracy, in: *Journal of Theoretical Politics*.

Keman, H./Lehner, F. (1984)
Economic Crisis and Political Management: An Introduction to Political Economic Interdependence, in: *European Journal of Political Research*, 12/2: 121-130.
Keman, H./Paloheimo, H./Whiteley, P.F. eds. (1987)
Coping with the Crisis, Alternative Responses to Economic Recession in Advanced Industrial Society, London, Beverly Hills, Sage.
Keman, H./Dijk, T. van (1987)
Policy Formation as a Strategy to Overcome the Economic Crisis, in: Keman et al. eds.: 127-162.
Keohane, R.O. (1984)
After Hegemony, Cooperation and Discord in the World Political Economy, Princeton (NJ), Princeton UP.
Kersbergen, K. van (1991)
Social Capitalism and Christian Democracy, PhD Thesis EUI, Florence.
King, A. (1981)
What Do Elections Decide? in: Butler, D./Penniman, H.R./Ranney, A.: 293-324
Kirchheimer, O. (1932)
Verfassungsreaktion 1932, in: *Die Gesellschaft*, IX, 415-427.
Kirkpatrick, J.J. (1981)
Democratic Elections, Democratic Government and Democratic Theory, in: Butler, D./Penniman, H.R./Ranney, A. eds.: 325-348
Kiser, K.L./Ostrom, E. (1987)
Reflections on the Elements of Institutional Analysis, Workshop in Political Theory and Policy Analysis, Indiana University, Bloomington.
Kohler, R.E. (1989)
Funding Policies and Research Programs, The Case of the Rockefeller Foundation, Discussion-paper, University of Pennsylvania.
Kohn, M.L. (1989)
Cross-national Research in Sociology, London etc., Sage
Korpi, W. (1983)
The Democratic Class Struggle, London, Routledge & KeganPaul.
Krasner, S.D. (1988)
Sovereignty - An Institutional Perspective, in: *Comparative Political Studies*, 21: 66-94.
Kuechler, M. (1991)
Issues and Voting in the European Elections 1989, in: *European Journal of Political Research*, Vol. 19, no. 1: 81-104
Lane, J-E. ed.(1985)
The Public Sector, Concepts, Models and Approaches, London, Sage.
Lane, J-E./Ersson, S.O. (1987)
Politics and Society in Western Europe, London, Sage.
Lane, J-E./Ersson, S.O. (1990)
Comparative Political Economy, London, Pinter.

Lane, J-E./Nyen, T. (1992)
Economic Organization Theory and the State, in: Foss ed.,*Economic Organization Theory*, Oslo, Universitetsforlaget (forthcoming).
LaPalombara J./Weiner, M. eds. (1966)
Political Parties and Political Development, Princeton, Princeton UP.
LaPalombara, J. ed. (1963)
Bureaucracies and Political Development, Princeton, Princeton UP.
Lasswell, H.D. (1968)
The Future of the Comparative Method, in: *Comparative Politics*, 1: 3-18.
Latour, B./Woolgar, S. (1979)
Cycles of Credit, in: Latour/Woolgar eds.,*Laboratory Life*, The Social Construction of Scientific Facts, Beverly Hills/London, Sage: 187 - 234.
Latour, B. (1987)
Science in Action, How to Follow Scientists and Engineers Through Society, Cambridge (Mass), Harvard UP.
Latour, B. (1988)
The Pasteurization of France, Cambridge (Mass)/London, University Press.
Laumann, E./Knoke, D. (1987)
The Organizational State, Madison, The University of Wisconsin Press.
Laver, M. (1981)
The Politics of Private Desires, Harmondsworth, Penguin.
Laver, M. (1986)
Social Choice and Public Policy, London, Basil Blackwell.
Laver, M./Schofield, N. (1990)
Multiparty Government, The Politics of Coalition in Europe, Oxford, Oxford UP.
Lehmbruch, G. (1967)
Proporzdemokratie: Politisches System und Politische Kultur in der Schweiz und in Oesterreich, Tübingen, Mohr.
Lehmbruch, G. (1984)
Concertation and the Structure of Corporatist Networks, in: Goldthorpe ed.: 60-80.
Lehmbruch, G./Schmitter, P.C. eds. (1982)
Patterns of Corporatist Policy-making, London etc., Sage.
Lehner, F. (1987)
Interest Intermediation, Institutional Structures and Public Policy, in: Keman et al. eds.: 54-82.
Lerner, D., (1958)
The Passing of Traditional Society: Modernizing the Middle East, Glencoe, Free Press.
Lewis, P.G./Potter, D.C./Castles, F.G. eds. (1978)
The Practice of Comparative Politics, A Reader, London, Longman.
Lijphart, A. (1971)
Comparative Politics and the Comparative Method, in: *American Political Science Review*, 65: 682-693.

Lijphart, A. (1975)
The Comparable Cases Strategy in Comparative Research, in: *Comparative Political Studies*, 8: 158-176.
Lijphart, A. (1977)
Democracy in Plural Societies, A comparative exploration, New Haven/London, Yale UP.
Lijphart, A. (1984)
Democracies, Patterns of Majoritarian and Consensus Government in 21 Countries, New Haven/London, Yale UP.
Lijphart, A. (1968a). Typologies of Democratic Systems, in: *Comparative Political Studies*, 1: 3-44.
Lijphart, A. (1968b)
The Politics of Accommodation: Pluralism and Democracy in the Netherlands, Berkeley, University of California Press.
Lijphart, A. (1993)
Electoral Systems and Party Systems in 26 Democracies, Oxford, Oxford UP.
Lindberg, L.N. (1985)
Models of the Inflation-Disinflation Process, in: Lindberg/Maier eds.: 25-50.
Lindberg, L.N./Maier, C.S. eds. (1985)
The Politics of Inflation and Economic Stagnation, Washington D.C., The Brookings Institution.
Lindberg, L.N./Scharpf, F.W./Engelhardt, G. (1987)
Economic Policy Research, Challenges and a New Agenda, in: Dierkes et al.
Linz, J.J./Stepan, A. eds. (1978)
The Breakdown of Democratic Regimes, Baltimore, Johns Hopkins, 4 vols.
Lipset, S.M. (1963)
Political Man, The Social Bases of Politics, New York, Doubleday Anchor Books.
Lipset, S.M./Rokkan, S. (1967)
Party Systems and voter Alignments, Cross-National Perspectives New York/London, The Free Press & Collier MacMillan.
Lowell, A.L. (1896)
Government and Parties in Continental Europe, London, Longmans.
Luhmann, N. (1968)
Die Knappheit der Zeit und die Vordringlichkeit des Befristeten, in: *Die Verwaltung*, 1: 3-30.
Luhmann, N. (1971)
Soziologische Aufklärung, Vol. 1, Opladen, Westdeutscher Verlag.
Luhmann, N. (1974)
Selbststeuerung der Wissenschaft, in: Luhmann ed., *Soziologische Aufklärung*, Aufsätze zur Theorie sozialer Systeme, Band 1, Opladen, Westdeutscher Verlag: 232-252.
Luhmann, N. (1986)
Ökologische Kommunikation, Opladen, Westdeutscher Verlag.

Luhmann, N. (1990)
Essays on Self-reference, New York/Oxford, Columbia UP.
Luthardt, W. (1990)
Sozialdemokratische Politik- und Verfassungstheorie während der Weimarer Republik, *Journal für Sozialforschung*, 30: 117 - 131.
MacIntyre, A.C. (1978)
Is a Science of Comparative Politics Possible?, in: Lewis et al. eds.: 266-284.
MacPherson, S./Midgley,J. (1987)
Comparative Social Policy and the Third World, Sussex, Wheatsheaf.
Macridis, R.C./Cox, R. (1953)
Research in Comparative Politics, (Report of the SSRC Interuniversity Research Seminar on Comparative Politics, Evanston 1952), in: *American Political Science Review* 47: 641-675.
Macridis, R.C. (1955)
The Study of Comparative Government, New York, Random House.
Macridis, R.C./Ward, R.C. eds. (1963)
Modern Political Systems, Englewood Cliffs, Prentice Hall, 2 vols.
Macrids, R.C./Brown, B.E. (1961; 1986)
Comparative Politics: Notes and Readings, Homewood, Dorsey.
Maddison, A. (1982)
Ontwikkelingsfasen van het kapitalisme, Utrecht/Antwerpen, Het Spectrum.
Maddison, A. (1991)
Dynamic Forces in Capitalist Development, A Long Run Comparative View, Oxford/New York, Oxford UP.
Mandell, M.P./Porter, D.O. (1991)
Institutional Structures and Rationales: Seeking a new Paradigm, in: *Discussion paper*, prepared for the Conference on Games in Hierarchies and Networks, Max-Planck-Institut für Gesellschaftsforschung, Köln.
Mansbridge, J. ed. (1983)
Beyond Adversarial Democracy, Chicago, Chicago UP.
Mansbridge, J. ed. (1990)
Beyond Self Interest, Chicago, University of Chicago Press.
March, J.G./Olsen, J.P. (1989)
Rediscovering Institutions, The Organizational Basis of Politics, New York, Free Press.
Mayer, L.R. (1972)
Comparative Political Inquiry, Homewood (Ill), The Dorsey Press.
Mayer, L.R. (1983)
Practicing What We Preach: Comparative Politics in the 1980s, in: *Comparative Political Studies*, 16/2: 173-194.
Mayer, L.R. (1989)
Redefining Comparative Politics, Promise Versus Performance, Beverley Hills/London, Sage.

Mayntz, R. (1988)
Funktionelle Teilsysteme in der Theorie sozialer Differenzierung, in: Mayntz ed., *Differenzierung und Verselbständigung*, Zur Entwicklung gesellschaftlicher Teilsysteme, Frankfurt aM/New York, Campus: 11-44.
Mayntz, R./Scharpf, F.W. (1990)
Chances and Problems in the Political Guidance of Research Systems, in: Krupp, *Technikpolitik angesichts der Umweltkatastrophe*, Heidelberg, Physica: 61-83.
McLean, I. (1989)
New Technology and Direct Democracy, Cambridge, Polity Press.
McLean, I. (1991)
Rational Choice and Politics, in: *Political Studies*, XXXIX: 496-512.
Meinecke, F. (1962)
Weltburgertum und Nationalstaat, Munchen, Oldenbourg Verlag.
Merkel, W. (1991)
After the Golden Age: Is Social Democracy Doomed to Decline?, in: Maravall et al., *Socialist Parties in Europe*, Barcelona, ICPS: 187-222.
Merritt, L./Rokkan, S. eds. (1966)
Comparing Nations, the Use of Quantitative Data in Cross-National Research, New Haven, Yale UP.
Merton, R.K. (1973)
The Sociology of Science, Theoretical and Empirical Investigations, Chicago, The University of Chicago Press.
Milner, H. (1989)
Sweden: Social Democracy in Practice, Oxford, Oxford UP.
Morel, J./Bauer, E./Meleghy, T./Preglau, M./Niedenzu (1989)
Soziologische Theorie, Abriß der Ansätze ihrer Hauptvertreter, München/Wien, R.Oldenbourg.
Morgenthau, H.A. (1948)
Politics Among Nations, New York, Knopf.
Müller, D.C. (1989)
Public Choice II: A revised edition, Cambridge, Cambridge UP.
Musgrave, R.A./Jarrett, P. (1979)
International redistribution, in: *Kyklos*, 32: 541-558.
Neumann, S. ed. (1956)
Modern Political Parties: Approaches to the Study of Comparative Politics, Chicago, University of Chicago Press: 395-421.
Nie, N.H./Verba, S. (1975)
Political Participation, in: Greenstein/Polsby eds., *Handbook of Political Science* (vol. 4), Reading (Mass), Addison/Wesley: 1-53.
Niskanen, W.A. (1971)
Bureaucracy and Representative Government, Chicago, Aldine-Atherton.
Nohlen, D. (1983)
Vergleichende Methode, in: Nohlen/Schultze eds., *Pipers Wörterbuch zur Politik*, München, Piper Verlag (1. Teil): 1079-1085.

North, D.C. (1981)
Structure and Change in Economic History, New York, Norton.
North, D.C. (1990)
Institutions, Institutional Change and Economic Performance, Cambridge, Cambridge UP.
O'Donnell, G.A. (1979)
Modernization and Bureaucratic Authoritarianism, Studies in South American Politics, Berkeley, Institute of International Studies/UCLA.
O. Donnell, G./Schmitter, Ph. C./Whitehead, L. eds. (1986)
Transitions from Authoritarian Rule, Baltimore, Johns Hopkins, 4 vols.
OECD, (1990)
Economic Studies no. 15 (autumn), Paris, OECD.
OECD, (1991)
Choosing Priorities in Science and Technology, Paris, OECD.
O'Grady, F. (1990)
Valediction, in: *Department of Health and Social Security*, DH Yearbook of Research and Development 1990, London HMSO: 1-5.
Olsen, J.P. (1991)
Political Science and Organization Theory, Parallel Agendas but Mutual Disregard, in: Czada/Windhoff-Héritier eds.: 87-120.
Olson, M. (1965)
The Logic of Collective Action, Cambridge (Mass), Harvard UP.
Olson, M. (1982)
The Rise and Decline of Nations, New Haven/London, Yale UP.
Olson, M. (1986)
An Appreciation of the Tests and Criticisms, in: *Scandinavian Political Studies*, 9/1: 65-80
Ordeshook, P.C. (1986)
Game Theory and Political Theory, Cambridge, Cambridge UP.
Organski, K. (1965)
The Stages of Political Development, New York, Knopf.
Ostrom, E. (1990)
Governing the Commons, The Evolution of Institutions for Collective Action, Cambridge: Cambridge UP.
Ouchi, W. (1980)
Markets, Bureaucracies, and Clans, in: *Administrative Science Quarterly*, 25: 129-141.
Oxford English Dictionary, Compact Edition, Oxford, Oxford UP.
Padgett, S./Paterson, W.E. (1991)
Social Democracy in Postwar Europe, London/New York, Longman.
Paloheimo, H. (1987)
Explanations of the Economic Crisis and Divergent Policy Responses: An Overview, in: Keman et al. eds.: 1-19.

Panebianco A. (1988)
Political Parties: Organization and Power, Cambridge, Cambridge UP (Italian original: Modelli di Partito, Bologna, 1982).
Pelassy, D. (1992)
Qui gouverne en Europe? Paris, Fayard.
Pennings, P. (1990)
Changes in Welfare Statism, paper presented at the ECPR Joint Sessions, Essex.
Pope, W. (1986)
Alexis de Tocqueville, London, Sage.
Porter, D.O. (1989)
Structural Pose as an Approach for Implementing Complex Programs, Discussion-Paper, San Bernardino, California State University.
Powell Jr., G.B. (1982)
Contemporary Democracies, Participation, Stability and Violence, Cambridge (Mass)/London, Harvard UP.
Powell jr., G.B. (1989)
Constitutional Desing and Citizen Electoral Control, in: *Journal of Theoretical Politics*, Vol. 1: 107-130
Pratt, J.W./Zeckhauser, R.J. eds. (1989)
Principals and Agents, The Structure of Business, 5. Aufl. Part One, Boston (Mass), Harvard Business School Press.
Prechtel, H./Sica, A. (1986)
Demonstrating Dependency, A Critique of Ideologies, educational Development and Quantitative Test, in: *Political Power and Social Theory*, 6.
Pridham, G. ed. (1986)
Coalitional Behaviour in Theory and Practice: An Inductive Model for Western Europe, Cambridge, Cambridge UP.
Przeworski, A./Sprague, J. (1986)
Paper Stones, A History of Electoral Socialism, Chicago & London, The University of Chicago Press.
Przeworski, A./Teune, H. (1970)
The Logic of Comparative Social Inquiry, New York, Wiley Press.
Przeworski, A. (1985)
Capitalism and Social Democracy, Cambridge, Cambridge UP/Éditions de la Maison des Sciences de l'Homme.
Przeworski, A. (1987)
Methods of Cross-National Research, 1970-1983, in: Dierkes et al.
Pye, L.W./Verba, S. (1965)
Political Culture and Political Development, Princeton, Princeton UP.
Pye, L.W. (1966)
Aspects of Political Development, Boston, Little Brown.
Pye, L.W. ed. (1963)
Communications and Political Development, Princeton, Princeton UP.

Ragin, C. (1987)
The Comparative Method, Moving Beyond Qualitative and Quantitative Strategies, Berkeley (Cal), University of California Press.
Ragin, C. ed. (1991)
Issues and Alternatives in Comparative Social Research, Leiden: E.J. Brill.
Renwick Monroe, K./Barton M.C./Klingemann M.J. (1990)
Altruism and the Theory of Rational Action: An Analysis of Rescuers of Jews in Nazi Europe, in: Renwick Monroe ed.: 317-351.
Renwick Monroe, K. ed. (1991)
The Economic Approach to Politics, A Critical Reassessment of the Theory of Rational Action, New York, Harper Collins.
Riker, W. (1962)
The Theory of Political Coalitions, New Haven, Yale UP.
Roberts, G. (1978)
The Explanation of Politics: Comparison, Strategy, and Theory, in: Lewis et al. eds.: 287-304.
Robertson, D. (1976)
A Theory of Party Competition, London, John Wiley.
Romein, J. (1971)
Historische lijnen en patronen, Leiden, Querido.
Rokkan, S. (1970)
Citizens, Elections, Parties, Approaches to the Comparative Study of the Processes of Development, Oslo, Universitetsforlaget.
Rokkan, S. (1975)
Dimensions of State-formation and Nation-building, in: Tilly ed.: 562-600.
Rokkan, S./Urwin, D. eds. (1982)
The Politics of Territorial Identity: Studies in European Regionalism, London etc., Sage.
Rokkan, S./Urwin, D. (1983)
Economy, Territory, Identity: Politics of West European Peripheries, London etc., Sage.
Rose, R. ed. (1974)
Electoral Behavior: A Comparative Handbook, New York, Free Press.
Rose, R./Massawir, H. (1967)
Voting and Elections: A Functional Analysis, in: *Political Studies*, 15/2: 173-201
Rose, R./Urwin, D. (1970)
Persistence and Change in Western Party Systems since 1945, in: *Political Studies*, Vol. 18, no. 3: 287-319
Rosenthal, U. (1978)
Political Order, Rewards, Punishments and Political Stability, Alphen a/d Rijn, Sijthoff & Noordhof.
Rueschemeyer, D./Stephens, E./Stephens, J.D. (1992)
Capitalist Development and Democracy, Cambridge, Polity Press.

Rustow, D.A. (1967)
A World of Nations: Problems of Modernization, Washington, Brookings.
Sartori, G. (1970)
Concept Misformation in Comparative Politics, in: *American Political Science Review*, 64: 1033-1053.
Sartori, G. (1976)
Parties and Party Systems, A Framework for Analysis (volume 1), Cambridge, Cambridge UP.
Scharpf, F.W. (1984)
Strategy Choice, Economic Feasibility and Institutional Constraints as Determinants of Full Employment Policy during the Recession, in: Gerlach/Peters/Sengenberger eds., *Public Policies to Combat Unemployment in a Period of Economic Stagnation*, An International Comparison, Frankfurt/New York, Campus Verlag. 67-114.
Scharpf, F.W. (1987)
A Game-Theoretical Interpretation of Inflation and Unemployment in Western Europe, in: *Journal of Public Policy*, 7: 227-258.
Scharpf, F.W. (1989)
Politische Steuerung und Politische Institutionen, in: *Politische Vierteljahresschrift*, 30/1: 10-21.
Scharpf, F.W. (1991)
Political Institutions, Decision Styles, and Policy Choices, in: Czada/Windhoff-Héritier eds.: 53-86.
Scharpf, F.W. (1992)
Crisis and Choice in European Social Democracy, Ithaca, Cornell UP
Scheuch, E.K. (1980)
Analysis of Historical Materials as the Basis for a new Cooperation between History and Society, in: Clubb/Scheuch eds., *Historical Social Research*, Historisch-Sozialwissenschaftliche Forschungen (vol. 6), Stuttgart, Klenn-Cotta: 25-45.
Schimank, U. (1985)
Der mangelnde Akteurbezug sytemtheoretischer Erklärungen gesellschaftlicher Differenzierung, in: *Zeitschrift für Soziologie*, 14, 6: 421-434.
Schmidt, M.G. (1982a)
The Role of the Parties in Shaping Macroeconomic Policy, in: Castles ed.: 97-176.
Schmidt, M.G. (1982b)
Does Corporatism Matter? Economic Crisis, Politics and Rates of Unemployment in: Lehmbruch/Schmitter eds.: 237-258.
Schmidt, M.G. (1983)
The Welfare State and the Economy in Periods of Economic Crisis: A Comparative analysis of Twenty-three OECD Nations, in: *European Journal of Political Research*, 11/1: 1-26.
Schmidt, M.G. (1985)
Die Schweizerische Weg zur Vollbeschäftigung, Frankfurt/New York, Campus.

Schmidt, M.G. (1987)
The Politics of Labour Market Policy, in: Castles et al. eds.: 4-53.
Schmidt, M.G. (1991)
Policy-Analyse, in: Mohr, G. ed., *Grundzüge der Politicologie*, Heidelberg.
Schmitt, H./ and R. Mannheimer, R. eds. (1991)
The European elections of June 1989, in: *European Journal of Political Research*, 19/1 (Special Issue)
Schmitter, Ph. C. (1981)
Interest Intermediation and Regime Governability in Contemporary Western Europe, in: Berger ed.: 287-330.
Schmitter, Ph.C. (1986)
Neocorporatism and the State, in: Grant, W. ed., *The Political Economy of Corporatism*, London, Macmillan: 32-62.
Schmitter, Ph. C./Lehmbruch, G. eds., (1979)
Trends Towards Corporatist Intermediation, London etc., Sage.
Schneider, V. (1988)
Politiknetzwerke der Chemikalienkontrolle, Eine Analyse einer transnationalen Politikentwicklung, Berlin, De Gruyter.
Schumpeter, J.A. (1942)
Capitalism, Socialism and Democracy, New York, Harper & Row.
Shonfield, A. (1982)
The Use of Public Power, Oxford, Oxford UP.
Sica, A. (1988)
Weber, Irrationality, and Social Order, Berkeley, University of California Press.
Sigelman, L./Gadbois, G. (1983)
Contemporary Comparative Politics: An Inventory and Assessment, in: *Comparative Political Studies*, 16/3: 275-307.
Simon, H. (1959)
Theories of Decision Making in Economics and the Behavioural Sciences, in: *American Economic Review*, 49: 253-283.
Skocpol, T. (1979)
States and Social Revolutions, A Comparative Analysis of France, Russia and China, Cambridge, Cambridge UP.
Skocpol, T. (1985)
Bringing the State Back In: Strategies of Analysis in Current Research, in: Evans et al. eds.: 1-45.
Smelser, N.J. (1976)
Comparative Methods in the Social Sciences, Englewood Cliffs, Prentice-Hall.
Smith, G. (1972; 1989)
Politics in Western Europe: A Comparative Analysis, London, Heinemann.
Steiner, J. (1986)
European Democracies, New York, Longman.

Steiner, J. A. (1974)
Amicable Agreement versus Majority Rule: Conflict Resolution in Switzerland, Chapel Hill, University of North Carolina Press.
Strange, S. (1988)
States and Markets, An introduction to International Political Economy, London, Pinter.
Streeck, W. (1983)
Between Pluralism and Corporatism: German Business Associations and the State, *Journal of Public Policy*, 3: 265-284.
Streeck, W./Schmitter, P. eds. (1985)
Private Interest Government, Beyond Market and State, London, Sage.
Strom, K. (1990)
A Behavioral Theory of Competitive Political Parties, in: *American Journal of Political Science*, 2: 565-598.
Strümpel, B./Scholz, J. (1987)
The Comparative Study of the Economy, Dimensions, Methods and Results, in: Dierkes et al. eds.
Summers, R./Heston, A. (1988)
A New Set of International Comparisons of Real Product and Price Levels Estimates for 130 Countries, 1950-1985, *Review of Income and Wealth*, 34: 1-25.
Szporluk, R. (1988)
Communism and Nationalism, Karl Marx versus Friedrich List, New York, Oxford UP.
Tarschys, D. (1983)
The Scissors Crisis in Public Finance in: *Policy Sciences*, 15: 205-224.
Taylor, C.L./Hudson, M. (1972)
World Handbook of Political and Social Indicators, New Haven, Yale UP.
Taylor, C.L./Jodice, D.A. (1983)
World Handbook of Political and Social Indicators, New Haven, Yale UP.
Therborn, G. (1986)
Why Some Peoples Are More Unemployed Than Others, London, NLB/Verso.
Thomassen, J.J.A. (1976)
Kiezers en gekozenen in een representatieve democratie, Alphen aan den Rijn.
Tilly, C. (1984)
Big Structures, Huge Comparisons, Large Processes, New York, Russell Sage Foundation.
Tilly, Ch. (1990)
Coercion, Capital and European States AD 990-1990, Cambridge (Mass), Harvard UP.
Tilly, Ch. ed. (1975)
The Formation of National States in Western Europe, Princeton, Princeton UP.
Tocqueville, A. de (1969)
Democracy in America, (1835; 1840), New York, Doubleday.

United Nations (1990)
Development Programme 1990, Human Development Report 1990, New York, Oxford UP.
United Nations (1991)
Development Programme 1991, Human Development Report 1991, New York, Oxford UP.
Van den Daele, W./Krohn, W./Weingart, P. eds. (1979)
Geplante Forschung, Vergleichende Studien über den Einfluß politischer Programme auf die Wissenschaftsentwicklung, Frankfurt aM, Suhrkamp.
Vanhanen, T. (1990)
The Process of Democratization, A Comparative Study of 147 States, 1980-88, New York, Crane Russak.
Verba, S./Nie, N.H./Kim, J. (1978)
Participation and Political Equality: A Seven-Nation Comparison, New York, Cambridge UP
Verba, S. (1986)
Comparative Politics, Where Have We Been, Where Are We Going?, in H.J. Wiarda ed.: 26-40.
Von Beyme, K. (1970)
Die Parlamentarischen Regierungssysteme in Europa, Munich, Piper Verlag.
Von Beyme, K. (1982)
Once again: Do Parties matter? in: *Politisches Vierteljahresschrift*, 23/2: 205-210.
Von Beyme, K. (1985)
Political Parties in Western Democracies, Aldershot, Gower.
Vris, J. de ed. (1983)
The Rise and Decline of Nations: Symposium, in: *International Studies Quarterly*, 27: 11-16.
Waarden, F. van (1992)
Dimensions and types of policy networks, in: *European Journal of Political Research*, 21/1-2: 29-52.
Wallerstein, I. (1974-1989)
The Modern World System, New York, Academic Press, 3 vols.
Ward R.E./Rustow, D.A. ed., (1964)
Political Modernization in Japan and Turkey, Princeton, Princeton UP.
Wheare, K.C. (1963)
Legislatures, Oxford, Oxford UP.
Whiteley, P.E. (1986)
Political Control of the Macro-economy, London, Sage.
Whiteley, P.E. (1987)
The Monetarists Experiments in the United States and the United Kingdom: Policy Responses to Stagflation, in: Keman et al. eds.: 182-204.
Wiarda, H.J. (1986)
Comparative Politics: Past and Present, in H.J. Wiarda ed.: 3-25.

Wiarda, H.J. ed. (1986)
New Directions in Comparative Politics, Boulder/London, Westview Press.
Wilensky, H. (1975)
The Welfare Sstate and Equality, Structural and Ideological Roots of Public Expenditures, Berkeley, University of California Press.
Wilensky, H. (1981)
Democratic Corporatism, Consensus and Social Policy: Reflections on Changing Values and the 'Crisis' of the Welfare State, in: OECD: 185-195
Williamson, O.E. (1975)
Markets and Hierarchies, Analysis and Antitrust Implications, A study in the Economics of Internal Organization, New York, Free Press.
Williamson, O.E. (1986)
Economic Institutions of Capitalism, Firms, Markets, Relational Contracting, New York, Free Press.
Willke, H. (1989)
Systemtheorie entwickelter Gesellschaften, Weinheim/München, Juventa.
Windhoff-Héritier, A. (1991)
Institutions, Interests, and Political Choice, in: Czada/Windhoff-Héritier: 27-53.
Wittfogel, K. (1957)
Oriental Despotism: A Comparative Study of Total Power, New Haven, Yale UP.
Woldendorp, J.J./Keman, H./Budge, I. (1993)
Handbook of Democratic Government. Party-composition of Government and Parliaments in 20 Democracies. In: *European Journal of Political Research*, Special Issue, June 1993 (forthcoming)
Wolfinger, R.E./Rosenstone, S.J. (1980)
Who Votes? New Haven, Yale UP
World Bank (1983)
World Tables, 3rd ed., Baltimore, Johns Hopkins UP.
World Bank (1991a)
Social Indicators of Development 1990, Baltimore, Johns Hopkins UP.
World Bank (1991b)
World Development Report 1991, New York, Oxford UP.
Zolberg, A.R. (1966)
Creating Poltitical Order: The Party States of West Africa, Chicago, Rand McNally.
Zysman, J. (1984)
Governments, Markets, and Growth, Ithaca/London, Cornell UP.

About the Editor and the Authors

Dr. **Hans Keman** is Professor of Political Science at the Vrije Universiteit in Amsterdam. He has previously taught at the University of Amsterdam, the European University Institute (Florence, Italy), the University of Leyden and was a Research Fellow at the Australian National University (Canberra). He has published on comparative politics, public policy formation, the welfare state, economic policy-making and on party systems and the functioning of governments.

Dr. **Dietmar Braun** is lecturer at the University of Heidelberg and has been researcher at the Universities of Amsterdam and Leyden as well as a Research Fellow at the Max Planck-Institut für Gesellschaftsforschung. He has published on the politics of unemployment and health care policy-making.

Dr. **Ian Budge** is Professor of Government at the University of Essex since 1966. He has published on democratic theory, party behavior, elections and party systems, and government formation from a comparative perspective. He is director of the 'Manifesto Research Project' on party programs, government declarations and public policy formation in Western democracies.

Dr. **Roland Czada** is a Research Fellow at the Max Planck-Institut für Gesellschaftsforschung and has previously taught at the University of Konstanz. He has published on corporatism, environmental policy-making and comparative political economy.

Dr. **Hans Daalder** is Professor of Political Science at the University of Leyden since 1964. He has been Head of Department at the European University Institute (Florence, Italy), and is at present Chairman of the Graduate School of Political Science in the Netherlands. He has published widely on comparative and Dutch politics as well as on topics of political history.

Dr. **Svante Ersson** is currently working at the University of Umeå. His main research concerns empirical comparative politics, and the development of comparable data on political behavior and institutions.

Dr. **Cees van der Eijk** is Professor of Political Science at the University of Amsterdam. He has published numerous articles and books on electoral behavior and elections in the Netherlands as well as from a comparative perspective.

Dr. **Jan-Erik Lane** is Professor of Political Science at the University of Oslo and the Norwegian School of Management and has previously taught in Umeå and Lund. He has published widely on topics of comparative political economy and sociology as well as on public administration and public policy formation.

Dr. **Adrienne Windhoff-Héritier** is Professor of Political Science at the University of Bielefeld and has previously taught at the University of Konstanz. She is an expert on policy analysis and on the comparative analysis of public policy formation.